PIECED
BORDERS
The Complete Resource

by

Judy Martin & Marsha McCloskey

CROSLEY-GRIFFITH
PUBLISHING COMPANY, INC.
GRINNELL, IOWA

To lifelong friendships
and the quilting threads that connect us

ACKNOWLEDGMENTS: Thanks to Steve Bennett, Denise Harris, and Jean Nolte. I couldn't have done it without your help. J.M.
Special thanks to all the quilters who have participated in classes, bought the books and given me so much encouragement over the years. M. Mc.

Written and illustrated by Judy Martin and Marsha McCloskey
Photography by Steve O'Connor, O'Connor Photography, Grinnell, Iowa
Printed in the United States of America

ISBN 0-929589-03-3
Published by Crosley-Griffith Publishing Company, Inc.
1321 Broad Street, Grinnell, Iowa 50112
(515) 236-4854
First Printing 1994
15 14 13 12 11 10 9 8 7 6 5 4 3

Contents

Talking Quilt

Judy: Marsha and I have been quilting friends for more than twenty years. Between us, we have written two dozen books. We have both collaborated with other quilters, yet this is our first book project together. I can't imagine what took us so long to get around to it!

Marsha: We met in the early '70s in Eugene, Oregon at a weekly craft fair called the Saturday Market. There weren't many quilters then and since both of us were selling patchwork, we began talking. I admired Judy because she made full-size quilts (comforters, really) and I only made potholders, pillows, patchwork toys and an occasional baby quilt. She was familiar with a lot more patterns than I was and used smaller pieces. I was virtually homebound with little kids and a husband in graduate school. Patchwork and the Saturday Market were my only outside activities. I was

so eager to share what I was experiencing with the patchwork (and to talk to another adult), that it's likely I made a pest of myself. Judy probably *had* to talk to me because I wouldn't go away.

Judy: I don't remember Marsha pestering me, but I can understand the need for adult conversation. Now that I have toddlers, I am always so grateful for the quilt talk that Marsha has trouble getting me off the phone so we can get our work done.

Marsha: We shared everything we knew about making quilts in 1973, and we still do.

Judy: I credit Marsha with that openness. I wasn't sure how to approach her as a "competitor" at the Saturday Market in 1973. She seemed perfectly willing to share her secrets, and I was happy to have someone to talk to about quilts. We have to chuckle now about the quilter at Saturday Market who didn't have any desire to talk quilts with us.

Marsha: She certainly missed out on a lot!

Judy: It was quilting that brought us together and quilting that keeps us in touch even though we haven't lived in the same state for 19 years. During the first year and a half of our acquaintance, when we both lived in Eugene, we seldom spent time at one another's homes. We never did anything together socially. We didn't even go fabric shopping together. We just talked quilts. But boy, did we talk quilts!

Marsha: My husband, not tuned in to our conversations nor understanding the terms, labeled it "the language of quilt" as if we were speaking a foreign tongue.

Judy: Realize that we met in 1973 when there were few quilting books, virtually no quilting shops, no guilds, no symposia (certainly no quilt cruises), and no classes until we taught them ourselves. The only quilt magazine back then was a fledgling *Quilter's Newsletter,* and it would be another year before I even heard of it.

Marsha: In those early years, we were both flying by the seat of our pants. With no one to teach us, we were making up quilting techniques and patterns as the need arose. We shared sewing tips and patterns and our love of patchwork. Judy introduced me to graph paper for drawing quilts and making templates. And I was mightily impressed with her sewing machine; the little black Singer Featherweight was just about the cutest thing that I had ever seen. After she moved to San Diego, Judy found a Featherwight for me at a flea market and shipped it to me in Seattle by Greyhound Bus. And even though I have other sewing machines now as well, I still use the one Judy found for me to piece most of my quilts.

Judy: Though we have developed different styles over the years, back in 1973 our work was very similar. One day my sister, with whom I lived, came home and asked me if I had some new patchwork pillows at a local consignment shop. It turned out she had seen some of Marsha's pillows and thought they were mine. That is not really surprising considering the dearth of fabric available then. In the days of polyester pant suits, once you weeded out the knits, there was scarcely any fabric left to buy. Colors tended toward the primary. I remember lots of red, yellow, and black calicoes.

Marsha: And don't forget the kelly green and the orange pin dots.

Judy: One thing you could say for the fabric: it was certainly a good buy! At $1.29 per yard, I could make a bed-size quilt, batting and all, for $15. Alas, quilt prices were low, too, and I sold my creations for $60 or $80.

Marsha: The first quilting workshop I ever taught was with Judy. We rented the recreation room at the University of Oregon married student housing, signed up over thirty interested people and set about teaching them in one day everything we knew about quiltmaking. Admittedly our knowledge of quilting was limited, but it still was an ambitious task. We were nearly manic, I think, and covered drafting, template-making, cutting, machine piecing, setting the quilt together, adding borders, marking for quilting, hand quilting, tying and binding. That was a lot of material to cover, and there were plenty of beginners in the class.

Judy: I remember a young man in that class was having trouble cutting fabric with scissors. Every time he squeezed the handles, the fabric bent rather than cut. I was so naive that I didn't realize that left-handed people would have trouble using right-handed scissors. I was at a loss about how to help him.

Marsha: In spite of the rough spots, the class was a success. Some of the people in that first class are still our friends and tease us about the impossibility of teaching so much in such a short time.

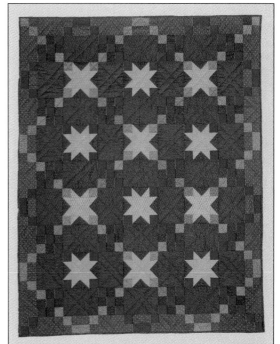

Star Matrix by Marsha McCloskey, 1989. Pieced completer borders keep this quilt from ending abruptly.

Judy: Quilters know so much more now than we did back then. It's almost embarrassing to recall some of our learning experiences.

Marsha: I can recall one such experience vividly. Judy calls this "The Seam Ripper Story." We were both making patchwork items to sell and I received a custom order for a queen size comforter. I had never made anything that large, and I asked Judy to teach me how to put the layers together and make the ties. We agreed on a time and place to get together, and she told me to add borders and prepare the backing in the meanwhile. Well, I lived in married student housing with my husband and two small children. The whole apartment was about 500 square feet with two bedrooms, a living area and kitchen. The queen-sized quilt top was larger than any of our rooms and though I could piece it, I couldn't really lay it out to measure it properly for borders. I had made a design with blocks set diagonally; the borders were plain with squared corners. I had cut the edge triangles with the bias on the long sides. I was having trouble measuring the top, so I just cut the border strips longer than I knew they needed to be. To attach them to the quilt center, I simply started at one end of the quilt and sewed the border on, thinking that pinning was too time-consuming and I didn't have room to do it anyway.

When Judy met me at my mother-in-law's house where there was enough room to baste the layers, we laid the quilt on the floor and Judy studied it with some concern. She asked for a tape measure and proceeded to measure. One side of the top was fully seven inches longer than the other! What a mess: I hadn't measured, I hadn't pinned and the bias edges along the outside of the quilt had stretched!

May Festival by Judy Martin, 1978. A double chain-of-squares border adds the perfect finishing touch to this quilt.

I forget exactly how long it took us, but we got out the seam rippers and took the border strips off. Then, Judy showed me how to measure the quilt properly (see page 80 for complete instructions). With the border strips cut to the correct lengths, we pinned thoroughly to ease in all the stretched-out edge triangles and sewed the borders on again. The quilt was stuffed and tied that day, thanks to Judy, and I had learned three valuable lessons: don't place bias edges along the outside because they're liable to stretch, always measure borders and cut them to the proper length, and pin borders in place before you stitch them to the quilt.

Judy: I've learned a thing or two from Marsha, as well. I often tell the story of how she introduced me to chain piecing. That may be the most valuable patchwork tip I ever learned, but I hesitated to try it for months. You see, Marsha described how she would sew one pair of patches together and then, without stopping to lift the presser foot, continue right on stitching the next set of patches. She said that her daughter would ready the pairs of patches and hand them to her. "Fine for her," I thought, "but I don't have a helper. Who is going to get my next set of patches ready while I'm holding on to the one I'm sewing?" I know this sounds really dumb, but it didn't occur to me that I could take my foot off the pedal and stop stitching while I readied the next pair of patches myself. As soon as I figured that part out, I was sold on chain piecing.

Marsha: Our careers as quiltmakers have run remarkably similar courses. We both took up quilting, started selling our wares, began teaching, and wrote our first quilt books at about the same times. And we have both ended up publishing our own quilting books.

Judy: In our personal lives, Marsha and I have always taken different paths. When we met, Marsha was a young wife with small children. I was single and struggling to find a job. We understood each other perfectly, though. We had a lot in common in spite of the obvious differences. I think our friendship works so well partly because the focus is on quilting, not on our personal lives. Certainly, we care about each other. We just skip over the little bumps along our personal roads and stay in touch about the general course of travel.

Marsha: And we talk quilt as often as possible.

Introduction

What is it about pieced borders that appeals to us so? Why does a grand design such as a Feathered Star or Goose in the Pond look so much better with the addition of a simple sawtooth border? And why does a humble Nine-Patch look suddenly special surrounded by a chain of squares? Some liken a pieced border to a picture frame. The frame lends dignity and finality and makes the picture look worthy. A pieced border is like the final couplet of a sonnet or the coda of a symphony. The rhythm changes to signal that the end is coming. It gives us the opportunity to anticipate the ending rather than being startled to find ourselves there. The poem or the concert or the quilt ends on a much more satisfying note.

A pieced border is a patchwork of shapes joined in long rows to make a design around the edge of the quilt. Usually, these designs are simple and repetitive. The linear arrangement of the patches provides a contrast to the quilt center, which is usually made of repeated squares. Further contrast can be achieved with color, fabric and scale. Any quilt (elaborate pieced patterns, simple ones, and even appliqué) can be attractively framed with the right pieced border. Though not *every* quilt *needs* a pieced border, a great many quilts are improved by them and some need them desperately. You should not consider your quilt complete until you have given some thought to its borders.

A simple sawtooth border completes a grand quilt. Goose in the Pond by Marsha McCloskey, 1985, is an intricate design perfectly framed with the most basic of pieced borders. Most patterns, plain or fancy, look wonderful with simple sawtooth or dogtooth borders. This block pattern is in Marsha's book, *Christmas Quilts*.

Your Quilts Are Begging For Pieced Borders

We've all admired those gorgeous antique quilts with the intricate borders. Have you ever noticed how many of the truly memorable quilts that you see have pieced borders? There's no question about it: pieced borders make a quilt special. Yet, admit it, most of us have slapped on four ordinary strips to finish a quilt, even when we knew that it would look better with a pieced border. Sometimes you just want to be done with it.

People are so used to thinking of borders as something you add on to a finished quilt that it is easy to see why they wouldn't want to be bothered. Here is a typical scenario: You stitch the final block, and you begin to feel that your quilt is finished. Obviously, a pile of blocks is not a quilt, so you go on sewing until the last row is joined. Now this is beginning to look like a quilt! Psychologically, you are ready to be done. You have been feeling almost done since you completed the last block. Slapping on four plain strips is beginning to sound pretty good. You don't relish the idea of going back and cutting more patches out of your pile of fabrics. Your quilt is begging for pieced borders. But pieced borders seem like a lot of trouble, so you declare your quilt complete.

Pieced Borders can save time. This Prairie Rambler quilt has 300 fewer pieces with pieced borders than it would have had with another row of blocks. A larger photo is on page 35; the pattern starts on page 112.

Make Fewer Blocks With Pieced Borders

There is another way to look at pieced borders. Pieced borders are not as much work as you might think. Do you realize that quilts with pieced borders don't necessarily require any extra patches? When you plan for pieced borders from the outset, you can make fewer blocks. Often the bordered quilt has no more patches than the ordinary quilt that you would have made. Sometimes, a pieced border even saves time and work. Prairie Rambler (at left and on page 35) would be the same size with an extra row of blocks all around instead of the border, but the border has 300 fewer pieces! The extra row of blocks would have been just more of same, but the pieced border makes the quilt special. Spectacular quilts with pieced borders are easily within your reach. You just need to rearrange your thinking.

Think of your borders as an important part of your quilt. Plan for borders from the beginning. You could even cut out the border patches when you cut out the rest of the quilt and sew the border units first. Then when you stitch the last block, and you begin to feel almost done, your quilt really is almost finished, and finished with a flourish! You'll love the satisfaction you derive from making such a unique and memorable quilt.

Beautiful Quilts Are Within Your Reach

Don't be intimidated by pieced borders. Generally, they are constructed from the most basic of shapes. The sewing couldn't be easier. The trick has always been in knowing how to make the border fit the quilt, both physically and aesthetically. We'll teach you the keys to a natural fit, and we'll even tell you how to make a success of your quilt if your cutting and sewing don't quite measure up. No matter what your background is, beautiful quilts are within your reach with *Pieced Borders*. The techniques you learn here, along with the wealth of border ideas and patterns, are all you need.

Go As Far As You Want with Pieced Borders

We realize that as a quilter you have unique talents, interests, and experiences. We've organized this book with plenty of photos, illustrations, captions, subheads, and tip boxes to make it easy to find the information you need. Go as far as you care to go. Just enjoy the pictures and patterns if you want and skip the sections that deal with designing and drafting borders. However, you probably can't resist sneaking a peek at the stock borders starting on page 44. If these intrigue you, you'll want to read the chapters, Border Design Basics and Keys to Border Fit. We've done everything in our power to make border planning easy and enjoyable. If you can figure out how many blocks to make for your quilt, you can figure out how to plan an appropriate pieced border from the bounty of designs here. We've done all the drawing and drafting for you, and most of the figuring, as well.

You will find everything you need to know about pieced borders in this book. If you want to learn some nifty math and drafting tips, you will find them here. Whether you are looking for creative design ideas or tried-and-true shortcuts and techniques, you will find what you need. We're excited about pieced borders. We think you will be too. So let's get started.

Border Design Basics

Pieced borders can be used to make a quilt larger, but if all you wanted were a larger quilt, an extra row of blocks could accomplish the same thing. Pieced borders add something special. They can change the look of a quilt and add a wonderful, finishing touch.

In preparation for this book, and for years before that, we have been making quilts and paying attention to the effect of pieced borders. As we studied the subject, we found a tremendous variety of pieced border looks. The border look you choose reflects your personality and gives your quilt style. You can add grace, spontaneity, sophistication, whimsy, sentimentality, dignity or any effect you desire, simply by adding pieced borders. Your choice of colors and fabrics, your use of rhythm and repetition, and your use of visual space are style elements that you can use in pieced borders to create unique and beautiful quilts.

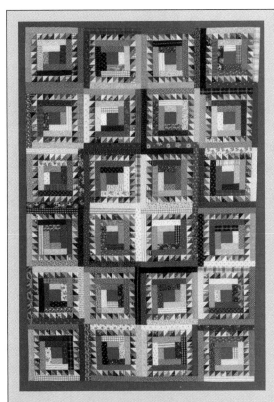

Before and after pieced borders. Here are two versions of the same Feathered Log Cabin quilt made by Judy Martin. Note how the pieced borders add impact as well as size to the quilt center. Even a simple design like a Log Cabin, which often is made without any borders, can benefit from the right pieced border.

Note also how the plain red borders on the before quilt highlight the red scraps and make the quilt seem predominantly red. In the after picture, you can see that the addition of a predominantly cream pieced border makes the quilt look lighter overall.

The total border area is equivalent to an extra row of blocks all around the quilt. The dark values and intricate piecing hug the quilt center, leaving an expanse of light contained by a narrow border of red. The spontaneously scrappy border suits the casual look of the quilt center. The quirky asymmetry of the stars counters the formality of the regimented sawtooth border. A larger photo is on page 37, and the pattern for this quilt is on page 118.

Border Colors Shift the Color Balance of the Quilt

Any border, whether pieced or plain, shifts the color balance of the quilt as a whole. Let's look at the simplest effects first. A plain border contrasts with the outer edge of the quilt top and makes a statement. Of all the colors of the quilt, one was chosen for the border. That color gains importance, and our eye will be drawn to that color wherever it appears in the quilt. A scrap quilt made from a rainbow of colors and bordered in blue will be perceived as a blue quilt.

The quilt binding can be considered to be the simplest type of border. Its color is important as it is the final design element of the quilt. Because it is narrow, a contrasting binding won't have as strong an effect as a wider border, but it will still change the overall impression of the quilt and highlight the binding color wherever it appears on the quilt surface. Of course, every quilt needs to be bound, and sometimes you don't want to make a new color statement with the binding. In such a case, you can simply bind the quilt to match the outer border.

Pieced borders affect the overall color impression in much the same way as plain borders and bindings do. You can include one or more pieced borders or a combination of pieced and plain. Plain borders calm down areas of busy piecing, providing a visual resting place.

Generally, pieced borders are somewhat lighter or darker than the quilt center. There is not much point, after all, in having a pieced border if it looks just like the rest of the quilt. Your pieced border should accent the quilt and alter its look. This can be accomplished using the same colors and fabrics that were used for the blocks. The overall effect changes because you use more of some fabrics and less of others than you used for the blocks. You might drop out most of the light values, for example, to make the border darker than the quilt center.

Feel free to introduce new values and fabrics in the border if you like. Some quilters recommend using fabrics in the border only if they have appeared in the quilt center. The rule was probably devised in order to prevent quilters from haphazardly adding completely new colors. In fact, we frequently and happily introduce new values and fabrics in our borders as long as they relate well to the quilt center.

Matching binding as a design choice. This Pinwheel quilt made by Marsha McCloskey in 1987 sports a binding to match the outer border. Marsha did not want to upstage the border with a contrasting binding here. The pieced border of shaded sawtooths repeats the shapes, colors and fabrics of the blocks. The blocks, however, are half light and the border is only one-quarter light. This change of color distribution helps make the border stand out as distinct from the quilt center. So does the linear rather than circular rhythm of the border. The pattern for this quilt appears in Marsha's book, *Lessons in Machine Piecing*.

Pieced Borders Alter the Rhythm and Repetition of the Quilt

Besides changing the color impression of the quilt, your border can change the rhythm of the visual composition. Pieced borders can alter the rhythm in a quilt in two ways. First, the border adds size without adding more blocks or more repetition of the established pattern. Second, the border adds its own new cadence. The pieced border will have a more linear look and a simpler structure than the blocks in the quilt center. It will serve as a frame, helping to focus attention on the quilt center. This change of rhythm provides a pleasant relief from the repetition of the blocks and adds interest and a sense of order.

Pattern and Space in Quilts with Pieced Borders

After bordering hundreds of quilts by trusting our instincts, we heard a bit of folk wisdom that opened our eyes to what we had been doing all along. It suggested that the total width of borders from one edge of the quilt center to the binding should be the same as the size of one quilt block in the quilt center. We proceeded to test the theory by comparing blocks and border widths of dozens of quilts. To our surprise, we found that most of our quilts fit this rule. We doubt that it is the only viable rule of proportion for borders on quilts, but it does provide a good starting point.

Too thin a border can look puny, while too wide a border can overpower the quilt center. Trust your own reactions on this one. Most of us have a pretty good sense of proportion. If you think a border looks good, it probably does. If you're not satisfied, try some different design solutions.

The pieced border accents the quilt and alters its look. In this Kayak quilt by Marsha McCloskey, 1993, the two borders, a sawtooth and a chain of Four-Patches, create a strong, dark edge for the light quilt center. The borders also introduce a change of rhythm and a change of color emphasis from black and white to red and pink. Note how the total space between the block and binding is roughly equal to the block size. This proportion is often a good choice for a quilt. The pattern for the Kayak block is in Marsha's book, *100 Pieced Patterns for 8" Quilt Blocks.*

Take your cue from the quilt center when you plan your borders. Some quilts need to be boxed in and framed by a strong border with a prominent pieced area and dark colors. Kayak, above, is a good example. Others seem to want breathing room and an airy, light border of wide plain areas complemented by small bands of simple piecing. Duck Paddle on the next page is a perfect example.

Generally, the entire border area is not pieced. One or more areas of piecing are joined by plain strips that offer visual relief. Pieced borders can be right up next to the quilt center for a cozy look. If you prefer, they can be nestled right up against the binding or outer plain border with a wide space separating the blocks and the pieced borders. In fact, you can put the pieced bands anywhere in between. The placement of your pieced border within the total border area is strictly a matter of personal taste and will reflect your style and the look you want for your quilt.

Pieced Borders Function As a Transition Area

Pieced borders can provide a delightful path linking plain outer borders with a pieced quilt center. The piecing echoes that of the quilt center, but the linear organization of the patches in the border has elements in common with the plain border, as well.

Use pieced borders to bridge one border area to the next. A pieced border of dark and light patches can take you gradually from a dark space to a light space. For example, a border could be pieced from red triangles and white triangles. Flanked by a red plain border and a white space, this border softens the change from white to red. Whenever you use the same value, color or fabric in the backgrounds of two neighboring areas, the backgrounds will blend. We use background blending often as you will see from the quilts in this book. It is a good way to obscure the line between different design areas. When you lose sight of this line, you can start to see the quilt as a whole, and it seems more natural and less rigidly structured.

A large print such as a floral chintz can be used as an unpieced border around the quilt or between design areas. Because the background color is interrupted by the colors of the flowers or other figures, the border edge is obscured. A large print, then, like a pieced border, softens the straight lines. Large floral prints also provide an organic, curving movement not easily achieved in pieced quilt designs. These prints can be used in conjunction with pieced borders for some lovely effects. In fact, one of Marsha's favorite border treatments is to use a large floral print 10"-12" wide for the outer border. Of course such a border needs to fit with the overall style of the quilt, but where appropriate, large prints add a complex, richly textured look with very little work.

The border can nestle up to the quilt center for a cozy look. In Marsha McCloskey's Duck Paddle quilt, 1991, the piecing occupies only a little bit of the total border space. The blocks appear to float on the quilt center, so a wide-open feeling in the border is perfectly suitable. However, for contrast, the pieced sawtooth crowds the quilt center. Background blending occurs where sawtooth triangles match the block backgrounds, softening the transition between design areas. The Duck Paddle pattern is in Marsha's book, *On to Square Two.*

Matching the Border Style to the Quilt

Generally, we like a very simple, repetitive quality to a border. The old border favorites serve our purpose most of the time. The classic look of a sawtooth can be paired with most quilts, even those with no triangles. A Log Cabin or a Lone Star, for example, looks good with a sawtooth frame.

An elaborate quilt center often looks good with a very simple pieced border. There is no need to make an intricate border to compete with a Feathered Star Sampler, for example. Likewise, a very simple quilt often looks best uncluttered and framed cleanly with a simple sawtooth or chain of squares. A fancy border can look ostentatious next to the simplicity of a Nine-Patch or Rail Fence. Between these extremes you will find a wealth of quilt patterns that can benefit from pieced borders, either plain or fancy. Marsha's Pinwheel quilt on page 10 has Pinwheel blocks set with alternate plain squares. The look is interesting, yet uncluttered. On the one hand, the

A wide space capped by a simple pieced sawtooth frames an intricate quilt perfectly. Marsha McCloskey's Feathered Star Sampler is a complex, formal pattern. The blocks are confined by contrasting sashes, yet the light backgrounds in the blocks and between sashes establish a precedent for the light space in the border. The pieced border echoes shapes found in a smaller size in the blocks. The red triangles cling to the edge of the quilt to give the center breathing room and a final flourish of color. The sawtooth border blends into the plain area because matching fabrics are placed side by side. The pattern for this quilt is in Marsha's booklet, *Feathered Star Sampler.*

Pinwheel quilt center is simple enough to benefit from a little embellishment, which the border treatment provides. On the other hand, it is complex enough to hold its own next to the fairly involved border design.

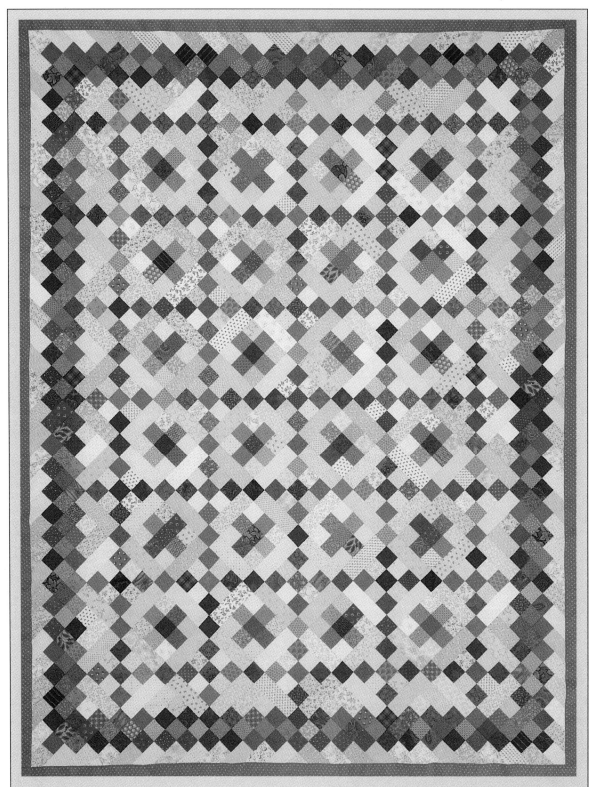

A simple border befits a humble quilt of Nine-Patch blocks. Judy Martin's Road to Colorado quilt, made in 1992, is an uncomplicated design. It doesn't call for a fancy border. All it needs is a little change of pace. The double chain of squares reorganizes the shapes and colors in the blocks in an orderly, linear arrangement that provides a fine finishing touch. This border was built in rather than added on. The pattern for Road to Colorado appears in Judy's book, *Yes You Can! Make Stunning Quilts From Simple Patterns.*

Finding Border Ideas in Block Shapes

The first place to look for border ideas is in the block used in the quilt center. You can single out a square, diamond, triangle, star, pinwheel, or any element or combination that you might want to repeat. A quilt center with a variety of shapes presents many design possibilities for the borders.

A block incorporating multiple shapes probably looks best with a border using some of the same shapes. Occasionally you may want to introduce new shapes in the border. For example, you could use a sawtooth border of triangles on a Log Cabin made of squares and rectangles. In such a case, it is a good idea to choose a border with similar angles to those in the block. A 45° triangle having a right angle would probably suit the right angles of a Log Cabin better than an equilateral triangle. A 60° equilateral triangle would suit a quilt made from 60° diamonds or hexagons.

After studying your block for possible border shapes, look through the Stock Borders chapter to see if you can find a border that you like which incorporates a shape or angle prominent in your quilt. Sometimes you may want to add or subtract lines of a standard pattern to adapt it to your quilt. Sometimes you may want to design a totally new, custom border. We will teach you how to do this starting on page 23.

Turning the Corners

The way the pieced borders flow around the corners is an important part of the quilt design. In antique quilts, pieced borders were often simply made sufficiently long and cut off without much thought. At the corner, one border strip would simply be cut off where it bumped square against its neighbor. This is certainly one way of dealing with the corners. However, it is not the only way. Cut-off borders have an unschooled, folk-art look. For a scrappy,

Block shapes and angles provide ideas for custom borders. In this Cabbage Rose quilt by Sara Nephew, 1988, the custom border of rosebuds is devised from shapes already found in the block. Since the block incorporates multiple shapes, there is no need to introduce unrelated shapes in the border. Block patches are enlarged to a size suitable for a border. Notice how the dogtooth border is made of equilateral triangles to echo the angles in the blocks. Center units and corner units help with border fit and graceful cornering. The pattern for this quilt is in Sara's book, *Stars and Flowers: Three-sided Patchwork,* available from Clearview Triangle, 8311 180th St. S. E., Snohomish, Washington 98290-4802.

casual quilt with a spontaneous quality, cut-off borders are perfect. For more formal quilts, you will want to find a way to go around the corners of your pieced borders gracefully.

Occasionally, pieced borders are centered carefully on each side of a square quilt and cut off at a 45° angle at the corners. The corners are then mitered, and because each border ends at the same point on the pieced pattern, the corners flow gracefully.

Sometimes there are square blocks in the corners, and the pieced borders conclude without going around the corner. In such cases, the pieced border strips need to be planned to start and end with complete motifs.

More often, the pieced design continues in some fashion around the corner. Sometimes the pattern will reverse at the corners. Sometimes a variation on the pattern may be required to make a graceful turn. It is usually easy to come up with an attractive way to flow around the corner of a pieced border. Study the quilts in this book and the designs in the Stock Borders chapter to see how we have accomplished this.

Block corners and well-planned repeats help pieced borders turn the corners gracefully. This Border Sampler quilt, made by Marsha in 1994, has a number of different pieced borders, each flowing around a corner gracefully. The checkerboard, dogtooth, and various chain-of-squares borders all accomplish their cornering with the simple addition of another border repeat. The key here is in fitting the border to the quilt center so that a border unit ends at each edge of the quilt. The outer border has blocks in the corners. No pattern.

Reverses

These are changes of direction of the border pattern. Many times, border motifs are asymmetrical, and you may want to achieve symmetry in your quilt by reversing the direction at the border corners or at the centers of each side.

Even a simple border such as a sawtooth can have myriad looks, depending on directional considerations. Units can be arranged to face the same direction throughout. Border units can run clockwise or counterclockwise. They can reverse directions at the corners or at the centers of each border. Border units can face toward or away from the center. Study the borders in the quilt photos throughout the book and in the drawings in the Stock Borders chapter to see the different effects you can achieve by playing with directional elements. The sawtooth border is particularly versatile.

Corner Units and Center Units

Some borders have different piecing units in the border corners or at the center of two or four sides of the border. These are called "corner units" and "center units" respectively. They may be required in order for the pattern to flow around the corners, to switch directions at the center of each side, or to fit when the border repeat does not naturally fit the dimensions of the quilt center. The Father's Fancy quilt below has these units.

Reversing the sawtooths at the center of each side makes a symmetrical border. In Father's Fancy, made by Judy Martin in 1992, the sawtooth border changes direction at the center of each side. This makes a balanced border from an asymmetrical border repeat. The direction of the sawtooths in the border echoes the triangles in the blocks. The Nine-Patches in the corners of the quilt and the plain white center units also repeat block elements. The center units allow the border to fit with an even number of repeats for balance. No pattern.

Natural-fit borders make planning easy. A good general rule for planning an appropriate pieced border for your quilt is to incorporate one or more patches from the block in the border. If your quilt has a 2" square, look for a border that can be made using a 2" square. This rule helps you plan an attractive border look, and if it is taken a step further, it can help you achieve an easy fit, too. Scrap Basket was made by Marsha McCloskey in 1988. The block measures 8"; the 2" border square is taken from the top corner of the block. The border look has a natural tie-in to the blocks. The fit is natural, too, because the patch orientation is the same in the blocks and border. Blocks are set diagonally, turning the squares diagonally. Squares in the border are also on the diagonal. The border repeat is the diagonal of a 2" square (two square roots of two, although we don't need to calculate this). The running dimension of one block on the diagonal is the same as four diagonals of a 2" square (eight square roots of two). Four repeats exactly fit alongside one block. No matter how many blocks are in the quilt, the border will fit with a minimum of fuss and figuring. The pattern for this quilt is in Marsha's book, *Lessons in Machine Piecing*.

Keys to Border Fit

Once you decide how you want the borders and corners to look, you must ensure that the border will fit the quilt center in such a way that the desired part of the pattern falls at the corner. We have some easy ways to accomplish this. Before you go off to enjoy the border illustrations, take a moment to learn the secrets here, as considerations of fit may affect your choice of borders.

This chapter covers key concepts that we use to make borders fit easily and naturally. For more details see the Design & Drafting chapter.

Border Repeats

Just as the quilt center is made from manageable units, usually blocks, pieced borders are made from manageable units. They are called border repeats. These units break down the border into small sections to help us design and construct it easily. A repeat can be a simple block or it can be some other shape. Study the illustrations in the Stock Borders chapter to see various pieced borders and the border repeats from which they are made. Repeats are sewn end to end down the length of the border. Sometimes the seams are perpendicular to the edge of the border. Sometimes they are at an angle other than 90°. For example, in a chain-of-squares border, such as the one in Scrap Basket at left, the border repeat is a unit comprising two right triangles sewn to opposite ends of a square. In this example, the seams joining border repeats are at a 45° angle to the edge of the border.

The running dimension of the border repeat is an important factor in quilt planning. Measure border repeats as finished sizes, not including seam allowances. The measurement is always from the beginning of one border repeat to the beginning of the next one, down the length of the border. In the chain of squares example, if the triangle measures 4" (finished) on the long edge, we say the pattern has a 4" border repeat because a new unit starts every 4" along the border. The patterns in the Stock Borders chapter list the sizes of the border repeats. Any pattern can be made from a variety of patch sizes, and the border repeat will be a different size when you use a different size of patch. You can choose a patch size having a border repeat that is compatible with your quilt. If you know the measurement of the quilt center, you can divide it by the size of the repeat to determine how many repeats you need for one side, not including corners.

Natural-Fit Borders

One easy way to ensure that your borders will fit your quilt center is to rely on natural fit. In this case, borders fit because the border patches are related to the block patches by virtue of a similar grid or size, shape and orientation of patches. A certain number of border repeats fits one block exactly. Suppose three border repeats fit your block exactly. Then, for every row of blocks you add to your quilt center, you add three border repeats to a border strip. With natural-fit borders, no matter how many blocks your quilt has, the border will fit. Because the shapes are drawn from the block, natural-fit borders mean less drafting and a natural tie-in to the quilt center.

Sometimes the border patches and block patches are different shapes or sizes. For example, in the Prairie Rambler quilt on page 35, the block has 2⅛" and 6" right triangles. The pieced border has 3" right triangles. In such a case, the borders may or may not fit the block naturally. Simple border repeats, such as checkerboards, sawtooths, and dogtooths often look best when they are sized to match the block's grid. When you relate the border repeat to the block's grid, you can easily achieve a natural fit. In our Prairie Rambler example, the 3" border repeat is perfectly compatible with the 9" block. Three border repeats fit exactly alongside each block, and the joints match on the blocks and borders.

Adjust the fit of made-to-measure borders with spacer strips if necessary. Carnival Ride was made by Judy Martin in 1990 and given as a pattern in her book, *Scraps, Blocks & Quilts.* Her husband, Steve, urged her to replace its plaid border with a pieced border for this book. Judy used the patch for the bright solid triangle from the block and added new shapes in prints and muslin to complete a shaded sawtooth unit. This border repeat has new shapes and a different orientation from the patches in the block; the fit is not natural. Judy made the borders 6"-7" longer than the quilt center's dimensions. The finished borders measured 65" and 78"; the center measured 58" x 72". To determine the width of spacer strips, she subtracted the quilt center from the border dimension and divided by two, calculating for length and width separately. Widths of 65" - 58" = 7" ÷ 2 = 3½"; lengths of 78" - 72" = 6" ÷ 2 = 3". She added 3½" spacer strips to the long sides of the quilt and 3" strips to the short sides. The difference is barely noticeable.

Made-to-Measure Borders

The other way to fit your borders to the quilt center is to make the parts conform to a suitable dimension. When the border patches are not directly related to the block or quilt center and the grids are not compatible, borders can still be made to fit. In this situation, we use made-to-measure borders.

Sometimes the border patches are the same size and shape as the block patches but the orientation differs. That is, they may be tilted differently. In

Spacer strips build the quilt center out to dimensions that work easily with made-to-measure border repeats. Marsha McCloskey finished California Star Medallion in 1991, three years after completing the 18¼" center block. She first added a narrow spacer strip to bring the awkward dimensions out to an even 20". The 2" sawtooth border brought the quilt out to 24", a wonderful number, being divisible by 2, 3, 4, 6, 8, and 12. The next border of stars with a 6" repeat, brought the dimensions out to 36".

The hourglass border with a 4" repeat fit next to the star border, but Marsha felt it looked crowded so she added spacer strips half the size of the repeat. She chose a large floral print for the spacers and used background blending of colors, as well, to break up the straight line between borders. The final pieced border divided the 48" space into six border repeats of 8" dogtooth triangles. The pattern for California Star Medallion is in Marsha's book, *On to Square Two.*

such a case, the fit will not be natural. You will need to make these borders according to measurements.

Sometimes blocks have no grid basis. Simply dividing the total finished block size by four or three or six (or whatever number you desire) will provide an appropriate size for the border repeat. Sometimes quilt centers are made without blocks. An example would be a Lone Star quilt. The Lone Star is not based on a grid. This is not a natural-fit situation. This is a case for making a border to match the measurement of the quilt center. Made-to-measure borders can be devised to fit block dimensions or whole quilt center measurements.

Spacer Strips

Plain borders can be included in your quilt design to separate the center of the quilt from the pieced border or a pieced border from another pieced border. This plain border is called a spacer strip because it can fill in whatever space you need. These plain border strips are employed to provide visual space. They can also adjust for discrepancies in measurements of pieced border strips and the quilt center. Spacer strips can be used simply to keep the border from visually crowding the quilt center. Sometimes you can anticipate a difference in measurements for the pieced border and quilt center and plan for a spacer strip from the outset. Occasionally you may have unexpected discrepancies due to less-than-perfect cutting and sewing. A spacer strip will provide an easy solution in such a situation, as well. Refer to the border construction chapter for complete instructions on figuring spacer strips.

Sashes the width of the border repeat keep the fit natural in sashed sets. When the block and border repeat enjoy a natural fit, don't spoil it with the wrong sash width. In Judy Martin's Summerfest quilt, made in 1992, the 2" sashes match the 2" border repeat, assuring a natural fit with the 12" blocks. In order to maintain the natural fit, any spacer strip desired for aesthetic reasons needs to measure some multiple of half the border repeat. Judy added a spacer strip of one inch, half the size of the 2" border repeat, to allow some breathing room between the sash and the sawtooth border. The Summerfest pattern is in Judy's book, *Yes You Can! Make Stunning Quilts from Simple Patterns.*

21

For square quilts and quilts with natural-fit borders, spacer strips are the same width on all four sides. For some other quilts, spacer strips may need to be made in two different widths, with top and bottom strips one width and side strips a slightly different width. Carnival Ride on page 19 is a good example of this.

Borders for Quilts with Sashes

It is easy to plan borders for quilts with sashes if you plan the borders before making the quilt. There are two ways to achieve a perfect fit. The first way, when the border repeat fits the block naturally, is to make the sash width relate to the border repeat. (You can make the sash width ½, 1, 1½, 2, 2½, 3, etc. times the border repeat.) For example, if your border repeat is 4", a good sash width would be 2" or 4". An example of a quilt sashed this way is Summerfest, page 21. With this solution, you can use sashes only between blocks or you can use sashes between blocks and around the perimeter of the quilt center as well.

The second way to achieve a good fit is to make blocks, sashes, and borders as desired and use spacer strips to adjust the

A spacer strip to match the sash fabric can adjust the fit when sash width and border repeat are unrelated. In Louise and Friends, 24" x 35", made by Country Threads in 1994, the blocks measure 7" x 9", sashes are ½", and the border repeat is 1". In this case, the blocks and border repeat fit naturally, but the sash width throws off the fit. With four block rows each having two blocks and one sash, the quilt center measures 18½" x 29½". This does not fit the 1" border repeat naturally. A spacer strip to match the color of the sashes and measuring ¾" wide adjusts the quilt's dimensions to numbers compatible with the 1" border repeat: 20" x 31". Louise and Friends is available as a pattern from Country Threads. Write to them at 2345 Palm Avenue, Garner, Iowa 50438.

fit. This was done in Louise and Friends, shown at left. Sometimes, the spacer strips may have to be different widths for the top/bottom and the side borders. When used with spacer strips, plan sashes between blocks but not around the outside edge. Cut spacer strips from the sash fabric and plan to make them slightly wider than the sashes.

Ideas for Custom Borders

Now that you know the basics of border design and fit, you are ready to use pieced borders to finish your quilts with flair. There are enough quilt patterns and border patterns in this book to keep you busy for quite some time. It never hurts to know about other possibilities, though. Just looking at the kinds of effects you can achieve with pieced borders can fuel your creativity. Even if you aren't ready to design your own custom borders now, read through this chapter to see what you can do if you take your border planning one step further. We'll teach you how to design and draft unique and new borders in the Design & Drafting chapter, but before we get into the details, let's look at some of the effects you can get with custom borders.

Custom Add-On Borders

Add-on borders are what you think of first when you picture pieced borders. Simple shapes are joined to form long, narrow pieced bands that are sewn to the edges of the quilt top. Stock add-on borders are standard patterns to mix and match with your quilt centers. We show many of these in the Stock Borders chapter beginning on page 44. Custom add-on borders are just add-on borders that you design yourself because you want to include certain shapes or motifs that you don't find in existing border patterns. You can simply adapt an existing pattern to do what you want. You'll learn more about this later in Design & Drafting.

Custom add-on borders regroup block parts to make an original border. In Judy's Flower Patch, all of the shapes needed for a beautiful border can be found in the blocks making up the quilt center. Each block in the quilt center has lozenge-shaped tulip units combined with a pair of triangles on each side to form a square. In the custom border, the same tulip units and triangles are rearranged with individual triangles in the four corners to make a rectangle. The borders frame the quilt with a closer, more linear arrangement of tulips. This quilt was designed to fit a double bed so that the triangles straddle the edge of the mattress and the tulips all stand upright around the sides and bottom of the quilt. The cut-off corners keep the quilt from dragging on the floor. For more information on designing quilts to fit specific beds, see page 89 of the Design & Drafting chapter. Judy Martin designed this quilt, which was pieced by Shirley Wegert and quilted by Phyllis Street in 1985. The pattern is in Judy's book, *Scrap Quilts*, published by Moon Over the Mountain.

Completer Borders

Sometimes a quilt has interesting design motifs that appear where the blocks are joined with their neighbors. The blocks around the edge of the quilt, in these cases, have only partial motifs. The quilt looks incomplete, or the design appears to crowd the edges. The quilt seems to need a custom border treatment that completes these designs around the edge and provides some finality. Often this kind of treatment won't appear to be bordered at all. You may still want to add a simple pieced border around this completer border.

Spontaneous Borders

These are borders that have a casual quality. Rather than being made from a predictable, repeating pattern, they change as they go along and give a contemporary or country folk art look to your quilt. If you're feeling somewhat adventurous, you'll enjoy making them.

You can map out spontaneous borders or you can let them design themselves. These are borders by instinct; they're so customized that you may not know what's coming next until you see it on a design wall. The sewing is usually very easy.

Pretty much free-form, spontaneous pieced borders are a good place to use up pieced blocks or strips of fabric left over from other projects. Join strips of

Completer borders put the finishing touch on designs where blocks combine with their neighbors to make a pattern. In two-block quilts and other patterns where a block borrows from its neighbor to make a design, the quilt center often looks truncated around the edges. Completing the blocks is not enough. You need to conclude the principal motifs, as well. In Marsha McCloskey's Sampler Quilt, 1985-1992, sampler blocks are set alternately with Chimneys and Cornerstones blocks. The backgrounds of the Chimneys and Cornerstones blocks run together with the sampler blocks' backgrounds, making the sampler blocks appear to be larger and set diagonally. A chain of navy squares frames each block. A special completer border of Chimneys and Cornerstones half-blocks alternated with custom-designed background half-blocks was needed to continue this illusion for the blocks around the edge. The pattern for this quilt is in Marsha's book, *100 Pieced Patterns for 8" Quilt Blocks*.

various lengths and widths to achieve the desired border size or make the border from an assortment of small blocks and other snippets that may or may not be related.

There are several examples of spontaneous border treatments in this book. In the Feathered Star Round Robin quilt on page 30, the outer border is made spontaneously from various strips of blue fabric. Spontaneous borders are not usually planned minutely; they simply happen. These borders suit the style of scrap quilts perfectly. Consider making every corner different or have only opposite corners match as in Long May She Wave on page 33 or the Feathered Log Cabin on page 37.

Spontaneous borders are so variable that we can't give you much concrete advice for planning or sewing them. Remember you can always add a snippet or a strip to achieve the fit you need, and you can work with a palette of related shapes and dimensions in order to make the fit come more naturally. If desired, simply chop off border sections as needed. Spontaneous borders can be combined with other border treatments, or they can stand alone. Their carefree look is perfectly compatible with an unschooled approach. Whatever you do, don't interfere with their natural growth.

Spontaneous borders and a mix of scraps in bright colors set a casual tone for a quilt. This Feathered Star quilt by Marsha McCloskey, 1993, could have been formal and elegant with another border treatment. Marsha chose, instead, a lively folk-art look with an unrestrained mix of colors, fabrics, and patterns. There is an artful randomness to this quilt. Borders are made from 8" blocks sewn into rows. A second row of blocks is sewn to two sides only; this surprising unevenness is made more obvious by the lone strip of navy running between pieced borders on the left. A similar Feathered Star block pattern begins on page 126. Use your choice of 8" blocks in the star's center and for the eclectic borders. Marsha's book *100 Pieced Patterns for 8" Quilt Blocks* is a good pattern source.

A simple change of coloring in the outer row of blocks creates a built-in border. This LeMoyne Star and Single Irish Chain quilt by Marsha McCloskey, 1990, appears to have a red chain-of-squares border surrounded by a subtle khaki dogtooth. Actually both "borders" are accomplished within the Single Irish Chain blocks. The center quilt block has eight small red squares. The corner blocks have four red and four khaki squares each; the remaining four edge blocks have six red and two khaki squares each. This simple change of coloring makes a built-in border. No pattern.

A change of background color for the outer row of blocks blends the blocks into the border. The central blocks in the Turkey in the Straw scrap quilt are made from various reds and creams. For the outer row of blocks, a single gold fabric was substituted for the creams. This change of color makes a built-in border that subtly frames the quilt. The plain gold border blends into the outer row of blocks and into the add-on border of sawtooths. The result is a quilt with no hard line between design areas. Turkey in the Straw was made by Judy Robinson in 1993. No pattern.

Built-In Borders

These often look like add-on borders, but they are pieced in blocks or half blocks that can be included with the center quilt blocks as they are set together, rather than added in long strips afterwards. Built-in borders often have a structure similar to the blocks in the quilt center, so they fit well even when your cutting and stitching are somewhat inaccurate.

Sometimes, the block from the quilt center can be simply adapted with a change of coloring to create a built-in border. The LeMoyne Star and Single Irish Chain wall quilt shown on page 26 appears to have a pieced border, but on closer inspection we see that the border effect is accomplished using Single Irish Chain blocks. It is the change of coloring that creates the chain-of-squares border. There is no extra drafting, piecing or figuring, just a little creative coloring.

Built-in borders are occasionally made from square blocks the same size as those in the quilt center, but in a different pattern. A few repeats of a stock add-on border could be joined to make a block. For a varied look, a couple of different add-on borders could be combined, with a few repeats of each making a block.

Often, built-in border units are triangular, made half the size of the quilt blocks. These triangles would be used to fill in the spaces around the edges of a quilt having blocks set diagonally. Edge triangles on diagonal sets are generally plain, but piecing can be

A built-in border adds needed detail in edge triangles. In Marsha McCloskey's Feathered Star Sampler, 1986, blocks are set diagonally and triangles square the edges. The intricate block calls for something special in the triangles. Embellished with pieced dogtooths, the triangles form a built-in border that befits the quilt. The pattern is in Marsha's book, *Feathered Star Quilts.*

included in this space to look like a pieced border. Without piecing, the edge triangles on the Feathered Star Sampler shown above would have been too large and plain in comparison to the intricate stars. Piecing in the edge triangles breaks up the space and helps tie the stars together in the composition.

With these triangular built-in borders the fit is automatic. You simply take a quarter-block or half-block triangle and run a length of border repeats parallel to the outside edge, placing it where it fits with complete repeats. Then you add plain border strips, if desired, and whatever background shapes are required to fill the shape.

Built-in borders can extend beyond the edge triangles for an uninterrupted motif. Quality Plus, made by Marsha McCloskey in 1991, has built-in borders in the edge triangles of this diagonal set. The border incorporates squares and strips similar to those in the quilt center. Marsha didn't want to crowd the navy squares, so she extended the built-in border units beyond the corners of the blocks. For construction, the units are still incorporated into the rows with the blocks. In terms of design, extended built-in borders allow the border pattern to weave into the spaces between blocks as well as to surround the blocks completely. The pattern is in Marsha's book, *On to Square Two*.

Sometimes built-in borders fill in the space of the edge triangles, and then extend a little beyond that as in the quilts Quality Plus on page 28 and Road to Colorado, page 14.

Triangular Add-on Borders

The popular Amish quilt pattern Diamond in a Square takes a square center and adds a large triangle to each of the four sides to make a square on point (the "diamond") within another square. Sets of four triangles can be added repeatedly to make a larger and larger square with more and more squares within it.

Triangular add-on borders follow this same Diamond-in-a-Square format, except that the triangles are pieced for a bordered effect. Triangular pieced borders, also called "cornering out," turn the center square on point and fill in the corners to make a new, larger square. Imagine the add-on border of your choice marching around the inside perimeter of this larger square. It can be right up against the edge or set a little inside by means of a spacer strip. Now imagine the center square in place and hiding part of your border. There you have a triangular add-on border.

The piecing goes around the two short sides of each triangle. Any stock border pattern can be used in this way. The fit is natural. You simply place the piecing in the triangle wherever it fits. Then you add strips and shapes as needed to fill the space.

Preview some triangular add-on border possibilities in the Stock Borders chapter (pp.44-79) by using a piece of

Use triangular add-on borders to frame a center square and turn it on point. These units are simply pieced triangles added to the corners of a square block or panel. In Judy Martin's Iowa Lone Star, started in 1987 and bordered in 1993, the borders feature half stars related to the central design. The remaining space is filled with spacer strips. Often, triangular add-on borders have a space first and a pieced border motif at or near the outer edge. Triangular add-on borders are easy to fit, since you simply place the pieced motif where it fits and surround it with background patches as needed. No pattern.

paper to cover up all but a triangle in the corner of an add-on border sketch. Triangular add-on borders can be combined in the same quilt with add-on borders, built-in borders, or spontaneous borders.

Medallion Quilts & Round Robins

Medallion quilts with multiple pieced borders surrounding a center block or panel are among the oldest pieced quilts found in museums in this country. Perhaps these antique quilts are still around for us to enjoy because medallion quilts have a uniqueness and grandeur that make people treat them with respect. Quilts receiving hard wear do not last two hundred years.

Design and construction of medallion quilts is basically the same as for any other quilt with a pieced border. The central design is generally smaller, and the pieced borders become the focal area. A mix of borders helps to keep a medallion quilt interesting without being too busy. Vary the border widths, employ background blending to break up the straight lines, and leave some visual space with plain borders as well. Use one or two borders with stars, pinwheels or other interesting motifs. For the rest of the borders, simplicity is the key, with checkerboards, sawtooths, dogtooths, chains of squares or diamonds and the like. Triangular pieced borders can be mixed with add-on borders to great effect.

Plan your medallion quilt on graph paper before you begin cutting and sewing, or after you see what you have so far, simply plan one border at a time.

Currently in the world of quilt-making, many groups are making round robin quilts as friendship projects. These quilts are often medallion quilts. Each quilter in a group of six or seven friends starts a quilt by making a block or center panel. Then each member of the group adds a border to each of the other quilt centers. Sometimes the quilts follow a general plan agreed upon beforehand. Often, "anything goes" is the rule. After each quilter has worked on every quilt, the finished quilt tops (now wall-hanging to bed-quilt size) are presented to the makers of the center squares.

In most round robins, templates and directions are not passed along to each successive quilter, so she must figure out for herself a way to make her border fit the existing project. The top comes to each quilter as is; the work that is already done can't be changed, only accepted and enhanced by new contributions.

Feathered Star Round Robin. This is a medallion quilt made jointly by friends Marsha McCloskey and Judy Martin in 1994. Marsha made the block from a pattern in *Feathered Star Quilts* and sent it to Judy. Judy added triangular pieced borders in a sawtooth design and an add-on border of parallelograms. Marsha got the quilt back and added an embellished dogtooth border and two rounds of spontaneous borders made from random strip lengths. Judy and Marsha enjoyed the shared experience and the challenge of working with each other's designs. Both agreed that playing with colors and fabrics that differed from their usual choices was the best part of all. No pattern.

The design and piecing of a round robin quilt is the same as that of a medallion quilt. You can use a variety of border approaches. You can't plan the entire quilt in advance; you can only plan the next border when it is your turn and you see what has come before. Working with other people's colors and designs can be both challenging and rewarding. It requires a willingness to break out of your old habits and design preconceptions. You'll need to be tolerant of others' workmanship, as well. Planning your own quilt with pieced borders is easier, but a round robin quilt project can be an enjoyable social activity and a good learning experience.

Individual differences in cutting and sewing can make it difficult to sew one person's pieced border to another's. We made two round robin projects in the course of writing this book, Calico Country Round Robin, below, and Feathered Star Round Robin shown on page 30. Where we chose not to use spacer strips, we found our piecing wasn't completely compatible. Marsha rotary cut her patches and finding them a little small (this is common with rotary cutting), corrected with skimpy seam allowances. Judy cut patches slightly larger to compensate for rotary cutting and took deeper seam allowances. Even when our patchwork ended up the right size, we had to stagger the seam allowances when joining our borders so Judy's deeper seams didn't cut off the points on Marsha's patches.

If the quilt comes to you in an awkward size, you can add spacer strips to accommodate easy border repeats. You might also employ paper folding as described on page 96 to achieve a proper fit.

Look for shapes and colors in the quilt center that can be used in your border to enhance and improve the project. You probably don't have the same fabrics in your stash that were used previously, but you likely can find similar colors and values. If not, a shopping trip with project in hand might be in order.

Pin the quilt up on the wall to study it over a period of days. Look for ideas and inspiration in the color photos and Stock Borders chapter in this book. You will probably come up with several design ideas and have to choose among them. Ego and competition have no place here, but cooperation and support do. Pay attention to what the quilt needs. It might turn out that your contribution will be only a simple sawtooth or checkerboard border, but if it will be better for the total quilt, you will be doing your share.

Calico Country Round Robin. Here is a second medallion quilt Judy and Marsha made together as a round robin in 1994. This one started with Judy's Calico Country block from her *Scraps, Blocks & Quilts* book. For this quilt, they agreed on a basic framework from the outset. The plan was to model the quilt after the Border Sampler quilt on page 16, with changes in the details to suit the block. Marsha added the first two borders; Judy added the last two. The borders include spacer strips, a dogtooth border, a chain-of-Nine-Patches border, and a sawtooth border. Nine-Patch center units and corner blocks derived from the quilt center complete the outer border. No pattern.

Gallery of Quilt Photographs

▲▲▲▲▲▲▲▲▲▲▲▲▲▲▲ F E A T U R E D P A T T E R N Q U I L T ▲▲▲▲▲▲▲▲▲▲▲▲▲▲▲

Columbia Square by Marsha McCloskey, 1994, 54¾" x 54¾". Marsha designed and made the center section of this quilt years ago as a sample for her Blocks and Borders class. By raiding Judy's fabric stash, she was able to make the final borders to complete the top for this book. The single Georgetown Circle block is framed first by very simply pieced triangular add-on borders. These border units comprise a navy triangle edged on two sides with an elegant striped fabric. The four pieced triangles turn the center on point and create a new, larger square. This square is framed by an add-on border of flying geese sewn end-to-end rather than side-by-side. A custom flourish embellishes the corners of this border. Another triangular add-on border surrounds this. Here, large, light triangles are bordered on two sides by a chain of squares. The next triangular add-on border is pieced of star blocks alternating with plain squares and edge triangles. An add-on dogtooth border and a striped navy outer border complete the quilt. The pattern is on pages 101-104.

Long May She Wave by Judy Martin, 1994, 59½" x 72¼". This original quilt has a built-in border of blocks the same size as those in the quilt center. Judy custom designed the border, adapting a natural-fit stock parallelogram border by incorporating a "spacer" divided into scrap squares. A plain spacer might have looked out of place with such a happy mix of scraps. The outer border is a sponta-neous border of random strip lengths joined end to end. This is a good border to make from fat quar-ters and fabric remnants. Two block corners and two squared corners add to the casual look of the quilt. The parallelogram border reverses at the bor-der centers, requiring an even number of repeats. This is easy to accomplish because the quilt looks better with an even number of blocks for a bal-anced arrangement of stars. The Long May She Wave pattern begins on page 105.

▲▲▲▲▲▲▲▲▲▲▲▲▲▲▲▲ **F E A T U R E D   P A T T E R N   Q U I L T** ▲▲▲▲▲▲▲▲▲▲▲▲▲▲▲▲

Meadow Lily by Marsha McCloskey, 1994, 45⅝" x 59⅝". In this quilt Marsha used her version of a traditional quilt block with a not-so-traditional border construction. Diagonally set Meadow Lily blocks are handsomely framed by a combination of chain-of-squares and chain-of-Four-Patches borders. The quilt appears to have an add-on border that is interrupted here and there by the block corners.

The look is complex, but the effect is achieved simply, not with add-on borders but with built-in borders. Square border blocks are added to the diagonal block rows of the quilt center. Each row is completed with an edge triangle, also pieced as part of the built-in border. The squares and triangles combine to make a graceful and attractive border. The Meadow Lily pattern starts on page 108.

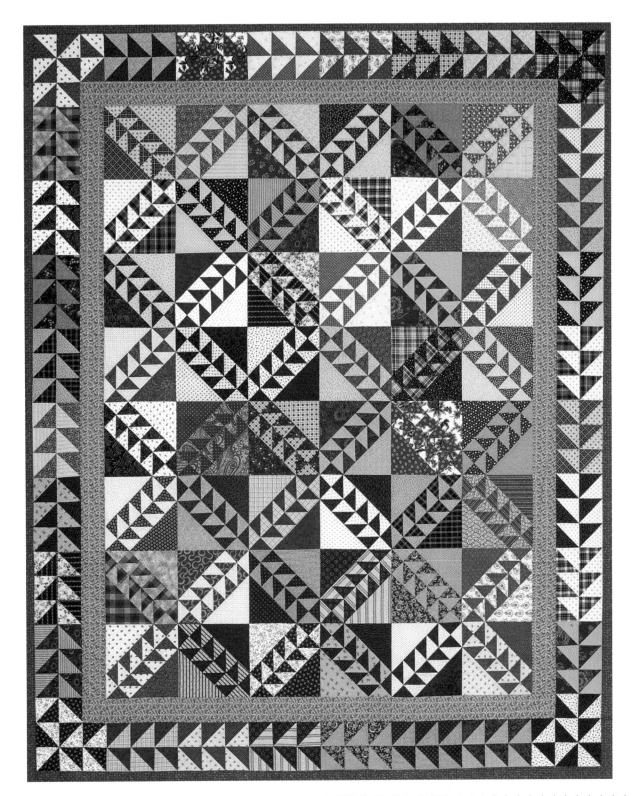

Prairie Rambler by Judy Martin, 1994, 75" x 93". The quilt block is an original variation of a traditional Rambler; add-on borders are made in a custom design taken from the block. The block motif was turned 45° and scaled up so that three border repeats fit alongside one block. A set of three border repeats was constructed of each pair of fabrics to echo the fabric usage in the blocks. A light strip was added for visual space, although it wasn't needed for a good fit. This necessitated adding a single border repeat to each end of each border, colored to match the Pinwheel block corners. While this border looks like the obvious choice for the quilt, Judy mulled border possibilities off and on for four months as she made other quilts. She drew half a dozen completely different border sketches on her computer before this solution came to mind. The quilt pattern begins on page 112.

▲▲▲▲▲▲▲▲▲▲▲▲▲▲▲▲ FEATURED PATTERN QUILT ▲▲▲▲▲▲▲▲▲▲▲▲▲▲▲▲

Swing Your Partner by Judy Martin, 1994, 66" x 81". This new quilt design has natural-fit add-on borders in two favorite old patterns, sawtooth and chain of squares. The border shapes are all found in the blocks, as well. A medium blue strip provides visual space between the borders. Its color is similar to the scrappy background triangles of the chain-of-squares border, so it blends the two areas a little. Because the value is lighter than most of the triangles, a line is apparent between the areas, as well. Judy considered sashing between blocks, but decided on a slightly different solution. For a natural fit, Judy had a choice of 1½" or 3" sashes to go with the 3" repeat of the chain-of-squares border. Judy felt that 1½" sashes put the blocks too close together and 3" sashes had patches that were larger and plainer than she intended. She chose to frame each block with 1½" strips instead. This puts two strips between neighboring blocks for more space without large patches. The pattern is on page 115.

Feathered Log Cabin by Judy Martin, 1992-1994, 62" x 82". This original Log Cabin design has a formal add-on border interrupted spontaneously by stars. Judy made the quilt center in 1992 and thought it was finished. In writing *Pieced Borders* Judy wondered why people seldom put borders, especially pieced ones, on Log Cabin quilts. She challenged herself to improve this quilt with a fitting border. In 1994 she cut two corners out of the existing bright red border to break the line, and added borders starting with a narrow spacer strip of light scraps to allow some breathing room

before the double sawtooth border. The border fit is natural, as the 1" sawtooth border repeats the sawtooth in the Feathered Log Cabin blocks. The 2" sawtooth echoes that motif and leads into a wide spacer strip with background blending. This area is pieced spontaneously of scraps. The stars in the two opposite corners add a spark of interest. Judy left two corners without stars so the sawtooth borders could turn the corner for continuity. Judy usually makes borders darker than the quilt, but she was happy with the effect of lighter borders here. The pattern is on page 118.

37

Italian Tile by Marsha McCloskey, 1994, 52" x 60". This medallion quilt was not planned ahead of time, but rather "grew" on the design wall. Marsha pieced her Italian Tile center block with easy rotary cutting dimensions, but the finished size was 10¼". As a center for a medallion, it needed to be enlarged with spacer strips to 12" before the 4" repeat border of Hourglass and Little Cedar Tree blocks (in the corners) could be added. Because of the low contrast of the colors used, the border looks like more of a background texture than an obvious repeating pattern. An extra row of Four-Patch blocks blends into the border at the top and bottom to elongate the quilt center. A dogtooth border sized to fit the grid of the block border comes next. A low-contrast single row of checks surrounds this, providing a straight line that juxtaposes nicely with the dogtooth. A few sawtooth triangles are spontaneously worked into the checkered border for added interest. A border of LeMoyne Star blocks gets extra definition and some adjustment to the fit thanks to sashes between some stars. A larger dogtooth border and single checkerboard complete the quilt. The pattern is on pages 122-125.

Feathered Star by Marsha McCloskey, 1994, 76" x 76". This is an intricate design in a favorite old pattern, subtly and simply bordered. The light pink background fabric of the blocks is eliminated from the borders to make a dark frame. The chintz floral still offers touches of pink, and it provides a justification for the two shades of green introduced in the border. Two staggered dogtooth borders combine to make a zigzag with an interesting shaded effect. The background of the pieced border blends with the sashes on one side and the outer border on the other to soften the straight lines established by the sashes. Marsha's trademark chintz border, with its bold scale and naturalistic curves, further softens the straight lines of the quilt. The Feathered Star pattern starts on page 126.

Devonshire Star by Marsha McCloskey, 1994, 50½"
x 63¼". In this original quilt design, Marsha set out
to make a quilt with built-in borders. The star
blocks in two different colorings alternate in a diagonal set. To create the built-in borders and complete the secondary square-in-a-square motifs of
the quilt center, Marsha repeated the large and
small triangles from the blocks in the edge trian-

gles. At this point the quilt design looked a little
incomplete, so she added a simple dogtooth border
to blend with the built-in border and form an
embellished zigzag. The plain outer border matches the background of the dogtooth border to blur
the line between borders. The wide, light outer border provides a visual resting place. The Devonshire
Star pattern is on pages 129-132.

▲▲▲▲▲▲▲▲▲▲▲▲▲▲▲▲ **FEATURED PATTERN QUILT** ▲▲▲▲▲▲▲▲▲▲▲▲▲▲▲▲

Starlight Log Cabin by Judy Martin, 1994, 55" x 69". This clever new quilt design combines two favorite old patterns, the Lone Star and the Log Cabin. Natural-fit add-on borders incorporate logs and checkerboards. The border is made from the same patches and fabrics as the blocks. However, in the border the light fabrics are small accents and the coral solid is more prominent. These changes in the distribution of colors help the border to contrast with the quilt center. The strong focal point of the Lone Star and the concentric rings of the barnraising set make this simply bordered quilt seem medallion-like. Judy made the pieced border wider at first, 7" to match the blocks, but she cut off the last two inches of the blue logs after studying the finished quilt top. Both Judy and Marsha feel you have to be open to changing your plans to suit the quilt. The pattern starts on page 133.

▲▲▲▲▲▲▲▲▲▲▲▲▲▲▲▲▲ FEATURED PATTERN QUILT ▲▲▲▲▲▲▲▲▲▲▲▲▲▲▲▲▲

Mountain Vistas by Judy Martin, 1994, 72" x 96". This quilt combines stock and custom add-on borders and a spontaneous outer border with an original quilt center. Judy originally planned the quilt without the stars. After making the quilt center and dogtooth borders, she was studying the quilt, trying to decide which fabric to use for spacer strips. The quilt seemed to need a little spark, so she revised her plans and added stars to complete the quilt. The fit is natural, with the staggered star border having a 6" repeat to match the central units. The dogtooth borders reorganize the same patches found in the quilt center. Judy wanted to add a 1½" spacer strip to keep the stars from crowding the center. Furthermore, she wanted to break the straight lines established in the quilt center by staggering the stars with 1½"-wide rectangular patches. To adjust for the amount of space these elements added, she could have added another spacer strip, but she preferred to "overlap" one square patch of the stars at the four corners of the quilt. This adjustment shaved three inches from the overall dimensions to allow the outer borders to fit next to the star border. The pattern is found on pages 137-139.

Harvest Time by Marsha McCloskey, 1994, 72" x 84". This simple quilt is framed by a series of simple borders to create a very striking composition. Evening Star blocks are set diagonally with alternate squares of plaid. The plaid is a similar value to the background of the stars, so the stars appear to float. Edge triangles are made from a slightly lighter plaid, and the difference suggests a border. A low-contrast dogtooth border and a dark spacer strip give the stars some breathing room. A chain-of-Pinwheels border has edge triangles that blend with the spacer strip on the inside edge and the shaded sawtooth border on the outside. The pattern for Harvest Time quilt begins on page 140.

Stock Borders

There are scores of traditional add-on borders that relate well with many blocks and quilts. We call these "stock borders." Many of the stock borders presented here are old favorites, loved for generations. Others are ones that we have devised for our own quilts through the years or that we made especially for this book. We focused on patterns that would be easy to mix and match with a variety of quilt blocks. We have done all the drawing and drafting for you, and on this and the following page you will find charts to help with the figuring.

Borders are arranged by families, based on construction. Read the introduction to each family for tips on planning and construction. Borders, with corners, are shown in scale drawings. Centers are indicated by an arrow for those borders where repeats reverse. Border repeats are indicated by a line ending with dots. Under each border, we list border repeat sizes that use patches in this book. Of course, you can make these borders in other sizes if you want to draft the patterns.

Full-size pattern shapes for stock borders begin on page 145. If you don't find your desired patch size here, don't worry. If you have made the blocks for the quilt center, chances are you already have the pattern pieces in the right size for your quilt. You can make a repeat and measure it, or you can base your figuring on the relationship to the block.

The border repeat sizes listed were chosen, wherever possible, to fit popular block sizes set straight or diagonally. A few borders, such as some of the diamond borders on page 74, probably will require a spacer strip. The repeat dimensions are not likely to fit naturally with typical quilt centers. Aside from these few, though, natural fit can be achieved simply by choosing a repeat compatible with the block in your quilt center. Some border repeats fit straight sets and others fit diagonal sets.

If you see a border repeat size with decimals or fractions, it was probably included because it fits a diagonal set. This does not mean that rotary cutting, sewing or planning will be tricky. See the chart on this page. Blocks in common sizes, when they are measured from point to point as they are in diagonal sets, have dimensions that include decimals or fractions. See the Finished Size of Patches chart on page 45. Common patches, such as the ubiquitous 2" triangle, T2, also have some dimensions with decimals or fractions. These same odd-looking numbers, such as 1.414 and 2⅛ come up again and again in patchwork. If you see a border repeat with an odd-looking dimension, you will probably find the same odd number in the charts here. Furthermore, you will likely find that the number is for a block or patch that is an old friend.

To find a border suitable for your quilt center, look up your block size in the chart below. Follow the box for your block size to the right to the column for straight or diagonal sets, whichever you used for your quilt center. Any of the border repeats listed in that box will fit naturally. Look for a border repeat having one of the same numbers.

Border Repeats to Fit Blocks in the Quilt Center

Block Size (side)	Fits Size of Repeat Straight Sets	Diagonal Measure of Block	Fits Size of Repeat Diagonal Sets	# Border Repeats per Block All Sets
6"	1"	8½"	1.414"	6
	1½"		2⅛"	4
	2"		2.828"	3
	3"		4¼"	2
	6"		8½"	1
8"	1"	11.314"	1.414"	8
	2"		2.828"	4
	4"		5.657"	2
	8"		11.314"	1
9"	1"	12¾"	1.414"	9
	1½"		2⅛"	6
	3"		4¼"	3
	9"		12¾"	1
10"	1"	14.142"	1.414"	10
	2"		2.828"	5
	2½"		3.535"	4
	5"		7.071"	2
	10"		14.142"	1
12"	1"	17"	1.414"	12
	1½"		2⅛"	8
	2"		2.828"	6
	3"		4¼"	4
	4"		5.657"	3
	6"		8½"	2
	12"		17"	1
14"	1"	19.799"	1.414"	14
	2"		2.828"	7

Finished Size of Patches from This Book

Patch Letter	Short Side	Long Side
D1	1.414"	
D2	1¾"	
D3	3"	
D4	1½"	
R1	2"	4"
R2	1"	2"
R3	1"	3"
R4	1"	4"
R5	1"	5"
R6	1"	6"
R7	1"	7"
R8	1"	8"
R9	1"	9"
R10	1"	10"
R11	1½"	12"
R12	1.333"	6"
R13	2⁹⁄₁₆"	21³⁄₁₆"
R14	1¾"	6"
R15	1.667"	6"
R16	2"	8"
R17	2"	10"
R18	1⅝"	21³⁄₁₆"
R19	1.714"	6"
R20	1½"	3"
R21	1½"	7½"
R22	1½"	4½"
R23	2⅛"	8½"
R24	1½"	6"
R25	4"	6"
R26	4"	8"
S1	1"	
S2	2"	
S3	3"	
S4	4"	
S5	10"	
S6	6"	
S7	1½"	
S8	2⅛"	
S9	4¼"	
S10	5⅝"	
S11	1¾"	
S12	8½"	
S13	8"	
S14	1⅝"	
S15	2⁹⁄₁₆"	
S16	12"	
S17	2.828"	
S18	2½"	
S19	0.943"	

Patch Letter	Short Side	Long Side
T1	1"	1.414"
T2	2"	2.828"
T3	3"	4¼"
T4	4"	5.657"
T5	5"	7.071"
T6	6"	8½"
T7	1½"	2⅛"
T8	2⅛"	3"
T9	4¼"	6"
T10	6½"	9³⁄₁₆"
T11	1¾"	2½"
T12	1⅛"	1⅝"
T13	2.828"	4"
T14	3.536"	5"
T15	1.414"	2"
T16	3.447"	4.592"
T17	7.071"	10"
T18	2½"	3.536"
T19	8½"	12"
T20	9"	12¾"
T21	5.657"	8"
T22	8"	11.314"
T23	1½"	3", 3.354"
T24	3"	6", 6.708"
T25	3"	3.354"
T26	3.354"	6"
T27	3"	5.543"
T28	2.296"	3"
T29	6"	6.708"
T30	1½"	2.772"
T31	1⅝"	3"
T32	6.364"	9"
T33	1⅝"	3", 3.920"
X1	3"	4¼", 8½"
X2	1.414"	1⅝"
X3	2⅛"	3"
X4	2"	2.828", 5.657"
X5	4"	8½", 14⅛"
X6	2"	5.657", 6"
X7	1", 1.414"	1.343", 2.343"
X8	1", 1.414"	3.343", 4.343"
X9	1", 1.414"	5.343", 6.343"
X10	1", 1.414"	7.343", 8.343"
X11	1", 1.414"	2.586", 3.586"
X12	1", 1.414"	3.172", 4.172"
X13	2⅛"	3", 6"
X14	2⅛"	6"
X15	2⅛"	9", 12"
X16	1½"	2⅛", 3"
X17	3"	6.708"

Checkerboard Borders

Checkerboard borders are made from only squares or rectangles or a combination of the two. The squares and rectangles can be any size. They can be modified to fit any grid found in your quilt center. Thus a border of any width and length you require can be divided into repeats using paper folding (page 96) or a calculator and ruler (page 98) to make a checkerboard.

A single band of squares or rectangles can be used, or two or more bands can be made separately and joined side by side, or made as a single, wide border having several patches in a row for a repeat.

Any of the checkerboard patterns shown can be adapted to rectangles having different proportions. A good example is border pattern #12, which can be made with longer or shorter rectangles as needed to fit your quilt center.

Natural Fit

For a natural fit, make the checkerboard to fit the grid of the block in the quilt center. If the block dimension is a multiple of the border repeat (or for diagonally set blocks, if the block's diagonal dimension is a multiple of the border repeat) the fit is also natural. For some checkerboards with gradated colors, the repeat is several squares wide. You can adjust the number of colors to make the repeat fit the quilt center. For other situations, add spacer strips to build the quilt center out to a dimension divisible by the repeat.

Graphing the Designs

The squares and rectangles for checkerboard designs and patterns can be drawn with all sides on the graph lines. For squares, count the same number of graph squares in length and width. For rectangles, count a different number of graph squares in length and width. Usually, but not always, the length of a rectangle is some multiple of the width. See some common squares and rectangles graphed on page 84.

Fabrics and Colors

Any of these designs can be made with just two colors or two fabrics that contrast highly. This produces a true checkerboard look. If you use more than two colors or values, different looks result. Colors can blend for gradated effects, or low contrast scrap fabrics can be combined for a subtle, tex-

tured rather than patterned look. When half of the squares on one edge match the neighboring design area, background blending softens the line between design areas.

Grainline and Cutting

Squares and rectangles are cut with the straight grain of the fabric along each side of the patch. We prefer lengthwise grain on the long edge of rectangles. If you need to cut squares or rectangles in dimensions not listed here, be sure to add ½" to the finished dimensions for ¼" seam allowances.

Border Repeats & Piecing

The repeating border unit comprises two or more squares or rectangles joined in one or more rows. Usually, all of the rows of squares or rectangles are joined together to make a unit before the units are sewn into border-length patchwork. Study the patterns here to see how a new repeat starts when a complete color sequence begins again.

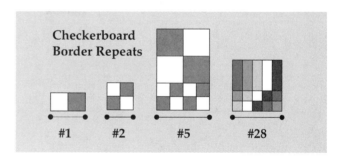

Checkerboard Border Repeats

#1   #2   #5   #28

Corners

In two-color checkerboards, the pattern is so uniform that it doesn't usually look out of balance with whole repeats and colors ending differently in two of the corners. If you are concerned about perfect balance, you may need a half repeat added to make all four corners match. For more elaborate colorings, an effective corner treatment may be to simply continue the established sequence to the corner at one end of a border strip and to interrupt it at the other end with a continuation of the adjacent sequence of colors. See border #20.

Pressing

Oppose seam allowances at the joints, generally pressing toward the darker fabric. Pin at each joint to keep the seam allowances controlled as you stitch across the joints.

1. Single Checkerboard

2": S1	4¼": S8
3": S7	5": S18
4": S2	6": S3

2. Double Checkerboard

2": S1	4¼": S8
3": S7	5": S18
4": S2	6": S3

3. Triple Checkerboard

2": S1	4¼": S8
3": S7	5": S18
4": S2	6": S3

4. Quadruple Checkerboard

2": S1	4¼": S8
3": S7	5": S18
4": S2	6": S3

5. Big & Little Checkerboard

4": S1, S2	8": S2, S4
6": S7, S3	

6. Big & Little Checkerboard

4": S1, S2	8": S2, S4
6": S7, S3	

7. Big & Little Checkerboard

4": S1, S2	8": S2, S4
6": S7, S3	

8. Big & Little Checkerboard

4": S1, S2	6": S7, S3

9. Big & Little Checkerboard

4": S1, S2	8": S2, S4
6": S7, S3	

10. Big & Little Checkerboard

4": S1, S2	8": S2, S4
6": S7, S3	

11. Nine-Patches & Rails
5": S1, R2   10": S2, R1
7½": S7, R20

12. Nine-Patches & Rails
6": S1, R3	10": S1, R7
8": S1, R5	12": S7, R21
9": S1, R6	14": S2, R16

13. Checks and Rails
8": S1, R2, R3
12": S7, R20, R22

14. Single Irish Chain
4": S1, R3   6": S7, R22

15. Double Irish Chain
8": S1, R3, R5
12": S7, R22, R21

16. Trip Around the World
4": S1   8": S2
6": S7   8½": S8

17. Trip Around the World
4": S1   8": S2
6": S7   8½": S8

18. Trip Around the World
5": S1   10": S2
7½": S7   12½": S18

19. Trip Around the World
5": S1   10": S2
7½": S7   12½": S18

20. Trip Around the World
5": S1   10": S2
7½": S7   12½": S18

21. Checkerboard & Logs
2": S1, R2, R3, R4, R5
3": S7, R20, R22, R24, R21

22. Keyboard
2": S1, R2, R3
3": S7, R20, R22

23. Zigzag & Logs
4": S1, R2, R3, R4
6": S7, R20, R22, R24

24. Zigzag & Logs
4": S1, R2, R3, R4
6": S7, R20, R22, R24

25. Checkerboard & Logs
2": S1, R3
3": S7, R22

26. Zigzag & Logs
4": S1, R2, R3, R4
6": S7, R20, R22, R24

27. Zigzag & Logs
4": S1, R2, R3, R4
6": S7, R20, R22, R24

28. Steps & Logs
5": S1, R3
7½": S7, R22

29. Single Checkerboard & Logs
2": S1, R3
3": S7, R22

30. Checkerboard & Logs
2": S1, R2, R3
3": S7, R20, R22

49

Chain-of-Squares Borders

Chain-of-squares borders are made of rows of squares set on the diagonal with triangles filling in along the edges. There can be single, double or even triple rows of squares. The squares can be plain or pieced; they can be all the same size or a combination of different sizes. The triangles along the edges also can be plain or embellished with piecing.

Coloring

In the plainer examples such as borders #31-38, various shadings can be employed to emphasize different aspects of the design. Adjacent squares can have high contrast to achieve a diagonal checkerboard look (#35), or they can gradate from light to dark for a softer look (#38). Edge triangles don't have to be all one shade. They can be dark on the outside and light on the inside or vice versa. In the pages that follow we have shown several variations. You could easily imagine more. Stay alert to opportunities to background blend the edge triangles with adjacent borders.

Design

In this border type, it is easy to pick up square design elements from blocks in the quilt center and incorporate them in the diagonally set squares. Border #51 is a chain of Nine-Patch squares, while Border #55 is a chain of Pinwheel squares. If these elements are found in your quilt, these borders would be a good choice. Actually, any square block design could be incorporated into a chain-of-squares border. You could choose simple blocks like the Shoo-fly (#54), Evening Star (#189), or Log Cabin (#57). You could even select more intricate designs like Judy's Long May She Wave (page 33) or a Feathered Star. Look through books that have lots of block ideas like *Judy Martin's Ultimate Book of Quilt Block Patterns* or Marsha's *100 Pieced Patterns for 8" Blocks.* Look for a block that you like and then imagine several of the same blocks set on the diagonal and strung out in a row. One interesting idea is to make your border a sampler of blocks and have every square in the chain be a different design.

Natural Fit

If you study the border sketches in this chapter, 50 you will see that the border repeats often start a half repeat from the corner. This is just a matter of construction units. (See the figures for the Piecing Border Repeats paragraph.) If your quilt center measurement is divisible by the border repeat, the fit will be natural. If you choose a design element from your quilt block for a chain-of-squares border, you can use patches from your blocks in the border to achieve a natural fit, providing patches are used in the same orientation. An easy fit can also be achieved if the border repeat matches or can be evenly divided into the block dimension. In other situations, a spacer strip could be added to the quilt center to bring it out to dimensions divisible by the repeat.

Graphing the Designs

The repeat of a chain-of-squares border is the length of the diagonal dimension of the square (also the long side of the edge triangle). It can be drawn on graph paper two ways: with the long side of the edge triangles on a line of the graph paper and sides of the squares on the invisible diagonal grid, or with the long side of the edge triangle on the diagonal grid and the sides of the squares on the graph paper lines. Once you have drawn the basic structure of the border, you can add some lines and drop out others to make design variations.

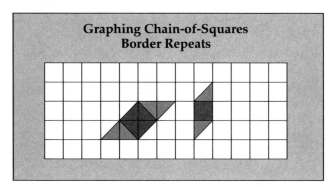

Graphing Chain-of-Squares Border Repeats

Grainline and Cutting

Squares should be cut with the straight grain along the edge. If squares are pieced blocks, straight grain should fall along the outside edges of the blocks. The edge triangles of the border repeat should be cut with the straight grain on the long side for stability and to permit accurate measuring of the completed border strip. If bias is placed on the long side of the triangles, the outside edge of the borders becomes stretchy and difficult to attach smoothly. The smaller triangles in the corners of the border have straight grain on the short sides.

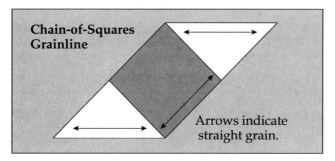

Chain-of-Squares Grainline

Arrows indicate straight grain.

Trimming Points

Trim the points of the edge triangles to align with square patches for ease of construction. Use the trim line indicated on the master patterns that is perpendicular to the short side of the triangle.

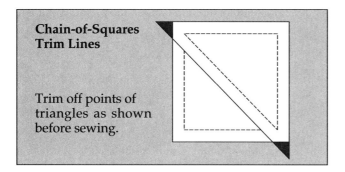

Chain-of-Squares Trim Lines

Trim off points of triangles as shown before sewing.

Piecing Border Repeats

The basic pieced repeat of a chain of squares is a square or block turned diagonally (on point) with triangles sewn to opposite sides to make a parallelogram. At times, two or three squares are sewn together in a row with triangles at either end.

Long pieced border strips are made by joining repeats along their long edges, opposing seams and pinning at each joint.

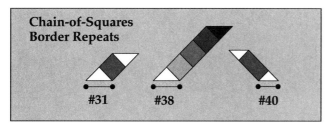

Chain-of-Squares Border Repeats

#31   #38   #40

Corners

After joining the border repeats, additional border units are needed at the corners of the quilt. See the corner diagram on this page. Unit A has a small triangle in place of one of the large triangles of a repeat. Unit B also has a small triangle, but it is positioned differently. Unit C has the two large triangles sewn to adjacent sides of the square. Unit D has two large triangles sewn to opposite sides of

the square, but turned differently from the repeat; a small triangle completes Unit D. Study the corners of the borders on the following pages. The first two strips to be sewn to the quilt center end with Units A and B as shown below. The last two border strips have a Unit C at one end. A Unit D at each corner completes the border.

Chain-of-Squares Corners

Pressing

Within a border repeat, press seams away from the square or block. If there are multiple squares in a repeat, as in a triple chain of squares, press seam allowances away from the first square, toward the second, away from the third, and so on. Seam allowances that join one repeat to the next should be pressed toward one side. This will mean that they turn away from one point on the edge triangle and toward the next point in the pattern. You are going to have to force seams one way or the other to keep them from twisting. Press them all to the right or all to the left. If you prefer, press toward one point and away from the next point. Pin at each joint to keep the seam allowances controlled when you stitch the border to the quilt.

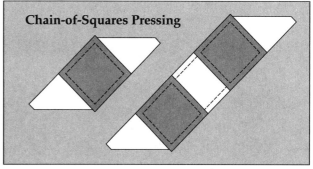

Chain-of-Squares Pressing

51

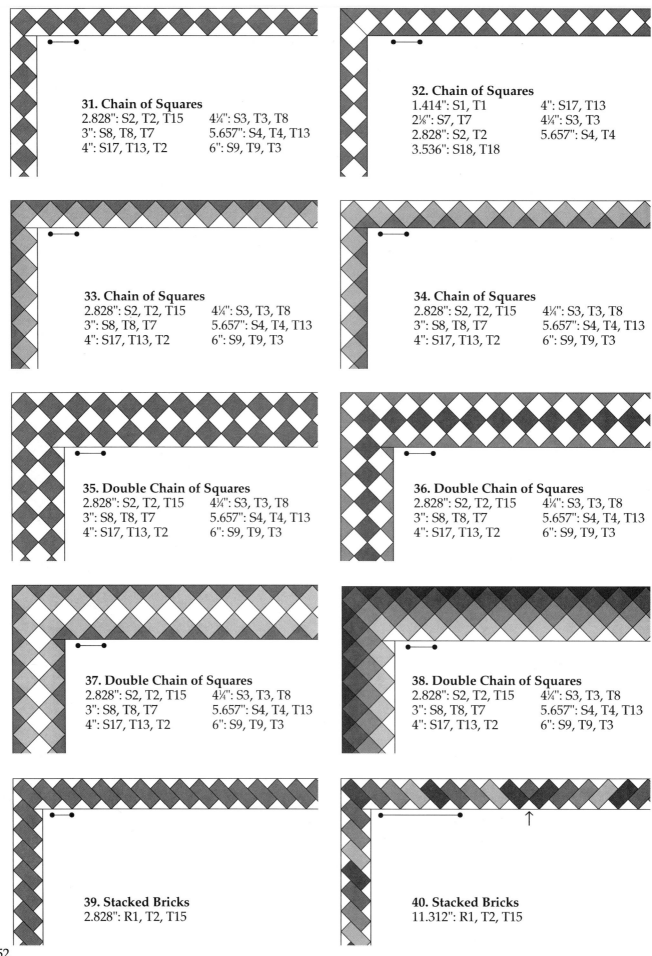

31. Chain of Squares

2.828": S2, T2, T15	4¼": S3, T3, T8
3": S8, T8, T7	5.657": S4, T4, T13
4": S17, T13, T2	6": S9, T9, T3

32. Chain of Squares

1.414": S1, T1	4": S17, T13
2⅛": S7, T7	4¼": S3, T3
2.828": S2, T2	5.657": S4, T4
3.536": S18, T18	

33. Chain of Squares

2.828": S2, T2, T15	4¼": S3, T3, T8
3": S8, T8, T7	5.657": S4, T4, T13
4": S17, T13, T2	6": S9, T9, T3

34. Chain of Squares

2.828": S2, T2, T15	4¼": S3, T3, T8
3": S8, T8, T7	5.657": S4, T4, T13
4": S17, T13, T2	6": S9, T9, T3

35. Double Chain of Squares

2.828": S2, T2, T15	4¼": S3, T3, T8
3": S8, T8, T7	5.657": S4, T4, T13
4": S17, T13, T2	6": S9, T9, T3

36. Double Chain of Squares

2.828": S2, T2, T15	4¼": S3, T3, T8
3": S8, T8, T7	5.657": S4, T4, T13
4": S17, T13, T2	6": S9, T9, T3

37. Double Chain of Squares

2.828": S2, T2, T15	4¼": S3, T3, T8
3": S8, T8, T7	5.657": S4, T4, T13
4": S17, T13, T2	6": S9, T9, T3

38. Double Chain of Squares

2.828": S2, T2, T15	4¼": S3, T3, T8
3": S8, T8, T7	5.657": S4, T4, T13
4": S17, T13, T2	6": S9, T9, T3

39. Stacked Bricks
2.828": R1, T2, T15

40. Stacked Bricks
11.312": R1, T2, T15

41. Big & Little Chain of Squares
2.828": S1, S2, T1, T15
4¼": S7, S3, T7, T8
6": S8, S9, T8, T3
8½": S3, S6, T3, T9

42. Big & Little Chain of Squares
2.828": S1, S2, T1, T15
4¼": S7, S3, T7, T8
6": S8, S9, T8, T3
8½": S3, S6, T3, T9

43. Chain of Hourglasses
2": T15, T1   4¼": T3, T8
2.828": T2, T15   5": T14, T18
3": T8, T7   6": T9, T3

44. Chain of Hourglasses
2": T15, T1   4¼": T3, T8
2.828": T2, T15   5": T14, T18
3": T8, T7   6": T9, T3

45. Big & Little Chain of Squares
2.828": S1, S2, T1, T15
4¼": S7, S3, T7, T8
6": S8, S9, T8, T3
8½": S3, S6, T3, T9

46. Big & Little Chain of Squares
2.828": S1, S2, T2   6": S8, S9, T9
4¼": S7, S3, T3   8½": S3, S6, T6

47. Big & Little Chain of Squares
2.828": S1, S2, T2   6": S8, S9, T9
4¼": S7, S3, T3   8½": S3, S6, T6

48. Double Chain of Sawtooths
2⅛": T8, T7, S7   4¼": T9, T3, S3
3": T3, T8, S8   6": T6, T9, S9
4": T4, T13, S17

49. Chain of Crosses
8½": T2, S2, R1, T15

50. Nonsense Chain
8½": T2, S2, R1, T15, S17

51. Chain of Nine-Patches
4": S19, T13, T2
4¼": S1, T3, T8

52. Chain of Squares & Nine-Patches
8": S19, S17, T13, T2
8½": S1, S3, T3, T8

53. Chain of Squares & Four-Patches
5.657": S1, S2, T2, T15
8½": S7, S3, T3, T8
11.314": S2, S4, T4, T13
12": S8, S9, T9, T3

54. Chain of Shoo-Flies
8½": T2, S2, T6, T9

55. Chain of Pinwheels
2.828": T1, T2, T15
4": T15, T13, T2
4¼": T7, T3, T8
6": T8, T9, T3
7.071": T14, T5, T18

56. Chain of Pinwheels
2.828": T1, T2
4": T15, T13
4¼": T7, T3
6": T8, T9
7.071": T18, T5

57. Chain of Log Cabins
7.071": S1, R2, R3, R4, R5, T5, T14

58. Chain of Log Cabins
7.071": S1, S18, R2, R3, R4, R5, T18, T5, T14

59. Chain of Nine-Patches & Stripes
8½": S1, R3, S3, T3, T8

60. Chain of Stars & Stripes
11.314": S1, R4, T1, T15, T4, T13, S2
17": S7, T7, T8, R24, S3, T9, T6
24": S8, T8, S9, T6, R23, T19, T3

Dogtooth Borders

Dogtooth borders are made from isosceles triangles (having two sides the same length). The straight grain of the fabric is placed along the third (the different) side, and triangles are joined to their neighbors turned head to foot. Dogtooth triangles are most commonly 1) isosceles right triangles, 2) equilateral triangles 3) narrow triangles having equal base and altitude or 4) wide triangles having a base four times the altitude as shown below.

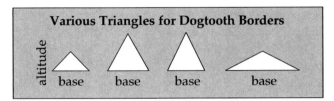

Various Triangles for Dogtooth Borders

altitude / base / base / base / base

However, any triangle having two equal sides can be used, even triangles having irregular numbers or odd angles. Thus a border of any width and length you require can be divided into repeats using paper folding (page 96) or a calculator and ruler (page 98) to make a dogtooth pattern.

A single band of triangles can be used, or two or more bands can be made separately and joined side by side. If two bands are staggered, we call the pattern a zigzag. Big and little triangles can be combined for more elaborate borders.

Any of the dogtooth patterns shown with right angles can be adapted to isosceles triangles having other angles. For example, a wide triangle could be substituted for the isosceles right triangle in a zigzag border as shown below. You may need to work out a new corner to suit the new angles.

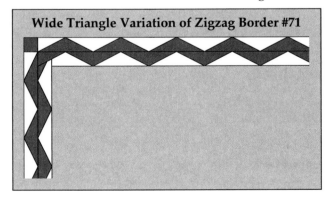

Wide Triangle Variation of Zigzag Border #71

Natural Fit

For a natural fit with one of these dogtooth borders, look for a block having the same patch in the same orientation. Natural fit is also possible if the block's grid matches the border repeat dimension. If the block dimension is a multiple of the border

repeat (or for diagonally set blocks, if the block's diagonal dimension is a multiple of the border repeat), the fit is also natural. For other situations, add spacer strips to make the quilt center a dimension divisible by the repeat, or custom design a border having a repeat that fits your quilt.

Graphing the Designs

The isosceles right triangle for dogtooth designs and full-size patterns is drawn with the long side on the graph lines and the two short sides on the diagonals. For every two graph squares on the base, draw one diagonal. The triangle's altitude is half the number of squares in the base.

If you don't have special graph paper, equilateral triangles can't be easily drawn on graph paper. Without it, you can draft the full-size pattern using a 60° angle and a ruler to mark off three equal sides and three 60° angles on plain paper. You can sketch your ideas roughly on plain paper or simply visualize them.

To graph the most common narrow dogtooth triangle, draw the base on two graph squares. From the middle of the base, go up two graph squares and make a dot. This is the top point of the triangle. Draw lines from this dot down to each end of the base, ignoring the graph lines and the graph's diagonals. For larger triangles, simply count out more squares, sticking to even numbers of squares and making the base and altitude the same.

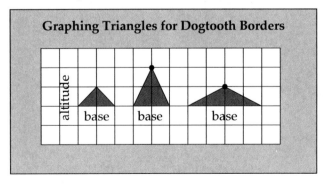

Graphing Triangles for Dogtooth Borders

altitude / base / base / base

Fabrics and Colors

Any of these designs can be made with the dark color on the outside edge or on the inside edge. A single dogtooth border is often made in just two fabrics, but scraps work well, too. When the triangles on one edge match the neighboring design area, background blending softens the line between areas. Multiple dogtooth borders or embellished dogtooth borders can be made with a 55 gradation of colors or several different colors rather than just two. We tried to show a few of the options for each border type. You can easily adapt these ideas to other specific border designs.

Grainline and Cutting

The base of a dogtooth triangle should be on the straight grain. For any half-size triangles in the corners, the straight grain should be on the two short sides. Any squares should be cut with the straight grain parallel with its edges. You can use our templates or cutting dimensions as listed in the charts or make your own. To rotary cut the isosceles right triangles for a dogtooth border, cut four triangles from a square that measures 1¼" more than the finished long side of the triangle. You may need to use templates or a template affixed to your rotary ruler to cut equilateral triangles or the patches for wide or narrow dogtooth borders.

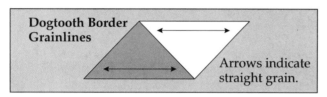

Dogtooth Border Grainlines

Arrows indicate straight grain.

Trimming Points

See the instructions for trimming points on page 146. When triangles are joined head to foot, as they are in a dogtooth border, if you trim the points you can easily align the patches properly for stitching. If the points are not trimmed, this can be tricky.

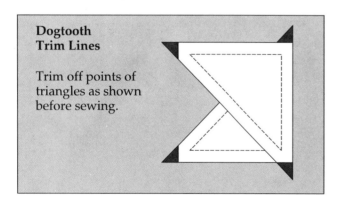

Dogtooth Trim Lines

Trim off points of triangles as shown before sewing.

Border Repeats & Piecing

The repeating border unit is angled, not square, except in the case of the split dogtooths, #95-98. The typical dogtooth repeat is made from two triangles sewn head to foot. The running dimension of the repeat is equal to the base of the triangle.

Multiple dogtooth borders can always be made and attached separately. When two neighboring dogtooth bands are staggered, as in a zigzag, this is

the only way to make them. Sometimes with other border designs, the repeating border unit follows straight through from one border band to the next, and you can piece a single wide border and attach it to the quilt all at once.

Embellished dogtooth designs are made from the same kind of slanted repeating border units as are plain dogtooth borders. Simply join the small patches to make triangles first.

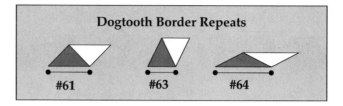

Dogtooth Border Repeats

#61   #63   #64

Corners

Borders #61 and 62 illustrate the principal corner treatments used for dogtooth borders. Often, you have a choice of corners. For staggered multiple dogtooth borders, such as the zigzags, you will need more than one kind of corner treatment.

Study the corner of your chosen design. Often, individual border strips are made from border repeats and a single triangle is added at one end. After the individual borders are attached to the quilt, corner units are added. These are triangular in shape, twice the size of the big triangle in the dogtooth. Sometimes the border strips end with a half-size triangle (and possibly a square patch) that squares the end. Sew these to the strips before attaching the borders.

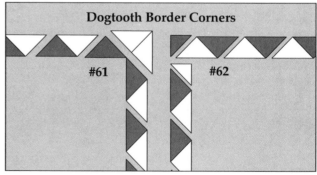

Dogtooth Border Corners

#61   #62

Pressing

Seam allowances naturally tend to turn away from the point of the triangle, and since that means they will be turning toward the next point in this pattern, you are going to have to force the seam allowances one way or the other to keep them from twisting. You can press them all to the right, all to the left or toward one point and away from the next point. Pin at each joint to keep the seam allowances controlled as you stitch.

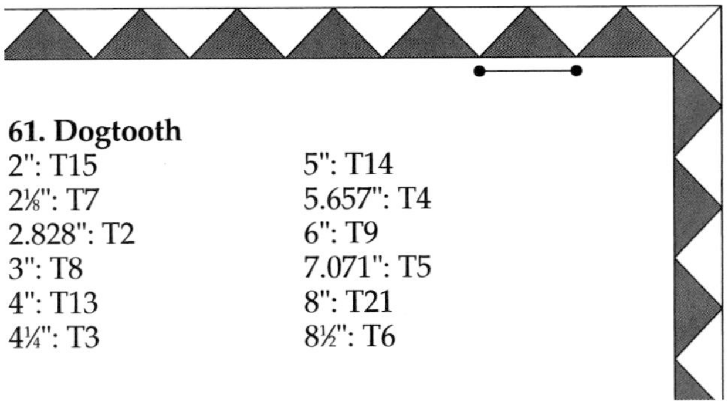

61. Dogtooth

2": T15
2⅛": T7
2.828": T2
3": T8
4": T13
4¼": T3
5": T14
5.657": T4
6": T9
7.071": T5
8": T21
8½": T6

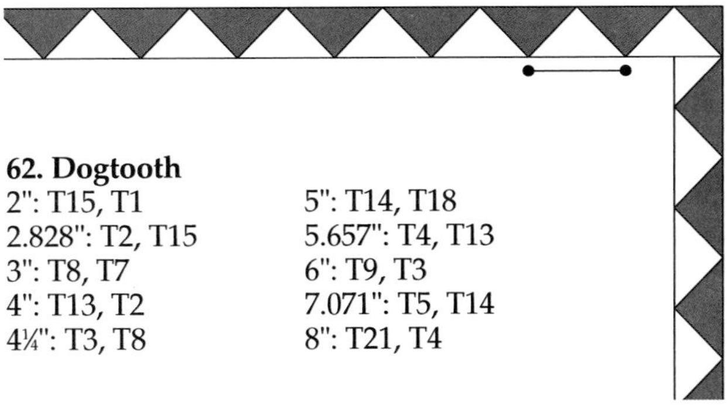

62. Dogtooth

2": T15, T1
2.828": T2, T15
3": T8, T7
4": T13, T2
4¼": T3, T8
5": T14, T18
5.657": T4, T13
6": T9, T3
7.071": T5, T14
8": T21, T4

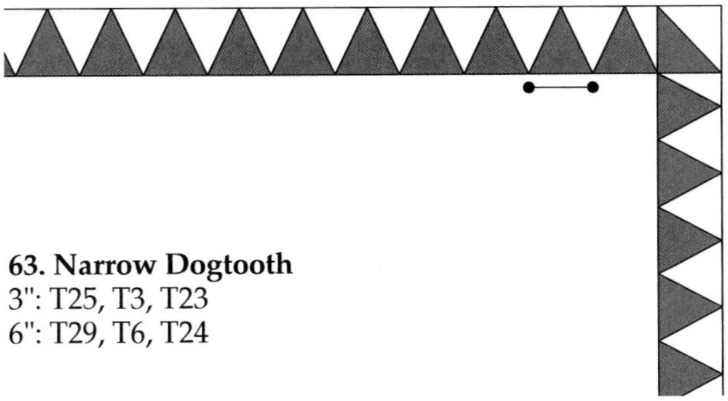

63. Narrow Dogtooth

3": T25, T3, T23
6": T29, T6, T24

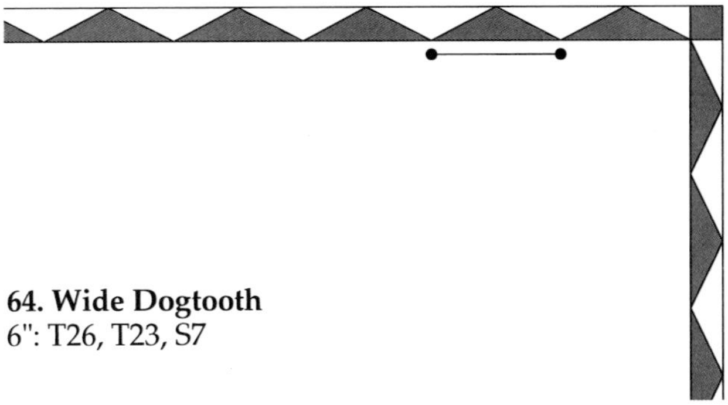

64. Wide Dogtooth

6": T26, T23, S7

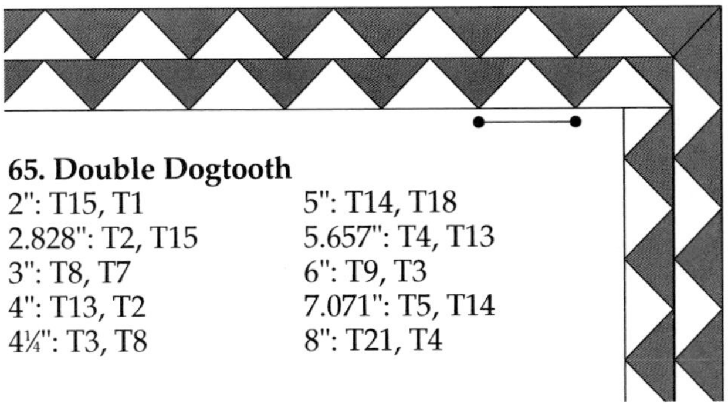

65. Double Dogtooth

2": T15, T1
2.828": T2, T15
3": T8, T7
4": T13, T2
4¼": T3, T8
5": T14, T18
5.657": T4, T13
6": T9, T3
7.071": T5, T14
8": T21, T4

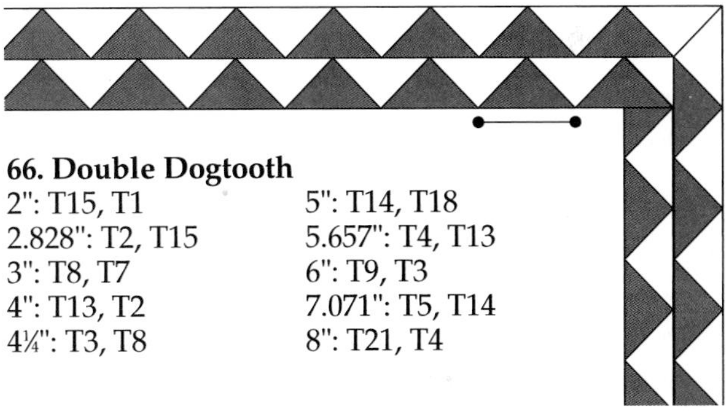

66. Double Dogtooth

2": T15, T1
2.828": T2, T15
3": T8, T7
4": T13, T2
4¼": T3, T8
5": T14, T18
5.657": T4, T13
6": T9, T3
7.071": T5, T14
8": T21, T4

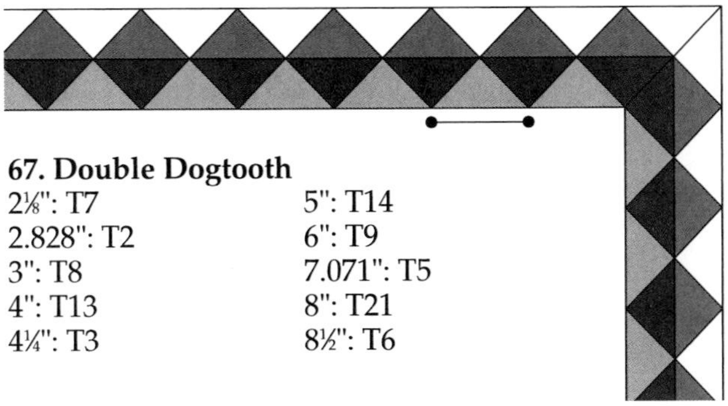

67. Double Dogtooth

2⅛": T7
2.828": T2
3": T8
4": T13
4¼": T3
5": T14
6": T9
7.071": T5
8": T21
8½": T6

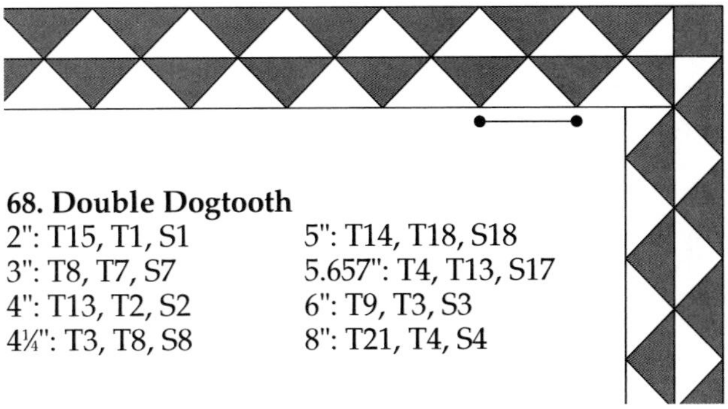

68. Double Dogtooth

2": T15, T1, S1
3": T8, T7, S7
4": T13, T2, S2
4¼": T3, T8, S8
5": T14, T18, S18
5.657": T4, T13, S17
6": T9, T3, S3
8": T21, T4, S4

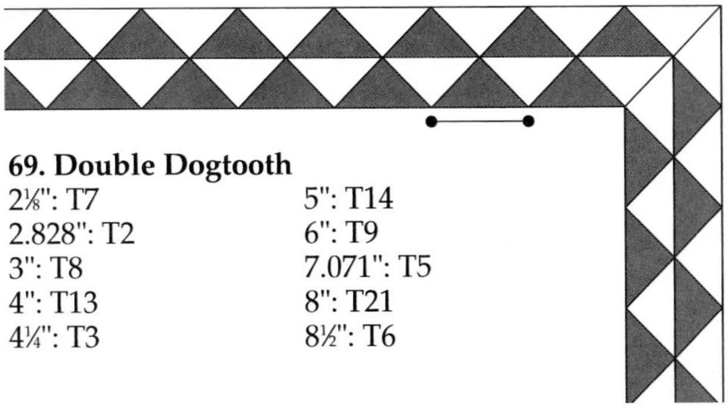

69. Double Dogtooth

2⅛": T7
2.828": T2
3": T8
4": T13
4¼": T3
5": T14
6": T9
7.071": T5
8": T21
8½": T6

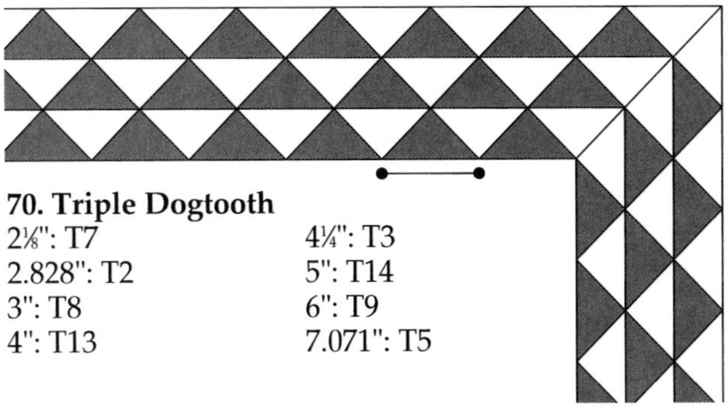

70. Triple Dogtooth

2⅛": T7
2.828": T2
3": T8
4": T13
4¼": T3
5": T14
6": T9
7.071": T5

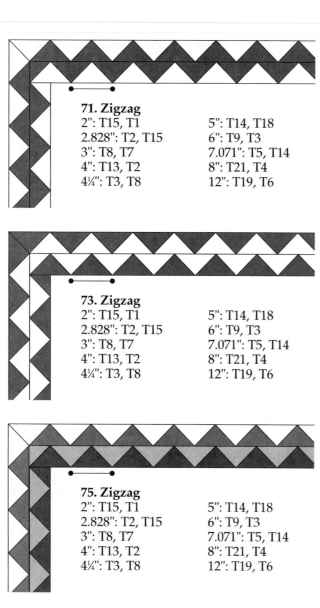

71. Zigzag

2": T15, T1	5": T14, T18
2.828": T2, T15	6": T9, T3
3": T8, T7	7.071": T5, T14
4": T13, T2	8": T21, T4
4¼": T3, T8	12": T19, T6

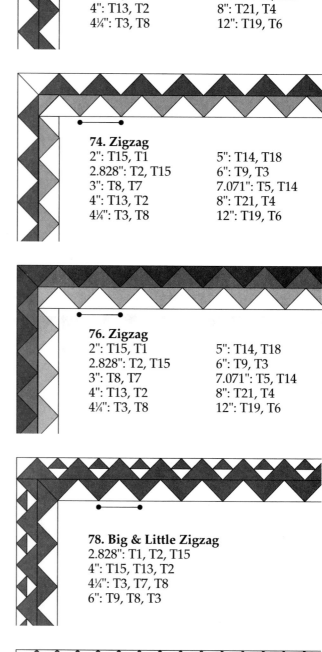

72. Zigzag

2": T15, T1	5": T14, T18
2.828": T2, T15	6": T9, T3
3": T8, T7	7.071": T5, T14
4": T13, T2	8": T21, T4
4¼": T3, T8	12": T19, T6

73. Zigzag

2": T15, T1	5": T14, T18
2.828": T2, T15	6": T9, T3
3": T8, T7	7.071": T5, T14
4": T13, T2	8": T21, T4
4¼": T3, T8	12": T19, T6

74. Zigzag

2": T15, T1	5": T14, T18
2.828": T2, T15	6": T9, T3
3": T8, T7	7.071": T5, T14
4": T13, T2	8": T21, T4
4¼": T3, T8	12": T19, T6

75. Zigzag

2": T15, T1	5": T14, T18
2.828": T2, T15	6": T9, T3
3": T8, T7	7.071": T5, T14
4": T13, T2	8": T21, T4
4¼": T3, T8	12": T19, T6

76. Zigzag

2": T15, T1	5": T14, T18
2.828": T2, T15	6": T9, T3
3": T8, T7	7.071": T5, T14
4": T13, T2	8": T21, T4
4¼": T3, T8	12": T19, T6

77. Zigzag & Dogtooth

2.828": T2, T15	5": T14, T18
3": T8, T7	6": T9, T3
4": T13, T2	7.071": T5, T14
4¼": T3, T8	8": T21, T4

78. Big & Little Zigzag

2.828": T1, T2, T15
4": T15, T13, T2
4¼": T3, T7, T8
6": T9, T8, T3

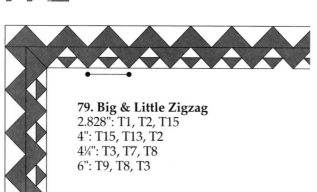

79. Big & Little Zigzag

2.828": T1, T2, T15
4": T15, T13, T2
4¼": T3, T7, T8
6": T9, T8, T3

80. Big & Little Zigzag

2.828": T1, T2, T15
4": T15, T13, T2
4¼": T3, T7, T8
6": T9, T8, T3

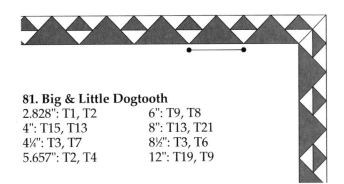

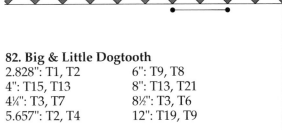

81. Big & Little Dogtooth

2.828": T1, T2	6": T9, T8
4": T15, T13	8": T13, T21
4¼": T3, T7	8½": T3, T6
5.657": T2, T4	12": T19, T9

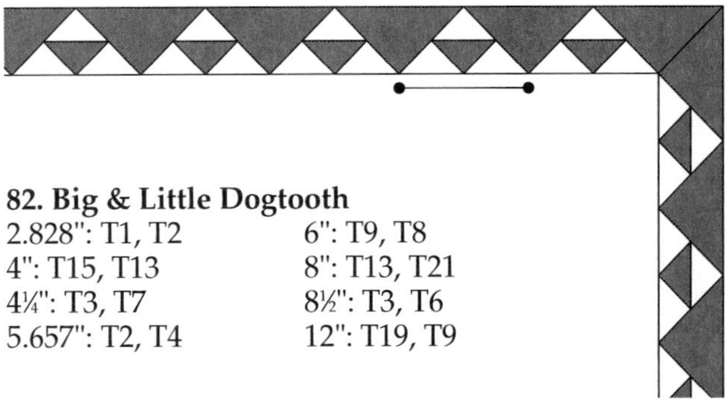

82. Big & Little Dogtooth

2.828": T1, T2	6": T9, T8
4": T15, T13	8": T13, T21
4¼": T3, T7	8½": T3, T6
5.657": T2, T4	12": T19, T9

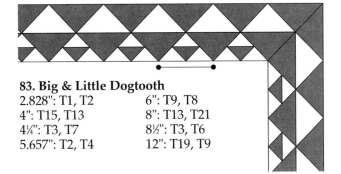

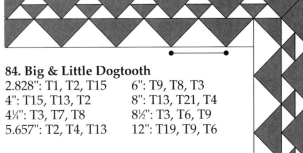

83. Big & Little Dogtooth

2.828": T1, T2	6": T9, T8
4": T15, T13	8": T13, T21
4¼": T3, T7	8½": T3, T6
5.657": T2, T4	12": T19, T9

84. Big & Little Dogtooth

2.828": T1, T2, T15	6": T9, T8, T3
4": T15, T13, T2	8": T13, T21, T4
4¼": T3, T7, T8	8½": T3, T6, T9
5.657": T2, T4, T13	12": T19, T9, T6

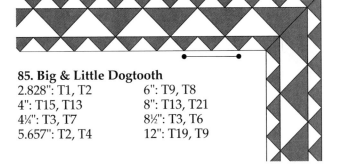

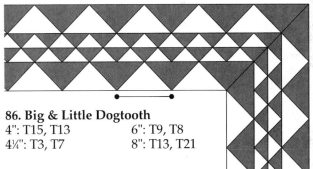

85. Big & Little Dogtooth

2.828": T1, T2	6": T9, T8
4": T15, T13	8": T13, T21
4¼": T3, T7	8½": T3, T6
5.657": T2, T4	12": T19, T9

86. Big & Little Dogtooth

4": T15, T13	6": T9, T8
4¼": T3, T7	8": T13, T21

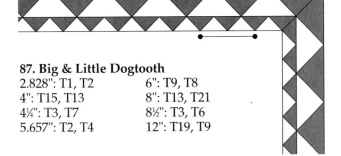

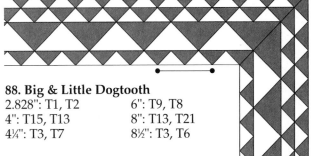

87. Big & Little Dogtooth

2.828": T1, T2	6": T9, T8
4": T15, T13	8": T13, T21
4¼": T3, T7	8½": T3, T6
5.657": T2, T4	12": T19, T9

88. Big & Little Dogtooth

2.828": T1, T2	6": T9, T8
4": T15, T13	8": T13, T21
4¼": T3, T7	8½": T3, T6

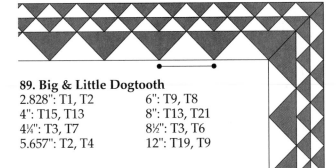

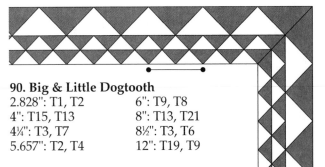

89. Big & Little Dogtooth

2.828": T1, T2	6": T9, T8
4": T15, T13	8": T13, T21
4¼": T3, T7	8½": T3, T6
5.657": T2, T4	12": T19, T9

90. Big & Little Dogtooth

2.828": T1, T2	6": T9, T8
4": T15, T13	8": T13, T21
4¼": T3, T7	8½": T3, T6
5.657": T2, T4	12": T19, T9

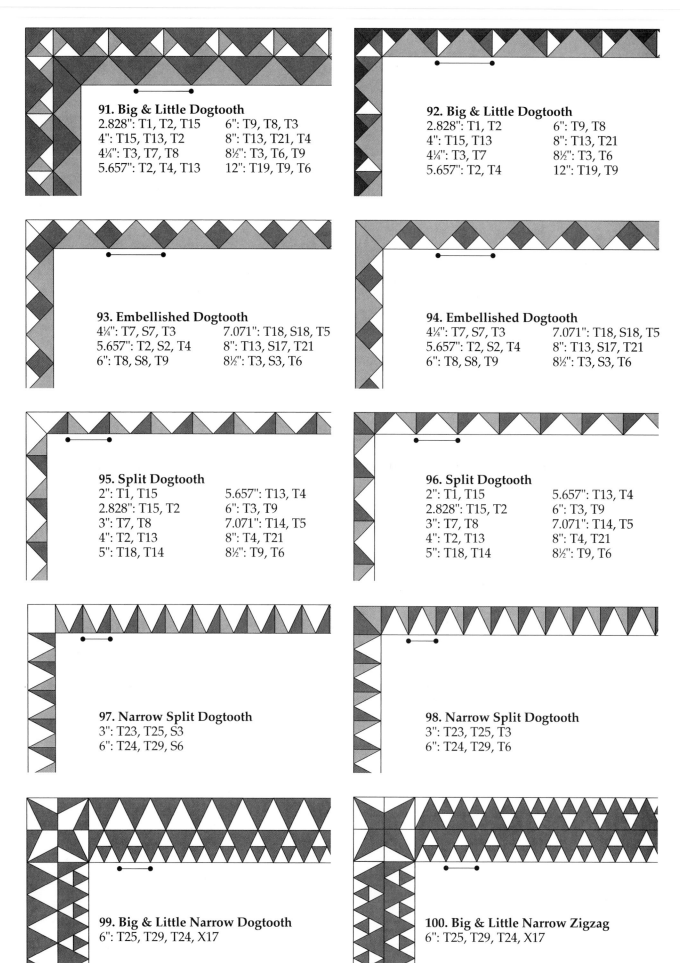

91. Big & Little Dogtooth
2.828": T1, T2, T15   6": T9, T8, T3
4": T15, T13, T2   8": T13, T21, T4
4¼": T3, T7, T8   8½": T3, T6, T9
5.657": T2, T4, T13   12": T19, T9, T6

92. Big & Little Dogtooth
2.828": T1, T2   6": T9, T8
4": T15, T13   8": T13, T21
4¼": T3, T7   8½": T3, T6
5.657": T2, T4   12": T19, T9

93. Embellished Dogtooth
4¼": T7, S7, T3   7.071": T18, S18, T5
5.657": T2, S2, T4   8": T13, S17, T21
6": T8, S8, T9   8½": T3, S3, T6

94. Embellished Dogtooth
4¼": T7, S7, T3   7.071": T18, S18, T5
5.657": T2, S2, T4   8": T13, S17, T21
6": T8, S8, T9   8½": T3, S3, T6

95. Split Dogtooth
2": T1, T15   5.657": T13, T4
2.828": T15, T2   6": T3, T9
3": T7, T8   7.071": T14, T5
4": T2, T13   8": T4, T21
5": T18, T14   8½": T9, T6

96. Split Dogtooth
2": T1, T15   5.657": T13, T4
2.828": T15, T2   6": T3, T9
3": T7, T8   7.071": T14, T5
4": T2, T13   8": T4, T21
5": T18, T14   8½": T9, T6

97. Narrow Split Dogtooth
3": T23, T25, S3
6": T24, T29, S6

98. Narrow Split Dogtooth
3": T23, T25, T3
6": T24, T29, T6

99. Big & Little Narrow Dogtooth
6": T25, T29, T24, X17

100. Big & Little Narrow Zigzag
6": T25, T29, T24, X17

Pineapple & Delectable Mountains Borders

Pineapple and Delectable Mountains borders are a combination of dogtooth and sawtooth triangles. In these pieced designs, large dogtooth triangles are edged with smaller sawtooth triangles. When the long sides of the small triangles are parallel to the long side of the large triangle, the design is called Pineapple (#101). When the long sides of the small triangles are perpendicular to the long side of the large triangle, the design is called Delectable Mountains (#106). These are traditional and somewhat formal border designs that are often paired with Feathered Star blocks because the small rows of sawtooth triangles echo those found in the star blocks. The traditional Delectable Mountains quilt design is made of several concentric borders that make the whole quilt design.

Fabrics and Colors

Using only two to four fabrics (a light and a dark, with one or two mediums if desired) will give a formal look to these borders. Scrap fabrics in two colors or several colors divided into light and dark will make the borders look casual and lively. High contrast between the light and dark fabrics gives a crisp look to the designs, while lower contrasts look softer. A large cabbage rose print paired with a plain-looking print or solid makes an elegant Pineapple or Delectable Mountains border. Cut the large print randomly, purposely trying not to center motifs in the fabric. When the pieces are sewn together, the look will be even lovelier and more interesting than the original large print, as the geometry of the piecing adds its structured rhythm to the more organic flow of the floral print.

Border Repeats and Natural Fit

With regard to the way they fit the quilt, these borders fall into two categories. In some designs (A in the top figure on this page) the repeat begins with a small triangle and ends with another just like it. In this case, the large triangle on the outer edge is the same size as the pieced triangle comprising the rest of the repeat (#104). The other border type (B) has shared end triangles, and the outer edge triangle is smaller than the rest of the border repeat (#103).

Either type of border can be used in conjunction with spacer strips. If you prefer to go without spacer strips, you will want to match the border

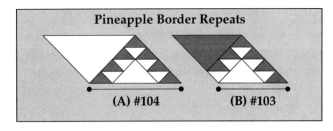

Pineapple Border Repeats

(A) #104   **(B) #103**

type to the quilt center as follows: For a natural fit with blocks set side by side, choose a border repeat of the A type, such as #104 or #109. If the block size is divisible by the repeat, the fit will be automatic. For a natural fit with blocks set with sashing, choose a border of the B type, such as #101 or #106. If the long side of the small triangle is the same dimension as the sash width and the long side of the larger inner triangle is the same measurement as the block, the fit will be natural. The border and quilt center also look their best related in this way.

Choose a patch size compatible with your quilt block. More or fewer small triangles can be incorporated in the border repeat, requiring larger or smaller edge triangles. Notice how in border #101, four small triangle pairs fit alongside one outer edge triangle. In border #102, three small triangles fit alongside one outer edge triangle. This is a good way to adjust the repeat to fit your quilt center. For diagonally set blocks, you can simply use the diagonal measurement of the blocks and sashes to plan a compatible border repeat.

Graphing the Design

The border repeat of a Pineapple or Delectable Mountains pattern can be drawn on graph paper two ways: with the long side of the edge triangles on a line of the graph paper and sides of the two-triangle squares on the invisible diagonal grid, or

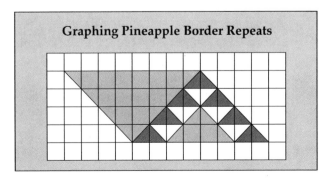

Graphing Pineapple Border Repeats

with the long side of the edge triangles on the diagonal grid and the sides of the two-triangle squares on the graph paper lines.

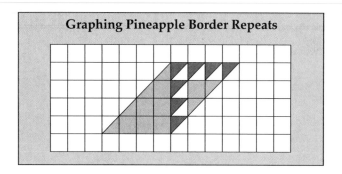

Graphing Pineapple Border Repeats

Grainline and Cutting

The large dogtooth triangles on the inner and outer edges of the border repeat should be cut with the straight grain on the long side to stabilize the edges of the border strip. Cut the small triangles with the straight grain on the short side. If you don't like cutting so many triangles, use your favorite rotary shortcuts, such as bias-strip piecing, to make the small two-triangle squares. (See Marsha's book, *On to Square Two*). We don't have room to describe this method here, but if you are familiar with strip-piecing methods for triangles or squares, by all means use them.

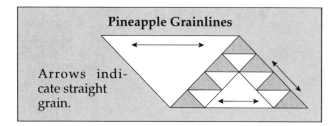

Pineapple Grainlines

Arrows indicate straight grain.

Trimming Points

In the rows of small triangles, trim points on the triangles to fit with neighboring patches for easy alignment and construction. Use the trim line indicated on the master patterns that is perpendicular to the short side of the triangle.

Piecing

Join pairs of small triangles to form squares. Then sew these into rows before attaching to the large dogtooth triangles. When sewing the rows of small triangles to the large dogtooth triangles, sew with the small triangles on top. You can see and sew right through the middle of the "X" where the previous lines of stitching intersect.

Corners

Corners for Pineapple and Delectable Mountains quilts are made from triangular units. These can sometimes be made from the same triangles used in the repeats, although some designs call for larger triangles. Leave off the large outer dogtooth triangle of one repeat in each corner. If you are making a type B design, add one small triangle to the end of the half repeat at each corner. Attach border strips. Join triangles as shown to make a triangular corner unit. Add the corner units.

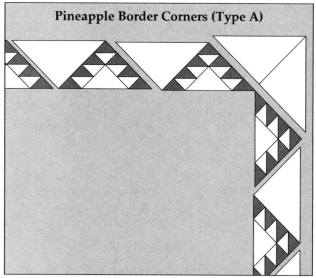

Pineapple Border Corners (Type A)

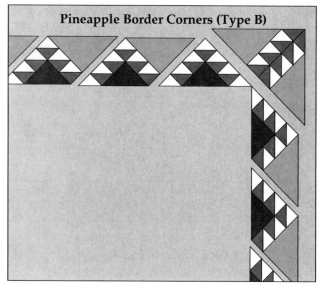

Pineapple Border Corners (Type B)

Pressing

When the finished size of the small triangles is 1¾" or smaller, consider pressing seam allowances open in the rows of small triangles. This will distribute the bulk of so many seams so close together and make a flatter piece of work with crisper-looking points. When sewing the small triangle rows to the larger triangles, press seams the way they want to go, which will be toward the larger triangles.

When joining border repeats, the long seams should be pressed toward the outer edge triangle and away from the small triangles. Pin at each joint to keep the seam allowances controlled when you stitch the border to the quilt.

101. Pineapple
5.657": T1, T3, T4
8": T15, T9, T21
11.314": T2, T6, T22

102. Pineapple
4¼": T1, T2, T3
6": T15, T13, T9
8½": T2, T4, T6

103. Pineapple
4¼": T1, T2, T3, T4
6": T15, T13, T9, T21
8½": T2, T4, T6, T22

104. Pineapple
5.657": T1, T2, T4
8": T15, T13, T21
12": T8, T9, T19

105. Pineapple
4¼": T1, T2, T3, T4
6": T15, T13, T9, T21
8½": T2, T4, T6, T22

106. Delectable Mountains
5.657": T1, T3, T4, S1
11.314": T2, T6, T22, S2

107. Delectable Mountains
4¼": T1, T2, T3, T4, S1
8½": T2, T4, T6, T22, S2

108. Delectable Mountains
4¼": T1, T2, T3, T4, S1
8½": T2, T4, T6, T22, S2

109. Delectable Mountains
5.657": T1, T2, T4, S1
12": T8, T9, T19, S8

110. Sawtooth Mountains
4¼": T1, T8
8½": T2, T9

Flying Geese Borders

Flying geese borders are made from units having an isosceles triangle flanked by two right triangles half the size of the center one. The three triangles form a rectangular unit. The two end triangles are joined to the center one head to foot. Center triangles for flying geese units are most commonly 1) isosceles right triangles, 2) equilateral triangles, 3) narrow triangles having equal base and altitude or 4) wide triangles having a base four times the altitude, as in the figures below.

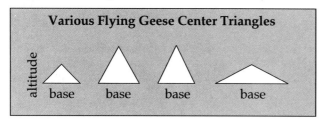

Various Flying Geese Center Triangles

altitude · base · base · base · base

In fact, any triangle having two equal sides can be used, even triangles having irregular numbers or angles. Thus a border of any width and length you require can be divided into repeats using paper folding (page 96) or a calculator and ruler (page 98) to make a flying geese pattern.

Usually, flying geese borders are made with the units joined along their long edges, with the point of one center triangle touching the base of the next center triangle. For a different and interesting effect, you can join the units with the right triangles side by side. Flying geese triangles can be embellished with additional piecing, or more triangles can be strung in a row within a unit to make more elaborate borders.

Any of the flying geese patterns shown can be adapted to isosceles triangles having other angles. For example, a wide triangle could be substituted for the large isosceles right triangle in border #112 as shown below.

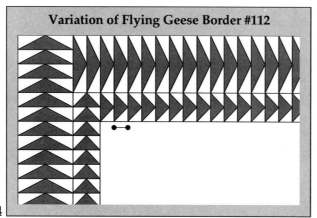

Variation of Flying Geese Border #112

Natural Fit

For a natural fit with one of these flying geese borders, look for a block having the same patch in the same orientation. Natural fit is also possible if the block's grid matches the border repeat dimension. If the block dimension is a multiple of the border repeat (or for diagonally set blocks, if the block's diagonal dimension is a multiple of the border repeat) the fit is also natural. For other situations, you can add spacer strips to make the quilt center a dimension divisible by the repeat, or you can custom design a border having a repeat that fits your quilt.

Graphing the Designs

The large isosceles right triangle for the center of the flying geese unit is drawn with the long side on the graph lines and the two short sides on the diagonals. For every two graph squares on the base, draw one diagonal. The triangle's altitude is half the number of squares in the base.

If you don't have special graph paper, equilateral triangles can't be easily drawn on graph paper. Without it, you can draft the full-size pattern using a 60° angle and a ruler to mark off three equal sides and three 60° angles on plain paper. You can sketch your ideas roughly on plain paper or simply visualize them.

To graph the narrow flying geese triangle, draw the base on two graph squares. From the middle of the base, go up two graph squares and make a dot. This is the top point of the triangle. Draw lines from this dot down to each end of the base, ignoring the graph lines and the graph's diagonals. For larger triangles, simply count out more squares, sticking to even numbers of squares and making the base and altitude the same.

To graph the end triangles, simply draw a vertical line from the top point of the center triangle to a point in the middle of its base to divide the triangle in half.

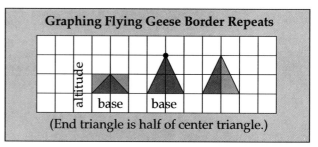

Graphing Flying Geese Border Repeats

altitude · base · base

(End triangle is half of center triangle.)

Fabrics and Colors

Most of these designs can be made with the dark color on the outside edges or in the center triangle of the unit. For units joined sideways, you will want to include a third value. A single flying geese border is often made in just two fabrics, but scraps work well, too. Background blending can be used to soften the line between design areas where the triangles on one edge match the neighboring design area. Flying geese borders can be made with a gradation of colors or several different colors rather than just two. Another interesting color effect is used in the Prairie Rambler border on page 35. Two fabrics are used for three consecutive repeats. Then two different fabrics are combined in the next three, and so on. We tried to show a few of the shadings and value options for each border type. You can easily adapt these ideas to other specific border designs.

Grainline and Cutting

The base of the large flying geese triangle should be on the straight grain. For the half-size triangles at the ends of the unit, the straight grain should be on the two shorter sides. Any squares should be cut with the straight grain parallel to its edges. You can use our templates or cutting dimensions as listed in the charts or devise your own patterns. To rotary cut four isosceles right center triangles for a flying geese border, cut two diagonals across a square that measures 1¼" more than the finished long side of the triangle. For two half-size isosceles right triangles for the ends of the unit, cut a single diagonal across a square that is ⅞" larger than the finished short side of the unit. You may need to use templates or a template affixed to your rotary ruler to cut other flying geese shapes.

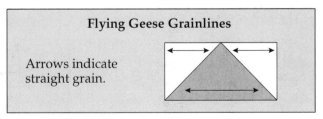

Flying Geese Grainlines

Arrows indicate straight grain.

Trimming Points

See the instructions for trimming points on page 146. In the typical flying geese border, you can easily align the patches properly for stitching without trimming points. However, trimming reduces bulk in the seam allowances and gets rid of distracting points that can interfere with making seams straight and true. When joining wide or narrow triangles, such as those in border #117, it is helpful to trim points as shown on our patterns.

Border Repeats & Piecing

The repeating border unit is a square or rectangle made from two right triangles attached to an isosceles triangle. Most of the time all three triangles are isosceles right triangles. Usually flying geese border repeats are joined with the point of one center triangle touching the base of the next one.

The running dimension of the repeat is equal to the altitude of the center triangle for the usual arrangement, and the base of the center triangle in sideways designs.

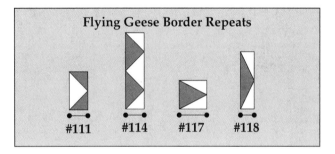

Flying Geese Border Repeats

#111   #114   #117   #118

Study the corner of your chosen design. Frequently, individual border strips are made from border repeats, and the border ends are simply squared corners as in border #111. Sometimes a square-within-a-square or some other simple patch is used to make block corners as in border #113.

Pressing

Because seam allowances naturally tend to turn away from the point of the center triangle, press them that way for each border repeat. Also press away from this point when joining border repeats to each other. Pin at each joint to keep the seam allowances controlled as you stitch.

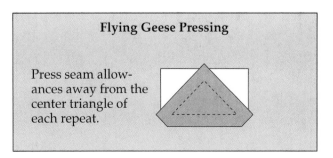

Flying Geese Pressing

Press seam allowances away from the center triangle of each repeat.

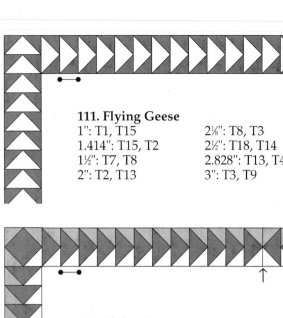

111. Flying Geese
1": T1, T15
1.414": T15, T2
1½": T7, T8
2": T2, T13

2⅛": T8, T3
2½": T18, T14
2.828": T13, T4
3": T3, T9

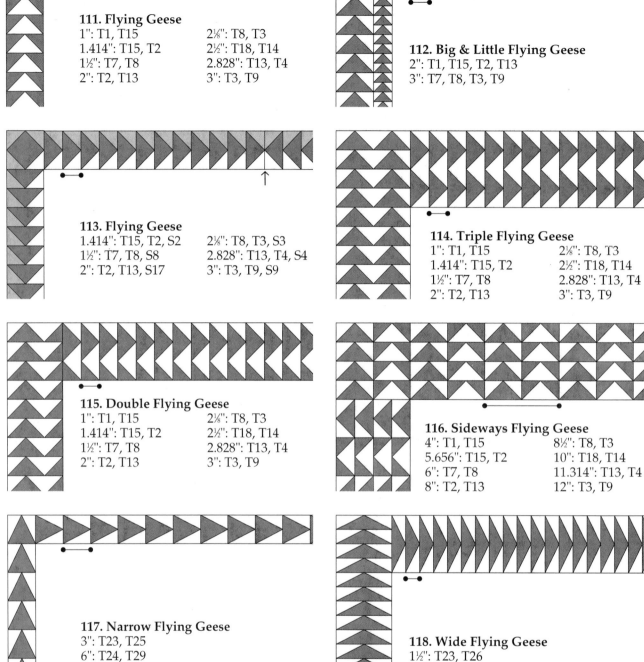

112. Big & Little Flying Geese
2": T1, T15, T2, T13
3": T7, T8, T3, T9

113. Flying Geese
1.414": T15, T2, S2
1½": T7, T8, S8
2": T2, T13, S17

2⅛": T8, T3, S3
2.828": T13, T4, S4
3": T3, T9, S9

114. Triple Flying Geese
1": T1, T15
1.414": T15, T2
1½": T7, T8
2": T2, T13

2⅛": T8, T3
2½": T18, T14
2.828": T13, T4
3": T3, T9

115. Double Flying Geese
1": T1, T15
1.414": T15, T2
1½": T7, T8
2": T2, T13

2⅛": T8, T3
2½": T18, T14
2.828": T13, T4
3": T3, T9

116. Sideways Flying Geese
4": T1, T15
5.656": T15, T2
6": T7, T8
8": T2, T13

8½": T8, T3
10": T18, T14
11.314": T13, T4
12": T3, T9

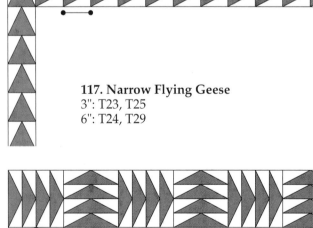

117. Narrow Flying Geese
3": T23, T25
6": T24, T29

118. Wide Flying Geese
1½": T23, T26

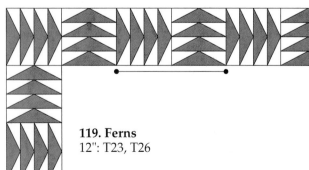

119. Ferns
12": T23, T26

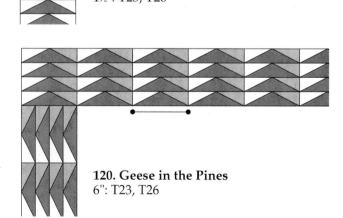

120. Geese in the Pines
6": T23, T26

66

Sawtooth Borders

Sawtooth borders are made from right triangles (having a 90° angle in one corner). The straight grain of the fabric is placed along the two perpendicular sides (the base and altitude), and triangles are joined to their neighbors to form squares or rectangles. Sawtooth triangles are most commonly 1) isosceles right triangles or 2) triangles having one side half the length of the side to which it is perpendicular as in the figures below.

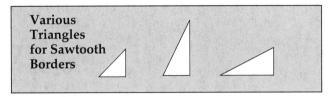

Various Triangles for Sawtooth Borders

Actually, any triangle having a right angle can be used, even triangles having "not nice" measurements. Thus a border of any width and length you require can be divided into repeats using paper folding (page 96) or a calculator and ruler (page 98) to make a sawtooth pattern.

A single band of triangles can be used, or two or more bands can be made separately and joined side by side. Big and little triangles can be combined for more elaborate borders.

Any of the sawtooth patterns shown can be adapted to right triangles having other angles. For example, a narrow triangle could be substituted for the isosceles right triangle. (Compare borders #121 and 147.) The dimensions of the corners may change, however. For clues to this, study the corners of other borders that use the same triangle.

Natural Fit

For a natural fit with one of these sawtooth borders, look for a block having the same patch in the same orientation. Natural fit is also possible if the block's grid matches the border repeat dimension. If the block dimension is a multiple of the border repeat (or for diagonally set blocks, if the block's diagonal dimension is a multiple of the border repeat) the fit is also natural. For other situations, add spacer strips to make the quilt center a dimension divisible by the repeat, or custom design a border having a repeat that fits your quilt.

Graphing the Designs

The right triangle for sawtooth designs and patterns is drawn with the two shorter sides on the horizontal and vertical graph lines and the long side at an angle. For isosceles right triangles, the most common used for sawtooth borders, draw the long side at a 45° angle, the true diagonal of the graph paper. For every graph square on the base, draw one square for the altitude.

To graph narrow right triangles, draw the base on one graph square. Draw the altitude up two or more squares from the corner of the base. Draw a line at an angle to connect the ends of the base and altitude.

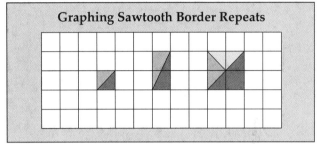

Graphing Sawtooth Border Repeats

Fabrics and Colors

Sawtooth borders are generally made from two colors or values, and often they are made from just two fabrics. They are also effective in a variety of scrap fabrics. We see a pronounced pattern when the contrast between the two values is high. We see just a hint of a pattern when the contrast is low. Any of the sawtooth designs in this chapter can be made with the dark color on the outside edge or on the inside edge. The colors can also be arranged as shown in border #124, although most sawtooths are not done this way. When the triangles on one edge match the neighboring design area, background blending softens the line between areas. Multiple sawtooth borders or embellished sawtooth borders can be made with a gradation of colors or several different colors rather than just two. We tried to show a few of the options for each border type. You can easily adapt these ideas to other specific border designs.

Grainline and Cutting

The base of a sawtooth triangle should be on the straight grain. Any squares should be cut with the straight grain parallel to its edges. You can use our templates or cutting dimensions as listed in the charts or make your own. To rotary cut the isosceles right triangles for a dogtooth border, cut two tri- 67 angles from a square that measures ⅞" more than the finished short side of the triangle. You may need to use templates or a template affixed to your rotary ruler to cut narrow right triangles.

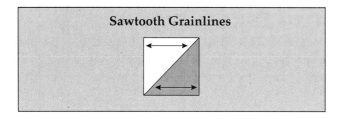

Sawtooth Grainlines

Trimming Points

See the instructions for trimming points on page 146. If you trim the points before joining triangles for a sawtooth border, it is easier to stitch a straight seam. Trimming is not necessary for aligning patches, but without trimming, the long extensions of the points can be bulky and distracting.

Border Repeats & Piecing

The basic repeating border unit is a square or rectangle composed of two triangles joined along their long sides. The running dimension of the repeat is equal to the base of the triangle.

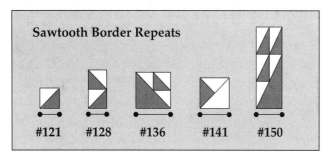

Sawtooth Border Repeats

#121   #128   #136   #141   #150

Multiple sawtooth borders can always be made and attached separately. Sometimes with sawtooth designs, the repeating border unit follows straight through from one border band to the next (#150), and you can piece a single wide border and attach it to the quilt all at once.

If you don't like cutting so many triangles, use your favorite rotary shortcuts, such as bias-strip piecing, to make the small two-triangle squares. (See Marsha McCloskey's book, *On to Square Two*). We don't have room to describe this method here, but if you are familiar with strip-piecing methods for triangles or squares, feel free to use them wherever applicable.

Embellished sawtooth designs are made from the same kind of repeating border units as are plain sawtooth borders. Simply join the small patches to make triangles first.

68

Corners

Study the corner of your chosen design. Often, individual border strips are made from border repeats, and squares the size of two triangles are used in the corners.

Sometimes the border strips end with another border repeat or a border repeat rotated 180°.

Reverses

Sawtooth units are asymmetrical, so they look different when they are turned. Sometimes sawtooth repeats reverse directions at the center of each side to achieve symmetry in the quilt. This requires an even number of repeats on each side. Other times the repeats meet in the corners as mirror images, but they do not reverse at the centers. Repeats face away from two opposite corners and they face toward the other two corners. This kind of sawtooth border can be made to fit quilts with even or odd numbers of repeats on a side. Sometimes, sawtooth units are turned to form half Pinwheels or other patterns.

Sawtooth Border Reversed at Centers

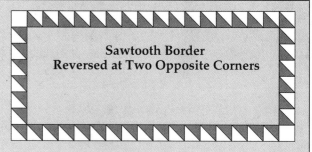

Sawtooth Border Reversed at Two Opposite Corners

Pressing

Generally, sawtooth border repeats are made from one light and one dark triangle, and you would press seam allowances toward the dark triangle. For very small sawtooth triangles, press the first seam open. This minimizes bulk in the seam. When joining one repeat to the next, press the seam toward the dark triangle again. When joining the sawtooth border to a plain strip, press away from the pieced border. Pin at each joint when you stitch the border to the quilt.

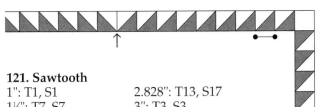

121. Sawtooth

1": T1, S1	2.828": T13, S17
1½": T7, S7	3": T3, S3
2": T2, S2	4": T4, S4
2⅛": T8, S8	6": T6, S6
2½": T18, S18	8": T22, S13

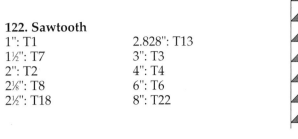

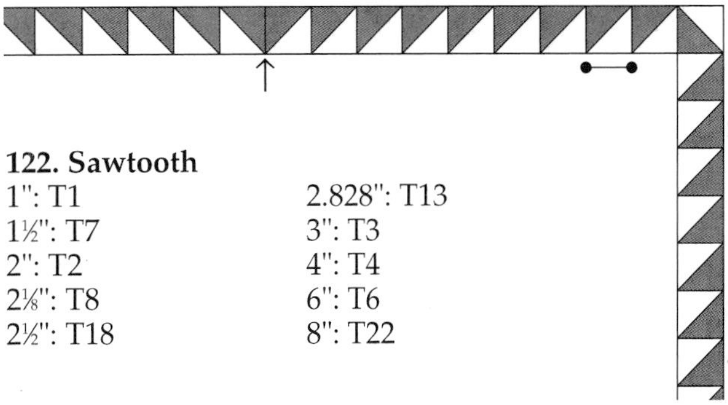

122. Sawtooth

1": T1	2.828": T13
1½": T7	3": T3
2": T2	4": T4
2⅛": T8	6": T6
2½": T18	8": T22

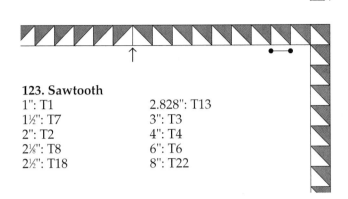

123. Sawtooth

1": T1	2.828": T13
1½": T7	3": T3
2": T2	4": T4
2⅛": T8	6": T6
2½": T18	8": T22

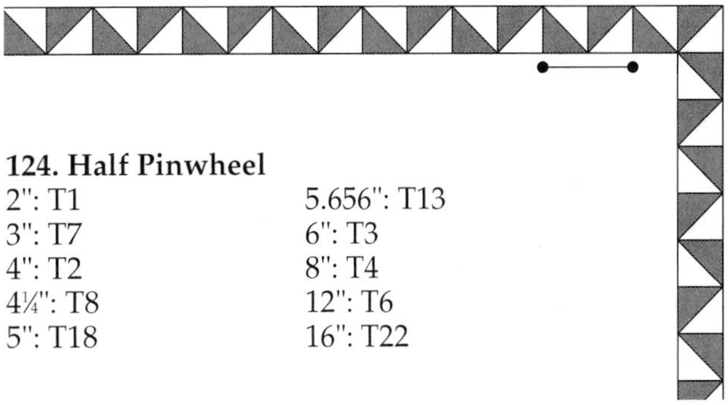

124. Half Pinwheel

2": T1	5.656": T13
3": T7	6": T3
4": T2	8": T4
4¼": T8	12": T6
5": T18	16": T22

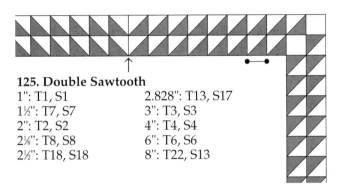

125. Double Sawtooth

1": T1, S1	2.828": T13, S17
1½": T7, S7	3": T3, S3
2": T2, S2	4": T4, S4
2⅛": T8, S8	6": T6, S6
2½": T18, S18	8": T22, S13

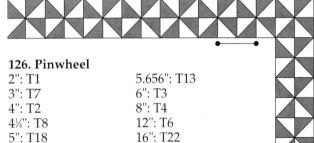

126. Pinwheel

2": T1	5.656": T13
3": T7	6": T3
4": T2	8": T4
4¼": T8	12": T6
5": T18	16": T22

127. Sawtooth Flying Geese

1": T1, S1	2.828": T13, S17
1½": T7, S7	3": T3, S3
2": T2, S2	4": T4, S4
2⅛": T8, S8	6": T6, S6
2½": T18, S18	8": T22, S13

128. Sawtooth Flying Geese

1": T1	2.828": T13
1½": T7	3": T3
2": T2	4": T4
2⅛": T8	6": T6
2½": T18	8": T22

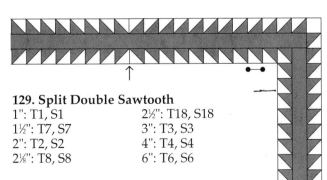

129. Split Double Sawtooth

1": T1, S1	2½": T18, S18
1½": T7, S7	3": T3, S3
2": T2, S2	4": T4, S4
2⅛": T8, S8	6": T6, S6

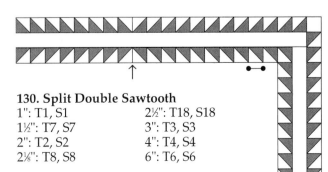

130. Split Double Sawtooth

1": T1, S1	2½": T18, S18
1½": T7, S7	3": T3, S3
2": T2, S2	4": T4, S4
2⅛": T8, S8	6": T6, S6

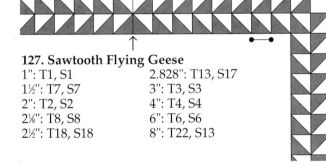

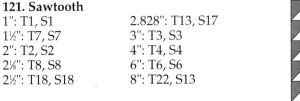

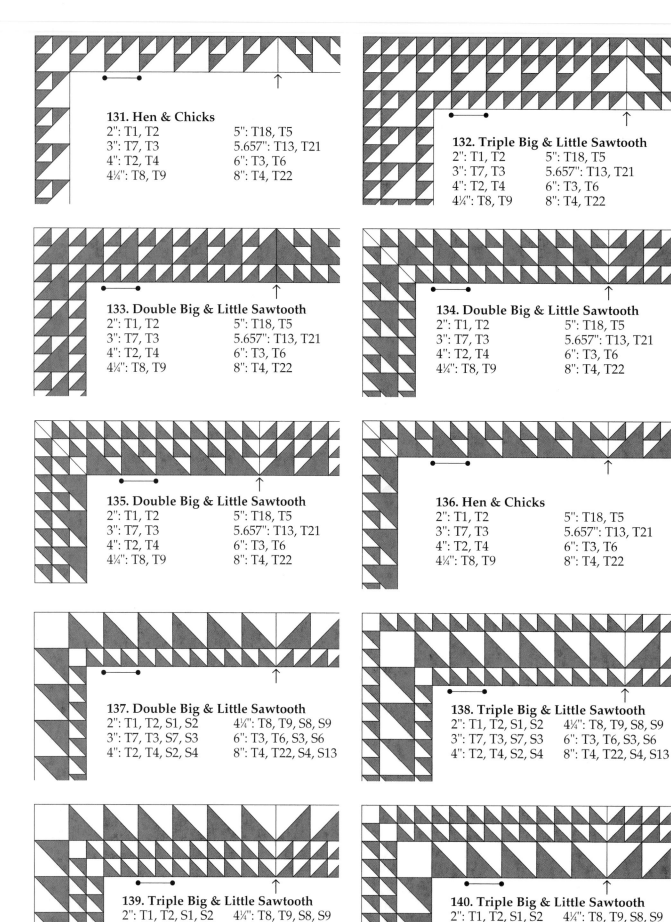

131. Hen & Chicks

2": T1, T2   5": T18, T5
3": T7, T3   5.657": T13, T21
4": T2, T4   6": T3, T6
4¼": T8, T9   8": T4, T22

132. Triple Big & Little Sawtooth

2": T1, T2   5": T18, T5
3": T7, T3   5.657": T13, T21
4": T2, T4   6": T3, T6
4¼": T8, T9   8": T4, T22

133. Double Big & Little Sawtooth

2": T1, T2   5": T18, T5
3": T7, T3   5.657": T13, T21
4": T2, T4   6": T3, T6
4¼": T8, T9   8": T4, T22

134. Double Big & Little Sawtooth

2": T1, T2   5": T18, T5
3": T7, T3   5.657": T13, T21
4": T2, T4   6": T3, T6
4¼": T8, T9   8": T4, T22

135. Double Big & Little Sawtooth

2": T1, T2   5": T18, T5
3": T7, T3   5.657": T13, T21
4": T2, T4   6": T3, T6
4¼": T8, T9   8": T4, T22

136. Hen & Chicks

2": T1, T2   5": T18, T5
3": T7, T3   5.657": T13, T21
4": T2, T4   6": T3, T6
4¼": T8, T9   8": T4, T22

137. Double Big & Little Sawtooth

2": T1, T2, S1, S2   4¼": T8, T9, S8, S9
3": T7, T3, S7, S3   6": T3, T6, S3, S6
4": T2, T4, S2, S4   8": T4, T22, S4, S13

138. Triple Big & Little Sawtooth

2": T1, T2, S1, S2   4¼": T8, T9, S8, S9
3": T7, T3, S7, S3   6": T3, T6, S3, S6
4": T2, T4, S2, S4   8": T4, T22, S4, S13

139. Triple Big & Little Sawtooth

2": T1, T2, S1, S2   4¼": T8, T9, S8, S9
3": T7, T3, S7, S3   6": T3, T6, S3, S6
4": T2, T4, S2, S4   8": T4, T22, S4, S13

140. Triple Big & Little Sawtooth

2": T1, T2, S1, S2   4¼": T8, T9, S8, S9
3": T7, T3, S7, S3   6": T3, T6, S3, S6
4": T2, T4, S2, S4   8": T4, T22, S4, S13

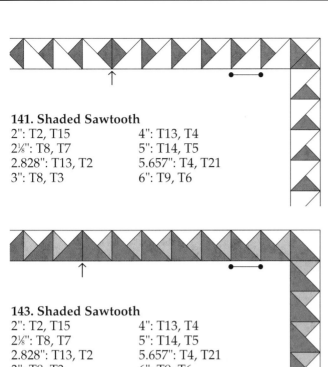

141. Shaded Sawtooth

2": T2, T15	4": T13, T4
2⅛": T8, T7	5": T14, T5
2.828": T13, T2	5.657": T4, T21
3": T8, T3	6": T9, T6

142. Shaded Sawtooth

2": T2, T15	4": T13, T4
2⅛": T8, T7	5": T14, T5
2.828": T13, T2	5.657": T4, T21
3": T8, T3	6": T9, T6

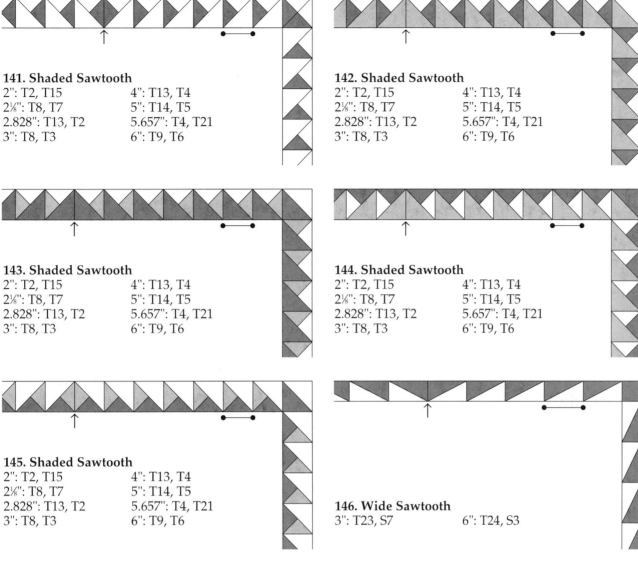

143. Shaded Sawtooth

2": T2, T15	4": T13, T4
2⅛": T8, T7	5": T14, T5
2.828": T13, T2	5.657": T4, T21
3": T8, T3	6": T9, T6

144. Shaded Sawtooth

2": T2, T15	4": T13, T4
2⅛": T8, T7	5": T14, T5
2.828": T13, T2	5.657": T4, T21
3": T8, T3	6": T9, T6

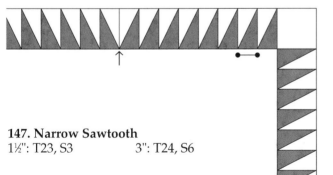

145. Shaded Sawtooth

2": T2, T15	4": T13, T4
2⅛": T8, T7	5": T14, T5
2.828": T13, T2	5.657": T4, T21
3": T8, T3	6": T9, T6

146. Wide Sawtooth

3": T23, S7	6": T24, S3

147. Narrow Sawtooth

1½": T23, S3	3": T24, S6

148. Narrow Big & Little Sawtooth

3": T23, T24, S3, S6

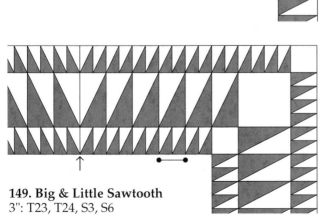

149. Big & Little Sawtooth
3": T23, T24, S3, S6

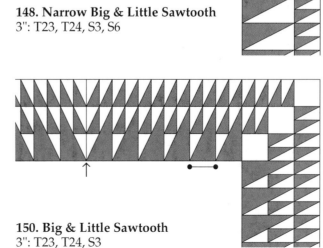

150. Big & Little Sawtooth
3": T23, T24, S3

Diamond & Parallelogram Borders

Diamonds have four equal sides, whereas parallelograms have two short sides and two long sides with opposite sides equal. In patchwork either of these shapes can work into myriad simple and effective border designs.

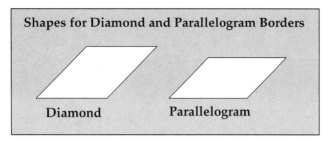

Shapes for Diamond and Parallelogram Borders

Diamond   Parallelogram

Design

Although the diamond borders we show here all have 45° diamonds, the same design ideas can be used with diamonds having other angles as well. You would probably want to make a border using the same kind of diamond that is in your quilt. Diamonds and parallelograms can be situated with a point on the edge of the border or with a side on the edge. Parallelograms act like two isosceles triangles back to back and often have nice repeat dimensions. Diamonds have a different geometry and work into repeat dimensions that are not always simple.

Coloring

In these borders, various shadings can be employed to emphasize different aspects of the design. Adjacent shapes can have high contrast to achieve a bold look (#172) or they can gradate from light to dark for a softer look (#153). Edge triangles don't have to be all one shade. They can be light on the inside and dark on the outside or vice versa. We have shown several variations. You could easily imagine more.

Natural Fit

Diamonds and parallelograms look nearly the same but the geometrical differences in the two shapes make a large difference in how they form repeats and fit your quilt. Once again, if you choose patches from the quilt design block in the same size and orientation, natural fit will result. An easy fit can also be achieved if the border repeat matches or can be evenly divided into the block dimension. 72 Parallelogram borders have many of the qualities

of borders made with squares and triangles, and they fit grids in the same way. With most of the diamond borders, however, repeat dimensions are usually unrelated to any grid because of the peculiar geometry of the shape. The most direct way to achieve a good fit with a diamond border is to add spacer strips to the quilt center to bring it out to dimensions that match the pieced border measurement. You can read about spacer strips on page 80. Diamond borders #158-161 will fit many quilt centers without spacer strips; other diamond borders may not.

Graphing the Designs

Imagine that a parallelogram is two right isosceles triangles back to back. It can be drawn on graph paper two ways: with the long side of each triangle on the diagonal grid and the short sides on the graph paper lines, or with the long side of each triangle on a graph line and the short sides on the invisible diagonal grid.

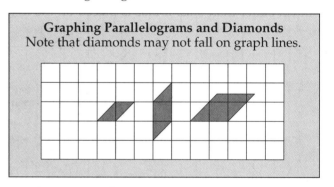

Graphing Parallelograms and Diamonds
Note that diamonds may not fall on graph lines.

See page 89 for how to draw an approximation of a 45° diamond on graph paper. The true shape cannot be drawn to follow a grid, but for sketching and design purposes, the technique works fine.

If you want to draw a diamond for a design such as #151-154 to fit a specific border repeat, simply mark two dots to indicate the desired diamond height on graph paper, from sharp point to sharp point. Draw a line from point to point. Midway between these points, counting graph squares, draw a line perpendicular to the first line. Count graph squares to equal half the border repeat to one side of the midline, and make a mark. Repeat on the other side of the midline. Draw four lines connecting the marked points to complete your diamond. This diamond is not necessarily a 45° or 60° or other common diamond. You can draw triangles to fill in the edges of a diamond border strip simply by dividing the diamond in half, either crosswise or lengthwise.

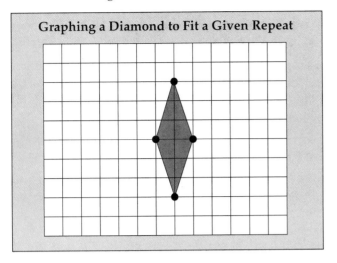

Graphing a Diamond to Fit a Given Repeat

Grainline and Cutting

Diamonds and parallelograms should be cut with straight grain along one set of parallel edges. Edge triangles should be cut with the straight grain on the side that falls on the outside edge of the pieced border. Multiplied the length of the border, this stable grain will hold the desired dimensions much better than bias. If bias is placed on the long side of the triangles, the outside edge of the borders becomes stretchy and more pinning is necessary for matching. In a few situations where triangle points must match precisely with points in adjacent pieced areas, a stretchy bias edge can be an advantage when pinning points for matching.

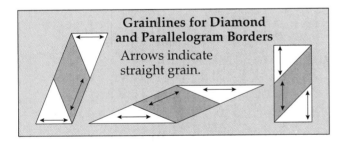

Grainlines for Diamond and Parallelogram Borders

Arrows indicate straight grain.

Trimming Points

Trim points on edge triangles and diamonds to align with adjacent patches for ease of matching and construction. Use the trim lines indicated on the master patterns .

Border Repeats and Piecing

Many of the diamond and parallelogram borders have a construction similar to chain-of-squares borders, where the repeating border units form parallelograms. Examples are #151, 155 and 163. Repeats are joined to make long rows that require

extra units at the ends in order to go around the corners. Matching the joints for parallelogram borders is fairly straightforward, but positioning pins will probably be necessary to match diamond joints as in borders #152 and 157. (See page 144.) A few borders, such as #158 and 159 require set-in seams. These could be eliminated by splitting the triangles in half to create repeat units consisting of a diamond with a triangle sewn on each end. This is similar to the repeat in #171.

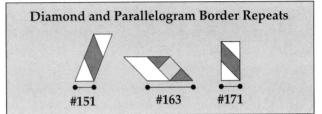

Diamond and Parallelogram Border Repeats

#151   #163   #171

Corners

Most of the parallelogram designs turn the corner easily by taking the same shapes that are used in the repeats and slightly reorganizing them in the corner square (#171). Some diamond borders, such as #155 and 159, have mitered corners. A few new patches or units may be required to complete the 45° angle in preparation for mitering. (See how to miter on page 81.) Many diamond borders, such as #151 and 152, have a wedge-shaped corner unit set in between the angled ends of the border strips. They are actually made with two wedges in each corner, one to switch the slant at the end of a border strip, and the second to fill the space in the corner. On parallelogram designs that are pieced with slanted border repeats, such as #163, the corner will be a pieced triangle that is sewn on after the border strips have been attached to each side.

Pressing

When joining repeat units, generally press toward the darker fabric. Press seams to oppose each other for easy matching. In smaller sizes, you may want to press the seams open within each border repeat in order to distribute the bulk.

Where seam allowances are pressed toward one side, they turn away from one point on the edge triangle and toward the next point in the pattern. You are going to have to force seams one way or the other to keep them from twisting. Press them all to the right or all to the left or toward one point and way from the next point. Pin at each joint to keep the seam allowances controlled when you stitch the border to the quilt.

151. Chain of Diamonds
2.296": D3, T28, T16

152. Double Chain of Diamonds
2.296": D3, T28, T10

153. Double Chain of Diamonds
2.296": D3, D4, T28, T10

154. Chain of Diamonds
2.296": D4, T28, T16

155. Chain of Diamonds
5.543": D3, T27, T33, T31

156. Chain of Diamonds
5.543": D3, D4, T30, T33, T31

157. Chain of Diamonds
5.543": D4, T27, T33, T31

158. Chevrons
2⅛": D4, S7, T7
2½": D2, S11, T11
4¼": D3, S3, T3

159. Chevrons
5⅛": D4, S7, T7
6": D2, S11, T11
10¼": D3, S3, T3

160. Double Diamond Ribbon
7.657": D1, T15
8⅛": D4, T7
9½": D2, T11
16¼": D3, T3

161. Diamond Ribbon
5⅛": D4, T7
6": D2, T11
10¼": D3, T3

162. Ribbon
4¼": X16, X13, T7, S7

163. Ribbon
4¼": X3, X13, T7, S7

164. Ribbon
4¼": X3, X13, T7, S7

165. Double Ribbons
4¼": X3, X13, T7, T3, S7

166. Double Ribbons
4¼": X14, X13, X15, T7, T8, R20, T3, S7

167. Chevrons
4¼": X3, S3, T3, S8

168. Chevrons
4¼": X3, S3, T3, S8

169. Chevrons
4¼": X3, T8, T3

170. Candy Stripes
4¼": X3, T3

75

171. Chain of Parallelograms
2⅛": X3, T8

172. Chain of Parallelograms
2⅛": X3, T8

173. Chain of Parallelograms
2⅛": X3, T8

174. Chain of Parallelograms
2⅛": X3, T8

175. Chain of Parallelograms
2⅛": X3, T8

176. Chain of Parallelograms
2⅛": X3, T8

177. Chain of Parallelograms
2⅛": X3, T8

178. Chain of Parallelograms
4¼": X3, T8

179. Chain of Parallelograms
4¼": X3, T8

180. Chain of Parallelograms
4¼": X3, T8

Stars & Other Block Borders

Block borders are fancier than the other border families we have included in this book and could easily become the focus of a quilt design rather than existing in a supporting role. Judy designed the #183 star border for her Mountains Vistas quilt pictured on page 42 to spark up an otherwise nice but everyday sort of quilt design. The Harvest Time quilt pictured on page 43 is another example of a fairly plain quilt center with fancy borders. This design idea of pairing plain quilt centers with knock-your-socks-off borders bears a lot of exploration. You could make a plain Nine-Patch, Four-Patch or Irish Chain quilt center and then add a wide and wonderful star border, perhaps in combination with some simpler stock borders. Don't feel limited to using just stars, either. There are hundreds of block designs that can be strung together in rows to make beautiful border designs. The Nonsense border (#50), which we included with the chain-of-squares borders because of its construction, was designed by drawing square design blocks in a row, dropping out some unnecessary seam lines and adding embellishments to the edge triangles.

The borders that follow are made of rows of quilt blocks either set straight (#191) or set on the diagonal with triangles filling in along the edges (#189). The blocks can be right next to each other or appear to overlap and share templates. They can be separated by alternate blocks or sashes (#188) or staggered with the addition of rectangles (#183) for a more dynamic look. When blocks are set on the diagonal, the triangles along the edges can be plain or embellished with piecing.

Design and Graphing

Look through books that have lots of block ideas, such as *Judy Martin's Ultimate Book of Quilt Block Patterns* or Marsha's *100 Pieced Patterns for 8″ Blocks*. Look for a block that you like; then imagine several of the same blocks strung in a row. Make graph paper sketches using the techniques described in the Design & Drafting chapter beginning on page 83. Be alert for opportunities to combine shapes to eliminate unnecessary patches as was done in star border #181, where triangles of adjacent stars were combined to make squares. This tactic might change the piecing sequence, but will usually save some work. However, there are times when leaving seams in, or even adding them, can simplify a border's construction.

Natural Fit

For block borders, you might approach fit from the opposite direction. Instead of choosing a border to fit the quilt center, you could design and choose a border first, and then choose a simpler design for the center, with patch sizes based on the border repeat. Patches from your border blocks could be used in a simpler arrangement in the quilt center. A natural fit results, provided you use the patches in the same orientation. An easy fit can also be achieved if the quilt center measurement is a multiple of the border repeat. In other situations, a spacer strip can be added to the quilt center to bring it out to dimensions that are readily divisible by the border repeat.

Other Considerations

Because of the variety in these borders and the limitless possibilities they offer, it is difficult to make specific recommendations as to color, grainline, piecing, and pressing. Refer to page 10 in the Border Design Basics section for a general discussion of color in borders.

See page 145 for more information about grainline. We show the border repeats on our border sketches, and these are usually a good indication of the construction units. To see how to piece your block border, look for long seams that begin at the inner edge of the border and continue to the outer edge of the border. If these seams are perpendicular to the edge of the border, square or rectangular repeating units are indicated. Seam lines at an angle to the edge of the border signal repeating units shaped like a parallelogram as in the chain-of-squares borders on page 52.

For corner units, also look for long seams that will show whether the corner is a square, as in sawtooth or checkerboard designs, or a triangular unit as in the dogtooth or the chain-of-squares borders.

When you stitch the border to the quilt, pin at each joint to keep the seam allowances controlled. Use the following guidelines for pressing these borders: Press generally toward darker fabrics. Look for opportunities to press for opposing seams (page 144), and press seams open where it is necessary to distribute bulk.

181. Evening Star
6": T7, T8, S3, S8, R20, S7
8": T2, T13, S4, S2, S17, R1

182. Evening Star
6": T7, T8, S3, S8, R20, S7
8": T2, T13, S4, S2, S17, R1

183. Staggered Stars
6": S7, S3, T7, T8, R24, R21
8": S2, S4, T2, T13, R16, R17

184. Staggered Stars & Chains
12": S7, S3, T7, T8, R20, R24
16¼": S2, S4, T2, T13, R16, R1

185. Star Dancer
9": T7, T8, S7, S3
12": T2, T13, S2, S4

186. Stars & Squares
9": T7, T8, S7, S8
12": T2, T13, S2, S17

187. Overlapping Stars
4": T15, S2, S17
6": T8, S3, S9
8½": T3, S9, S6

188. Ohio Stars
7": S2, T15, R6

189. Chain of Evening Stars
8½": T6, T9, T7, T8, S3, S7
12": T19, T6, T8, T3, S9, S8

190. LeMoyne Stars
6": D2, T11, S11
10¼" D3, S3, T3

191. Chimneys & Cornerstones
7": S1, S2, R2, R4, R6

192. Massachusetts Cross & Crown
6": T15, T2, S2
6⅜": T7, T8, S8
8½": T2, T13, S17
9": T8, T3, S3

193. Rosebud
6": T1, T2, T3
12": T2, T4, T6

194. Lost Ships
4": T1, T2
5.656": T15, T13
6": T7, T3
8": T2, T4

195. Jacob's Ladder
12": S1, T2
18": S7, T3
24": S2, T4

196. Flying Pinwheel
4": T1, T15, T2
5.656": T15, T2, T13
6": T7, T8, T3
8": T2, T13, T4
10": T18, T14, T5
12": T3, T9, T6

197. Grape Basket
4": T1, T2, R2
6": T7, T3, R20
8": T2, T4, R1

198. Windmill Star
8½": X3, T8

199. Ocean Waves
8": T1, T2
11.312": T15, T13
12": T7, T3
16": T2, T4
17": T8, T9
20": T18, T5

200. Fox & Geese
4": S1, T1, T2
6": S7, T7, T3
8": S2, T2, T4
8½": S8, T8, T9
10": S18, T18, T5

Special Tips for Border Construction

Handling long strips of pieced or plain fabric is different from normal block piecing. Here are a few simple techniques and strategies we use to accurately measure, cut and stitch our pieced and plain borders.

Measuring

If your cutting and sewing are always perfectly accurate, the only measuring you will need to do is to cut the spacer strips and plain borders to the proper length according to your quilt plan. You can tell your work is accurate if the sashes or alternate blocks consistently fit the more heavily pieced areas without one part extending beyond the other. If you feel your cutting and sewing are accurate, you can double check by measuring your quilt top. The number you get should not surprise you. If the measurement is within a quarter inch, trust your expected number rather than the measurement.

You know from your pattern or quilt plan what size the quilt center and borders are supposed to be. Often the cutting and piecing are neat and respectable, but the results may not measure exactly what they should. This means that you'll need to measure the quilt top and borders. When determining dimensions for plain borders (either spacer strips or outer borders), take the measurement across the center of the quilt as well as near the edges. If these measurements differ, try again and average if necessary. Pick a number halfway between the longest and the shortest. Not coming up with the expected dimension or the same measurements at the center and sides of the quilt is not uncommon. Fortunately, fabric is very forgiving, so don't worry.

If your quilt center and pieced borders don't measure quite as expected and spacer strips are in your quilt plan, you're in luck. You can make adjustments to assure a good fit. The pieced areas can be made to fit each other perfectly by altering the width and length of the spacers strips. See the discussion of spacer strips that follows. Refigure the lengths and widths of the spacer strips using the *actual measurements* of the quilt center and pieced borders in place of the original numbers.

If your pieced border will be sewn directly to the quilt center and the measurements are only slightly off, the difference can be made up with careful pinning, easing, pressing and quilting. If the actual measurements of the quilt center and border are significantly different from your plan, consider adding spacer strips for a better fit. It is possible you will want to add a repeat to your pieced borders to make the spacer strip a reasonable width.

The adjusted *length* of spacer strips and plain outer borders will depend on the type of corner treatment you choose: mitered, squared or block corners. Mitered corners meet at a 45° angle. Squared corners meet at a 90° angle. Block corners have an extra square at the corners where the borders meet. For each type of corner, you'll be measuring, cutting and sewing as you go. Refer to the detailed information on pinning and stitching on page 82.

Spacer Strip Calculations

Spacer strips can be used for natural-fit borders as well as made-to-measure borders. For natural-fit borders, the width of the spacer strip should be some multiple of half the size of the repeat.

You can figure the size of the spacer strip from your quilt plan. Nevertheless, it is better to wait and cut spacer strips *after* the quilt center and pieced border sections are complete. To plan the width of the spacer strip for a square quilt, calculate the quilt center and the pieced border dimensions. Do not include seam allowances in these dimensions. Subtract the quilt center's size from the pieced border's size. Divide the resulting number by two and you'll have the finished width of the spacer strip. You'll need to add ½" for seam allowances before cutting strips.

To arrive at a dimension for the width of the spacer strip for a rectangular quilt, you will have to figure dimensions separately for both the length and the width of the quilt center. Also calculate the length of one side pieced border and a bottom pieced border. Once again do not include seam allowances in these dimensions. The *long* measurements are going to tell you the width of the *short* spacer strips and the *short* measurements will tell you the width of the *long* strips. (The reason for this is that the width of a vertical spacer strip contributes to the total length of the horizontal borders, and the width of a horizontal spacer strip contributes to the total length of the vertical borders.) There are times when the widths of horizontal and vertical spacer strips will not be the same.

Subtract the long dimension of the quilt center from the dimension of the side pieced border. Divide the resulting number by two and you'll have the finished width of the top or bottom spacer strip. Subtract the short dimension of the quilt center from the short pieced border figure. Divide the resulting number by two and you'll have the finished width of the side spacer strip. Add ½" for seam allowances before cutting strips. Recall that the *length* of the spacer strips will depend on the type of corner treatment you choose. A discussion of the different corner options and how to figure spacer strip lengths for them follows.

Cutting Plain Borders and Spacer Strips

Border strips cut parallel to the selvedges can be seamless. They are more stable than strips cut across the grain, but they require continuous yardage, which can be expensive.

Frugal quilters may want to buy less fabric and plan borders cut following the crosswise grain of the fabric. Crosswise borders are a little stretchier and may require seams to reach the needed length. Seams should be pressed open and placed in the center of each side.

A strategy for scrap quilts might be to cut lengthwise strips from many fabrics in whatever fabric lengths you have. Seam these together to the desired total lengths. You won't need to buy extra fabric; the lengthwise grain adds stability; and the scrap look adds character.

Plain borders should be cut to fit the actual size of the quilt center, as measured. However, you will probably want to cut borders first, before cutting the patches from the same fabric. Since you won't be able to measure the quilt center until you have sewn it, start by cutting border strips longer than you think you'll need, then trim them later to fit the quilt.

It is important that the quilt end up "square" (with 90° corners) and true. Top and bottom border strips should be cut to match each other in length. Likewise, the two side borders should be cut to match each other.

Squared Corners

Squared corners are an easy option that usually requires a little less fabric than mitered corners. They are necessary when the spacer strips are uneven. Some quilt judges prefer mitered corners, but this shouldn't be a factor if you aren't entering your quilt in competition. Squared corners are per-

fectly acceptable. We use them for most of our own quilts.

Squared Corner

To find the proper length of borders with squared corners, first measure the length of the quilt, *including seam allowances.* Cut two borders to match this length. Pin and stitch them to the sides of the quilt, according to the directions on the next page. Press. Measure again, this time across the width of the quilt, including the borders just sewn. Cut a border this length for the top and another for the bottom of the quilt. Pin and stitch. It is not uncommon to have to ease one side of a quilt to fit a border and stretch the opposite side slightly to fit the same dimension.

Mitered Corners

Mitered corners require precision and a touch more fabric than squared corners, but in some situations they are the best choice. Miter when you have a striped fabric for the border and you want the stripe to turn the corner gracefully. Miter when you have multiple plain borders. (You can sew the different colored strips together before stitching them to the quilt center and it will be like sewing on a single border.) Finally, miter when formality is important to you.

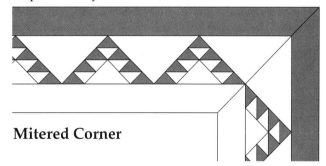

Mitered Corner

In preparation for mitered corners, cut the border strips about three inches longer than the dimensions in your quilt plan. Fold a long border strip in half to find its midpoint; press the fold lightly. Measure the corresponding side of the quilt center (without seam allowances) as described on page 80, and divide this number by two. On the border, measure this distance from the fold toward 81 one end and mark a point on the back side to indicate the end of the stitching line. Repeat from the fold to the other end. Match the border center fold to the center of the side of the quilt, and pin. Match marked points to points ¼" from the raw edge of the quilt center. Pin, then stitch the border to the quilt top. Be careful to stop and backtack ¼" from the ends of the quilt top, rather than stitching all the way to the cut edge. Repeat for the opposite side. Add borders to the remaining two sides of the quilt in the same way.

With your border face down, use your ruler to mark a line at a 45° angle from the end of the seam line to the corner of the border. This will be a sewing line. Lay the ¼" line of your rotary ruler on this line. With a rotary cutter, cut ¼" outside the marked line. Be careful not to cut the quilt top. Repeat for all eight border ends. Stitch a short seam at each border corner, starting exactly at the marked point, and proceeding along the marked line to the corner of the quilt.

Block Corners

Block corners are a traditional border treatment requiring a shorter length of fabric for border strips than the other methods. Block corners add interest and are easy to sew. The separate corner squares can be plain or pieced.

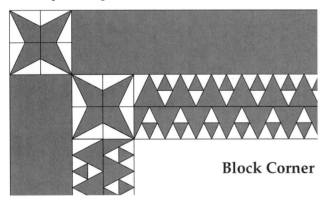

Block Corner

First make four corner squares according to your quilt plan. Cut border strips as *wide* as the corner squares including seam allowances. Cut border strips as *long* as the quilt center measurements including seam allowances.

Pin and stitch border strips to two opposite sides of the quilt center. Sew a corner square to each end of the remaining two borders strips. Oppose seams to match joints at the corners; pin and stitch to attach the last two border strips.

Pinning Borders

Sometimes pieced borders are sewn directly to the quilt blocks in the quilt center, and the joints of the seams will provide all the guidance you need to position the border perfectly. Pin at each joint to be matched, and pin further at intervals of about four inches if needed.

When the pieced border is sewn to a spacer strip or when the joints of the blocks and borders are unrelated, you'll need to make guides. Fold the quilt in half to find the center of one side and mark it with a pin. Then fold each half in half again and mark with a pin at the edge of the quilt. Do the same for the border strip. When you pin the border to the quilt, start by matching the center pins. Then match the other pins and the ends of the quilt and border. These matching pins will help you attach your border strip evenly.

Support the weight of the fabric when pinning long seams. Don't let your quilt droop and stretch out of shape. You may find it helpful to lay the quilt on the carpet or on a bed to pin the borders.

If you're working in a small space or need to do some easing, work at the ironing board. Pin the quilt to the board to keep it from slipping. Position the border on the quilt by matching centers, ends, and joints. Ease and generously pin everything in between. If necessary, press the border to the quilt center with a steam iron. This helps the two fit together and makes the sewing go more smoothly. Steam can shrink or stretch fabric, allowing you to adjust the fit as needed.

Stitching Borders

After pinning thoroughly, stitch borders to the quilt center with a ¼" seam allowance. Do not pull the fabric, rather, let it feed naturally. Don't let the weight of the fabric hamper the natural feed. For an even seam, you will need to support the weight of the quilt while you stitch. Stitch with the pieced side up so that you can see the points as you sew across them. Backtack at both ends of these long seams.

You might want to change the color of your thread before attaching a plain border strip. If the thread that you have been using for piecing is much lighter or darker than the border fabric, it is likely to show in a long seam. Change the bobbin thread to match the plain border.

Design & Drafting

When you want to adapt a stock border, design a custom border, or simply see how your border and quilt look and fit together, you may want to make a sketch of your quilt. This is usually done on graph paper.

Why Do I Want to Draw My Quilt on Graph Paper?

We use graph paper for two things: first, to make small sketches of quilt designs and second, to make full size drawings of shapes for templates or as guides to rotary cutting. Let's begin with a discussion of drawing a quilt plan on graph paper, then continue with how to translate that drawing to full-size usable shapes for templates or rotary cutting.

Realize that it is not difficult to draw on graph paper, but that if you prefer to skip this step, you can still make quilts, even quilts with pieced borders. Graph paper drawing is strictly optional. If you are adding a natural-fit border in a simple design such as a sawtooth, you can probably imagine how it will look, and you can figure how many border repeats you need without a sketch. The patches needed to construct the border are probably the same ones you used for the quilt center or they are presented with the stock border templates in this book.

> **10 Good Reasons for Drawing a Quilt Plan**
> 1. To adapt a stock border to your quilt
> 2. To design a custom border
> 3. To play with colors
> 4. To see how a border looks with your quilt
> 5. To work out the border corners
> 6. To eliminate some of the figuring
> 7. To be sure of the border fit
> 8. To map out a construction plan
> 9. To judge proportions of the design areas
> 10. To correct flaws before making the quilt

If you find the prospect of drawing on graph paper daunting, here's a little story. When Judy's young daughter graduated from diapers to training pants, she was not always easily convinced that she really ought to try sitting on the potty. Often, when it had been quite awhile between bathroom visits, yet she insisted she couldn't go, Judy would coax her by saying, "Just try it. You might surprise yourself." Inevitably, no sooner would she sit down on the potty than she would exclaim gleefully, "I surprised myself!" You might surprise yourself, too, if you try some of the design and drafting techniques described here. It is worth the effort. Even if you don't *need* a graphed quilt plan, there are many reasons why you might *want* one. Sometimes, you might want to play with different colorings. In that case, you will want to make a sketch of the quilt. A drawing helps when you want to be absolutely certain about the border fit and number of repeats. It can even eliminate some of the calculations. (You can simply count border repeats and such on your sketch.) Your graph paper picture is a map to which you can refer as you construct your quilt. It will help you see the relative proportions of the border and the quilt in order to judge the effect. Best of all, your sketch lets you preview your quilt and make improvements before you start cutting and sewing.

Basics of Graph Paper Drawing

If you have never before drawn on graph paper, don't be intimidated by it. The lines are not there to confound you; they are actually quite helpful. You have probably sketched a quilt block at one time or another. Perhaps you've seen a fabulous antique quilt at a show and wanted to make a note of it for future inspiration. If you're like us, you may have resorted to drawing on the back of a checking account deposit slip. Your sketch might be wobbly, but it gets the point across.

If you can rough out a block on a scrap of plain paper, you most certainly can draw one on graph paper. Graph lines are like the threads in counted cross stitch. You ignore them except when you are using them to count. It is actually much easier and neater to draw geometric shapes when you have that grid of light blue horizontal and vertical lines to guide you.

Where do you begin? Both for sketching and for choosing fitting borders, it helps to understand the basis of your quilt block. If you can't see obvious divisions such as the three rows across and three rows down on a Nine-Patch, start by looking for seams that go from edge to edge or corner to corner of the block. This may give you some idea of the block layout. Often the grid divisions are some multiple of the smallest patch.

Some blocks are not based on square graph grids at all. LeMoyne Stars, Lone Stars, and Grandmother's Flower Gardens are examples. The presence of true octagons, true diamonds, hexagons, and equilateral triangles are clues that your pattern is not based on a square grid. Actually, there is a trick for sketching approximations of true diamonds and true octagons to help you visualize many of these non-grid patterns. See page 89 if you are interested in drawing these shapes.

Most patterns *are* based on grids of squares. Once you can see the divisions of the block, you can outline an appropriate number of squares to represent the block perimeter on your graph paper. Within this, you simply copy the block's shapes onto your paper.

Even if you haven't been able to ascertain the block's grid structure, you can copy shapes in relation to each other. Simply start with a square or other easy patch. Then notice how the neighboring patch relates to it, and draw it in place. Usually, a block has two or four corners pieced the same, and you can simply copy what you drew for one corner when you draw the next one. Proceed in this manner until the block is complete.

Drawing Common Shapes on Graph Paper

To draw small square shapes, trace around the outline of one graph square. For larger square patches, skip some blue lines and outline an area of two by two graph squares or more. For isosceles right triangles, draw along two adjacent sides of a small or large square and then draw a diagonal line from corner to corner to connect the sides and complete a triangle. A small rectangle might be one square wide and and two squares long. Look constantly for dimensions one, two, three, four, or more times the size

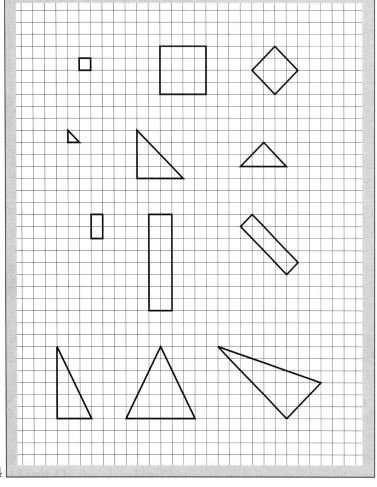

Drawing Basic Shapes on Graph Paper

Squares, rectangles, and various triangles can be easily drawn on graph paper. Simply count squares and follow the grid lines or the invisible diagonal grid. Shapes can be drawn straight or tilted on the diagonal.

of the smallest patch. Notice how the patches relate to each other in size. Follow the angles in the block. Lines usually follow the graph lines or the diagonals of the graph lines. Occasionally, a line will run at an angle such that you go to the right two squares for every one square down. These lines will start and end on graph square corners, and they usually start and stop at the corners of your block's divisions.

Right triangles can be drawn so they sit on their long side or they sit on their short side. We already described how to draw right triangles with the short sides on the graph lines and the long side on the diagonal. You can also draw right triangles with the long side following a line two graph squares long and each short side following the diagonal of one square.

Squares can be drawn following the graph lines. Squares tilted on the diagonal can be drawn guided by the corner points of the graph squares. Think of your graph paper as having not only blue horizontal and vertical lines but also an invisible grid of diagonal lines that you can easily follow. Any shape that you can draw following graph lines you can also draw diagonally following corner points where the graph lines intersect. If you have trouble following the invisible diagonal grid, lay a ruler diagonally on your paper so that it runs from corner to corner of the graph squares and draw along the ruler's edge. See the box at right for a handy use for drawing your patches at an angle.

As you are sketching your quilt on graph paper, don't worry about scale. Any accurate drawing will be a representation to scale, but sometimes the scale is not a nice number. You needn't worry about the number at this stage. Also note that it doesn't matter what size squares your graph paper has. Graph paper with 8 squares, 10 squares or 12 squares per inch usually yields quilt drawings that will fit on an 8½" x 11" sheet of paper and have patches of a suitable size for coloring. (Bigger squares are not necessarily better as they take longer to color.)

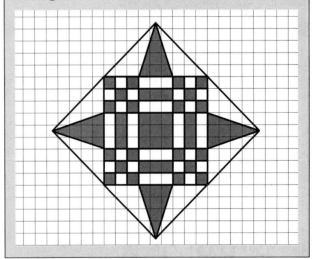

Draw Blocks at an Angle if it Helps

Any shapes can be drawn following the blue grid lines or the invisible diagonal grid. This means that you can draw your quilt block either on the diagonal or straight. Usually blocks are drawn straight, that is, with their edges parallel to the edges of the paper. This is the case even in diagonally set quilts. However, there are times when it is easier to draw a block diagonally. For example, when most of the patches follow a block's diagonals, it can be easier to draw the patches following the graph lines and draw the block's perimeter on the diagonal.

Planning the Quilt and Borders on Graph Paper

Drawing the quilt plan is much like drawing a block. You can draw the whole quilt if you want to visualize it fully or if you need a complete outline in order to plan your colors. You may want to draw the entire quilt to avoid calculations. However, usually it is sufficient to draw just part of the quilt. Judy usually draws about four blocks and a border with one corner. Marsha likes to draw most of the center, a corner and two whole sides of the quilt. You may want to draw much or all of the border but only a few of the blocks. The rest of the blocks could be a simple suggestion of their perimeter. You'll find the grid lines provide a great guide for drawing patchwork shapes and show size relationships clearly. Two quilt sketches of blocks and borders are shown on the following two pages as they would appear on graph paper. Take time to study these illustrations as they hold a wealth of information.

Graphed Border Plan for a Straight Set

Below is a quilt plan on graph paper. It represents 8" quilt blocks set straight with 2" sashes, 4" spacer strips, and a sawtooth pieced border. The border repeat is 2". All of the numbers are compatible. Four 2" border repeats naturally fit an 8" unit block, and one 2" repeat fits the 2" sash. The 4" dimension for the interior plain border or spacer strip was chosen because it equals two full 2" repeats of the border design for each side of the quilt or four total repeats. Two-inch spacers would have worked as well, but a wider look was sought. Since the sawtooth unit is asymmetrical and it changes direction at the center of each side, it was necessary to have an even number of repeats. An odd number of blocks in length and width yields an even number of blocks and sashes for an even number of border repeats.

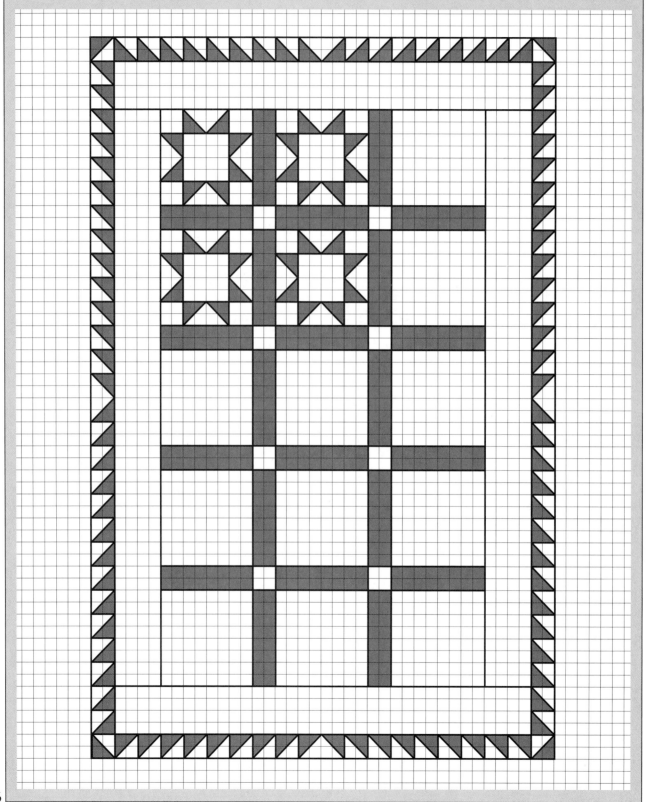

Graphed Border Plan for a Diagonal Set

Below is a second quilt plan on graph paper. It incorporates into a diagonal set the same 8" quilt blocks we saw in the plan on the previous page. Blocks are set side by side, and edge triangles square off around the perimeter of the quilt. The quilt center is framed by a natural-fit chain-of-squares border and a natural-fit embellished dogtooth border. The borders are made from patches found in the star blocks. The patches have the same orientation in the border as they have in the quilt center. (Patches that are straight within a block are turned diagonally in the border. Because the blocks are placed on the diagonal, their patches are turned diagonally, as well.) The relationships of natural-fit borders in a diagonal set are just as definite as they are in a straight set, but the border repeats must be compatible with the diagonal dimension of the block. You don't need to know what these diagonals measure at this stage, just how to draw them. To plan a project with a diagonal set, draw the quilt blocks straight, according to the lines on the graph paper. Draw the perimeters of the quilt center and borders following the diagonals. Turn the paper at a 45° angle to view the quilt plan.

Common Multiples Help You Draw Some Quilts

It seems, sometimes, that what you have in mind simply can't be drawn on graph paper. Perhaps the quilt is made of blocks with a 4 x 4 grid, and the border repeat is the same dimension as the block, but it is based on a 3 x 3 grid. You *can* draw this; you simply need to know the secret of common multiples. Multiply one grid by the other to find a number that is divisible by both numbers: 3 x 4 = 12, in our example. The resulting number, 12, is the number of squares across and down the block or border unit. If you can find a smaller number that is divisible by both numbers, so much the better. (Math majors will recognize that the least common multiple is the ideal number to use, but any multiple will work.) Draw each block on 12 squares with four divisions of 3 squares. Draw each border unit on 12 squares with three divisions of 4 squares. The drawing may be too large to fit the whole quilt on one sheet of paper. It helps to use a small grid such as $\frac{1}{10}$" or $\frac{1}{12}$" squares. To see the entire quilt, draw one quarter of it, including borders. Then make photocopies (reduced to a smaller size, if possible), and tape the sections together. Photocopy again to eliminate the tape and make coloring easy.

Composite Drawings Can Help

Sometimes when the fit is natural and usually when it is not natural, you may have trouble drawing the border and the quilt in their proper positions on graph paper. If the border and block are offset from one another, you don't want to have to draw an entire border that misses the graph lines. The solution here is to draw the quilt center on one sheet of graph paper, and the border on a separate sheet. Then you can cut out the quilt center and affix it to the border drawing in the proper place. If you have already begun a quilt plan and drawn much of it before realizing that you are going to need to adjust the placement of the border relative to the quilt center, you can salvage what you have done. Simply cut away the quilt center and complete the border, patching in with another sheet of paper, if necessary. Then position the quilt center properly over the border sketch. If you have drawn all of the parts to the same scale, you can still use this drawing to help you with your planning.

Occasionally you can draw your quilt plan to scale and draft your templates full-size by mixing two different kinds of graph paper. If it suits your purpose, you can draw the border on graph paper with squares of one size and draw the quilt center on graph paper having a different grid altogether. See an example at left.

Mixed Grids Example

Suppose you want to draw an Irish Chain quilt center of 10" blocks framed by a border of 10" Variable Star blocks. You can easily draw the star border on 8-squares-to-the-inch graph paper. One block covers one inch square, with four divisions of two squares each. It would be difficult to draw the 25-Patch Irish Chain block in 8 x 8 graph squares. Instead, draw the 10" block in one inch on 10-squares-to-the-inch graph paper. The Irish Chain blocks have five divisions of two squares each. The scale would be one inch (8 or 10 squares, depending on the graph paper) represents 10" for both the border and the quilt center; on the other hand, one square on the $\frac{1}{8}$ grid represents $1\frac{1}{4}$" and one square on the $\frac{1}{10}$ grid represents 1". Draw the quilt center on 10-squares-to-the-inch graph paper and draw the border on 8-squares-to-the-inch paper. Cut out the quilt center and affix it in position over the blank space in the middle of the border drawing.

For full-sized templates, multiply the number of squares on the edge of the patch by the scale. You will need 2 x 1" = 2" square shapes for the 10" Irish Chain and 2 x $1\frac{1}{4}$" = $2\frac{1}{2}$" square shapes for the 8" Variable Star. As it turns out, patches for both blocks can be easily drawn full size on the $\frac{1}{8}$ graph paper, which allows you to add seam allowances readily.

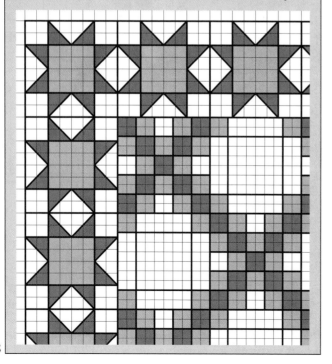

Graph Paper Approximation of True Diamonds and True Octagons

For quilt sketches involving true octagons or diamonds, you need to draw shapes having equal sides, with some vertical or horizontal sides and some diagonal sides. You cannot draw these shapes precisely by following the graph grid. The horizontal and vertical grid of the paper isn't the same size as the invisible diagonal grid. If you try to draw a diamond one square on each side, you will either end up with a parallelogram with two long sides and two short sides, or you will have to draw three of the sides in between graph lines, with the graph paper providing very little help. Here is a trick Judy devised for previewing the look and rough fit of blocks and quilts based on these shapes. This technique is not meant for making templates or taking measurements. Use graph paper and a ruler to draft accurate, full-size patterns for templates, and use your sketch as a map, but double check with accurate calculations for spacer strips, border repeats, patch dimensions and so on.

Use graph paper with a small grid, at least eight to twelve lines to the inch. For each straight side of a diamond or octagon, count out *three* graph squares. For each diagonal side, count out *two* diagonals. The resulting shapes look almost perfect, yet you can follow the graph lines and diagonals. On ⅛" graph paper, you can hardly see the ²⁄₁₀₀ of an inch difference in the supposedly equal sides.

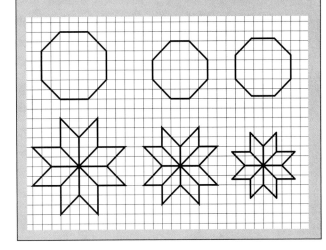

Approximating True Octagons & Diamonds		
1st Column: Approximated octagon & diamonds fit grid without much distortion.	2nd Column: Typical grid-drawn shapes are distorted.	3rd Column: True octagon & diamonds usually don't fall on the grid lines.

Designing a Quilt to Fit a Bed

Most of the time, borders are planned to surround a quilt evenly on four sides like a picture frame. This looks wonderful for a wall quilt or a throw. It usually looks great on a bed, too. However, a bed and a picture are viewed differently. The picture is basically two dimensional; the bed is three dimensional. It has four different planes: the mattress surface, the drop at the bottom, the drop at the left side, and the drop at the right side. Each of these, plus the pillow area, is a different design space. The drop at the sides and bottom is usually a continuous, uniform pattern. Often, the pillow area is treated the same, as well. Generally, any adjustment to the quilt size needed for your desired pattern is made in the pillow area. The pillows can be tucked under the quilt, placed over it, or placed directly on the sheet with the quilt folded back a little. A pillow tuck requires an extra 3"-12" in the length of the quilt. Placing the pillows on the sheet can take up to 12" off the quilt's length. This provides the flexibility you need to make an attractive design that fits naturally.

If you are planning a quilt for a specific bed, it will be difficult to anticipate the exact amount of take-up due to quilting. You can usually count on a finished bed-size quilt being 2"-4" shorter and narrower than the quilt top and the quilt plan. Thick batting and heavy quilting will result in the maximum take-up. Since this is somewhat variable, don't plan to have a focal design element fall exactly at the edge of the mattress. Plan for a spacer strip or simply pieced area here that will look good whether it falls on the mattress, in the drop, or straddling both.

You will need to start your plan by knowing the mattress size. Measure your bed or refer to the chart at the left. Then have an idea of how far down the sides you want the quilt to drop. Plan on at least 9" to cover the mattress for use with a dust ruffle. Plan on at least 16" to cover the box springs. Proceed by drawing the quilt center to scale, to roughly fill an area equal to the mattress size less any pillow area you choose to design differently.

Usually, a bed-size quilt having 15"-20" of borders on each side will place the central design clear of the pillows. If the quilt center is planned to be about the width of the mattress, the design will suit a double, queen, or king-size bed admirably. For a twin bed, the central design should be about 40" x 60" and surrounded by 15"-20" of borders on all four sides.

Next, design a transition area that is fairly plain. Finally, design borders to fill the drop and pillow areas.

Standard Mattress Dimensions	
Youth Bed	33" x 66"
Twin Bed	39" x 75"
¾ Bed	48" x 75"
Double Bed	54" x 75"
Queen Bed	60" x 80"
King Bed	76" x 80"
Calif. King	78" x 80"

Design and Drafting for Custom Borders

For most quilt projects, stock borders, such as those shown on pages 44-79 will serve admirably. Occasionally, however, you may want to venture beyond these into custom borders--borders you design specifically to suit your quilt. Most custom borders are derived from block parts strung into linear repeats. Just as the triangles from a Variable Star block can be used to make a sawtooth border, elements from your block can be put together to make unique borders to suit your quilt perfectly. Judy devised the border for her Prairie Rambler quilt on page 35 by taking the pieced band out of the center of the block, turning it 45°, and sizing it up to fit the block. Think of custom borders as special cases of stock borders that no one has gotten around to designing before.

Usually custom borders are simply variations or combinations of stock borders. If you can easily visualize how they will look on your quilt, and if you already have the patterns necessary to cut the patches, you won't need to do any drawing or drafting. However, for some custom borders, you will want to sketch the idea to see how it looks next to your blocks or to work out corner treatments. Sketching on graph paper is also a good way to generate new ideas for borders.

During the sketching phase of your quilt design is when you really can do some playing with shapes and ideas. Once you've sketched a center portion of a quilt, you can outline a space for the pieced border. In this space you can draw a simple design and then change it by adding lines or dropping them out and changing coloring until you are satisfied with the effect. Use the stock borders that begin on page 44 for inspiration, then change them to suit your fancy.

Keep in mind that whatever the design, you must be able to sew it together. Part of any border design is planning for the easiest construction by adding or eliminating seams as appropriate. Our stock borders are shown with the standard seaming. These versions look great in scraps, but if you are using just a few fabrics, some seams between same-colored patches could be eliminated.

Turning the Corner

Whenever you are planning a quilt, pay special attention to how your border design turns the corners. Many times, as in the symmetrical chain-of-squares border, the design turns the corner simply with the use of another repeat. But in the chain-of Four-Patches, the border design needs a different coloring in the corner unit to turn gracefully. Often the graph paper lines will suggest design solutions for different cornering situations. The designs are there, you just have to find them!

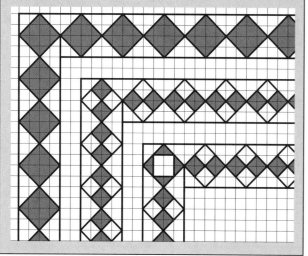

There has to be an element of play in this process of quilt planning and designing pieced quilt borders. Allow a piece to grow. Don't be afraid to break the frame or color outside the lines. Let colors and design lines extend to the next border area to soften the lines and provide a transition. Play with lines and make photocopies of your line drawings so you can try different colorings.

Once you have an idea you like, cut and stitch a sample swatch of the border section and study it next to the quilt center on the floor or on a design wall. What looks great on paper doesn't always translate well to fabric, so trust your own perception. If the border in relationship to the rest of the quilt looks good to you, it probably is good. If it seems wrong--too wide or too bright or too busy--try again until you have something you really like. Listen to those nagging doubts. If you aren't 100% pleased at the planning stage, you probably won't be any happier with the finished quilt. Give it time. Put your planning aside for a few days to give your subconscious a chance to play with the problem. You'll come up with a creative solution before long, and you'll be glad you waited. Once you have completed your quilt plan, don't follow it slavishly. Give yourself permission to make changes as the quilt grows and you begin to see it in fabric.

> ### Keep the Numbers Simple
> If you can count and do simple multiplication and division, you can plan pieced borders for your quilts. One way to make it go smoothly is to try to keep the numbers simple. For a pieced border to fit your quilt naturally, the finished dimensions of the central patchwork need to be divisible by the border repeat measurement. To use 2" repeats, for instance, the length and width of the quilt center must be divisible by 2". A 52" x 68" quilt center would be compatible with a 2" border repeat. A 53" x 68" quilt center would not. A 4" border repeat fits only measurements divisible by 4" and so on.
>
> Use numbers that work together. To design borders that go with 8" blocks, use 2" and 4" repeats, because 8 is divisible by 2 and 4. Use the same dimensions for spacer strips and sashes. Twelve inch blocks fit easily with 1", 1½", 2", 3", 4" and 6" border repeats because 12 is divisible by those numbers. Ten is divisible by 1, 2, 2½, and 5, so repeats of those dimensions would work with 10" blocks, and so on.
>
> Another reason for using easy numbers is to ensure cutting dimensions that will match standard markings on rotary cutting rulers. Though it is possible to cut any dimension with rotary tools, it is easier to cut dimensions that are already marked on your rotary rulers.

Your Quilt Plan Tells You the Dimensions of Patches and Border Strips

Your quilt sketch is a drawing of your quilt in miniature, a scale drawing, actually. If you assign a full-sized dimension to the small squares on the graph paper, you can use your sketch to help with figuring.

You may know the scale from the outset. For example, you may have drawn a Log Cabin quilt that you intend to make with logs that finish one inch wide. You probably drew the quilt on graph paper with logs one square wide. The scale, in that case, is one square equals one inch. Knowing this, you can figure the widths of spacer strips and the lengths of borders. Simply count the squares and that is the number of inches. You can also figure the lengths of the logs and the sizes of the pieced border patches the same way.

You can assign a scale after making the sketch. In this case, you can choose a number that will give you a quilt of the desired size, but it helps to consider the patch size, too. Try to keep the numbers nice and easy. Suppose your sketch is 70 squares long, and you want to make a quilt 90" long. 90" divided by 70 squares = 1.28" per square. You will have trouble drafting patterns this size or rotary cutting shapes of these dimensions. If you make the scale 1 square = 1¼", you can easily draft templates and rotary cut patches. The quilt would measure 70 squares x 1¼" = 87½" long. You can make the outer border 1¼" wider if you need the quilt to measure 90".

Each small graph square on your sketch could equal 1", or 1½" or 2" on your quilt; whatever *scale* you choose. By assigning a scale to the graph paper squares, you can figure the finished size of your quilt. Furthermore,

Figuring the Size of Spacer Strips
From Your Scale Drawing

Fill in this chart to figure the dimensions of spacer strips and plain borders for your quilt. Do four separate computations: 1) length of long border, 2) width of long border, 3) length of short border, and 4) width of short border.

_____ number of graph squares in the border (count the squares along the appropriate edge)

x _____ number of inches each graph square represents in your scale*

= _____ number of inches that dimension should be in your quilt

Measure and adjust for construction discrepancies before cutting strips.

*To determine the correct scale, do the computation below. Use the resulting number in the chart above.

_____ desired block size

÷ _____ number of graph squares per one edge of block in your drawing

= _____ number of inches each graph square represents in your scale--for use above

when it's time to put your design into action, your drawing will tell you cutting and sewing dimensions for all the parts.

A Little Math Provides Helpful Details

Your quilt plan is full of useful information. For example, it may tell you that you need four rows of five blocks and 40 border repeats on one long side. It will also tell you the dimensions of the patches and of the borders, spacer strips, and overall quilt, with just a little easy math. You could count the blocks to determine there are 20; it would be easier to simply count four blocks in width and five blocks in length and multiply four times five to get 20. A little multiplication will also reveal that 40 border repeats times 2" each = 80", the length of one spacer strip. If you would prefer to count rather than multiply, skip ahead to "Don't Figure Dimensions for Diagonals If You Don't Have To" on the next page.

Quilters often need to work with ¼" or ⅛" or other fractions. To make the math easy, use a calculator. Calculators don't have fractions. They use decimals instead. To use a calculator to do figures involving fractions, find the decimal equivalent in the chart below and enter it in place of the fraction. Then, when your calculations are complete, look on the equivalents chart again to convert back to fractions found on your ruler. Do all your figuring with as many decimal places as your calculator gives you. When you get a final answer, just look at three digits to the right of the decimal point. Ignore any numbers farther to the right. Look on this chart to see the equivalent in fractions. If the result is a number that is not in this chart, look to see which two numbers it falls between. Compare the result to the numbers in the chart. Choose the closer number if it is obvious. For example, if your calculator gives you a result of 4.13, compare .13 to the numbers in the chart. Our number, .13, carried out to three decimal places is .130. It falls between .125 and .156. It is closer to .125 than to .156, so we call it ⅛. Our answer is 4⅛. If it is not immediately obvious which number is closer, choose either number. The difference between the two listed numbers is just ⅟₃₂ of an inch. A number about halfway between the two listed numbers would be about ⅟₆₄" from either number. This is definitely close enough for patchwork purposes.

Decimal Equivalents Chart

⅟₃₂	.031	⁹⁄₃₂	.281	¹⁷⁄₃₂	.531	²⁵⁄₃₂	.781
⅟₁₆	.062	⁵⁄₁₆	.312	⁹⁄₁₆	.562	¹³⁄₁₆	.812
³⁄₃₂	.094	¹¹⁄₃₂	.344	¹⁹⁄₃₂	.594	²⁷⁄₃₂	.844
⅛	.125	⅜	.375	⅝	.625	⅞	.875
⁵⁄₃₂	.156	¹³⁄₃₂	.406	²¹⁄₃₂	.656	²⁹⁄₃₂	.906
³⁄₁₆	.188	⁷⁄₁₆	.438	¹¹⁄₁₆	.688	¹⁵⁄₁₆	.938
⁷⁄₃₂	.219	¹⁵⁄₃₂	.469	²³⁄₃₂	.719	³¹⁄₃₂	.969
¼	.250	½	.500	¾	.750		

Figuring Dimensions for Diagonals

Most quilt plans have some lines on the diagonal. This is not generally a problem, as usually the straight patch dimensions are known, and they are all you need to know. Sometimes, especially with diagonally set blocks, you may need to figure a dimension based on diagonals. If you have a quilt center of 8" blocks set diagonally and you want to figure the length of spacer strips needed to frame this, you will need to know the diagonal measurement. You can make a block and measure it from point to point (excluding the seam allowances), or you can figure the dimension from your quilt plan by multiplying the number of blocks times the side dimension of one block times 1.414 (the square root of 2), as described in the box at the right.

Don't Figure Dimensions for Diagonals If You Don't Have To

When your blocks are on the diagonal, the border repeats must be compatible with the block's diagonal dimension in order to achieve a natural fit. This does not necessarily mean that you have to *know* that dimension. You can simply devise a border from block patches if you are careful not to change their orientation. For example, you might make a quilt of 8" star blocks set on the diagonal, as in the quilt plan on page 87. A chain-of-squares border of the same patches fits the quilt center naturally, and you never need to know what the diagonal dimensions are.

Translating Sketches to Full Size Templates

After sketching a quilt or border design on graph paper and deciding on a scale, you can draw patches full size. You'll need graph paper, a sharp pencil, and a drawing ruler. Graph paper comes in different sizes and grids. Often the most useful measures 11" x 17" and has ⅛" squares, but sometimes other grid sizes are better for specific dimensions. (See the box on the next page.) For drafting, a fine-tipped mechanical drawing pencil is ideal, but an ordinary #2 lead pencil with a good sharpener will do just fine. If you are going to do a lot of drafting, choose a thin ruler. Marsha's favorite is a clear plastic ruler, 2" x 18" with a ⅛" grid of red lines. Rotary cutting rulers often don't work well for drafting because they are extra thick and throw a shadow on the paper, making it difficult to see where to draw lines.

Begin by copying a portion of the block and a section of border full size on the graph paper. Multiply your scale by the number of graph squares on one side of a patch. Use a ruler to mark off this dimension, and start drawing a portion of your block or border full size. Continue drawing the patches in relation to each other until you have included each different shape and size of patch. This often means drawing a portion of the block, a border repeat and a border corner as well.

You may want to start by marking off a grid of squares the size of your scale. For example, if your scale is one square = 1¼", count or measure to mark a grid of 1¼" squares on your graph paper. Now, ignoring the blue graph lines and following your penciled grid, copy your sketch, square for square, to the full-sized grid.

You'll only need one patch of each size and shape, so identify each shape that needs to be cut by lightly coloring it in with a colored pencil.

Example: Figuring Dimensions For Diagonals

To figure the diagonal dimension of any square or block or the hypotenuse of an isosceles right triangle, multiply the side of the square or the short side of the triangle by 1.414. (This is the square root of 2, also denoted by $\sqrt{2}$). For quick approximations, you can multiply by 1.4. Even better, use a calculator and then use the decimal equivalent chart on page 92 to convert to fractions suitable for sewing. In order to find the diagonal dimension of a 12" block, multiply 12" times the square root of 2. Using a calculator, punch the buttons as follows, treating the square root button ($\sqrt{}$) just as you would treat another digit in a number starting with 2. Punch "12," "x," "2," "$\sqrt{}$," "=." The result is 16.97. Be sure to give the calculator enough time to bring up the number before punching the equal sign.

Sometimes, when the square is on point on the graph paper, the diagonal is the known number. Likewise, the hypotenuse of an isosceles right triangle may be known. To determine the dimension of the side of a square or the short side of a triangle in this case, divide the diagonal measurement by the square root of 2. If a square has a diagonal of 4", we figure on the calculator as follows: Punch "4," "÷," "2," "$\sqrt{}$," "=." The result is 2.828.

Figure dimensions of border strips or whole quilts by multiplying the number of diagonals times the dimension of the short side times the square root of 2 (1.414).

Be sure to used finished dimensions in these calculations. To make templates based on these finished dimensions, add ¼" seam allowances after the calculations are complete.

Add a consistent ¼" seam allowance around each shape. (This seam allowance will overlap the neighboring patches and may overlap other seam allowances as well.) If your graph paper is 4, 8 or 12 squares to the inch, you can follow graph lines to add seam allowances to the horizontal and vertical sides of patches. For diagonals, measure the ¼" seam allowance with a ruler rather than following a diagonal of the invisible grid. You will also need to measure ¼" with a ruler to add seam allowances whenever you use graph papers that don't have lines spaced ¼" apart. After adding seam allowances, trace the completed template shapes to eliminate the overlap. Use them as cutting guides for no-template rotary cutting, or cut them out and prepare templates from them.

You Can Make Full-Size Templates Without Graph Paper

Sometimes the design we have in mind does not conform to a graph grid. Inspired design occasionally calls for some more flexible drafting solutions than ordinary graph paper techniques can provide. Should you ever need to foresake graph paper and easy numbers in pursuit of art, you will want to know about alternative ways of sketching a quilt plan and drafting full-size templates.

From here to the end of this chapter, we describe drafting strategies, any of which you can use instead of the graph paper technique already described. We will start with the methods that everybody will understand. Read through as many of these methods as you care to. If you want to avoid math whenever possible, skip the last two techniques.

The following techniques transcend the usual limitations of graph paper grids. They can result in patches that don't have nice, easy measurements that match the markings on your rotary cutting rulers. If this is the case, use tinted acetate film (Static Stickers ™) to make templates, including seam allowances. These will stick to the underside of your rotary ruler to use as a cutting guide. If you don't have this product, you can make a paper template and tape it to the ruler with removable tape.

Proportional Drawing

This method is a little casual, but it gets the job done with easy calculations. It is good for full-size templates, but it won't be of much help for sketching a whole quilt plan. You will find proportional drawing especially useful in drafting full-size shapes that can be easily graphed in miniature but that pose problems full-size because of oddball dimensions. This is a method that has been described by Jinny Beyer in her book *Patchwork Patterns* and that can also be found in a beginning mechanical drawing book. This method can be used to divide any square into any number of divisions. What this trick accomplishes is that it lets you measure nice numbers to draw a grid of not-so-nice numbers. This works because the drawing and the measurements represent two images that are proportional to each other. See the facing page for an example of proportional drawing.

Proportional Drawing Example

Suppose you want to make a 4" square into a Nine-Patch. You can draw this on graph paper having ½" squares. However, if you don't have this kind of paper, what can you do? You will need a nine-square grid in a 4" space. When 4" is divided by 3, the result is 1⅓". Standard rulers do not even have ⅓" markings.

1. Draw a square of the desired finished size (4"). The easiest way to make sure that your square is true is to draw it on graph paper. However, quilters who are unaccustomed to graph paper may want to trace this square onto plain, unlined paper because the graph lines will not relate to the grid lines we are going to draw next. (Some people find it confusing to draw on graph paper and ignore the lines.)

2. Select a measurement on your ruler that is longer than the side of the square (4"), shorter than the diagonal (about 5⅝"), and is easily divisible by the number of divisions desired (in this case, 3). In this situation, 4½" is a good number. So let's divide 4½" by 3 to equal 1½" intervals.

3. Hold the point of your pencil on the exact corner in the lower left of your square. Place the 0" or end of your ruler against the pencil point and pivot

the ruler until the mark for your chosen number (4½") on the ruler touches the right side of the square. Make a fine dot at the calculated interval (every 1½", that is, at 1½" and 3" marks on the ruler) as shown.

4. Use a gridded ruler or a right angle tool to draw a vertical line through each dot. Make sure that each line is perpendicular to the top and bottom of the square and is absolutely parallel to the sides. The lines you will draw will divide the square into equal sections. In this example two lines divide the square into three sections.

5. To make the horizontal divisions, place your ruler with the 0" at the same lower left corner, but this time pivot the ruler until the mark indicating your chosen number (4½") touches the top of the square. Again make dots at your calculated interval (1½") and use a ruler or right triangle tool to draw horizontal lines to complete the grid.

6. You can use this grid just as you would use commercial graph paper to draw triangles or other shapes needed for your design. For each size and shape of patch, add ¼" seam allowances as described on page 94. Make traditional templates or use this drafting as a guide for rotary cutting dimensions.

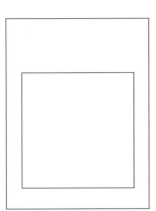

Draw a square the desired size of the block (4").

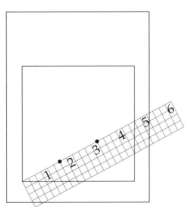

Place a ruler with "0" at corner and "4½" at side; make dots at 1½" and 3".

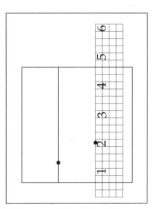

Use a ruler to draw a vertical line through each of the dots.

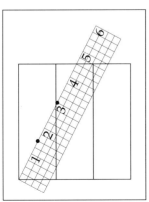

Place ruler with "0" at corner and "4½" at top; make dots at 1½" and 3".

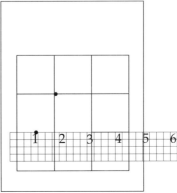

Use a ruler to draw a horizontal line through each of these two dots.

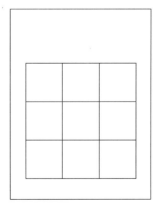

Your Nine-Patch grid in a 4" square is complete.

Paper Folding

With all of our modern resources--graph paper, fancy rulers and computers--sometimes the old-fashioned, low-tech solution to a problem is the best one for most people. Paper folding is just such a method. What it lacks in scientific precision, it makes up for in ease and practicality. The results are good enough for patchwork--and have been for generations. You can use paper folding for full-size templates, but it won't do you much good for drawing your whole quilt in miniature.

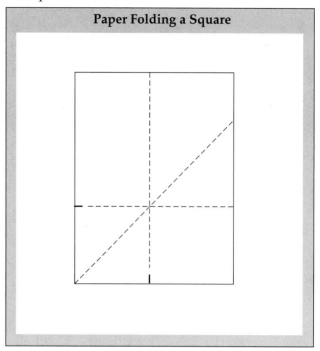

Paper Folding a Square

For this technique, in addition to plain paper (such as typing paper) and pencil, you may need adding machine tape, a ruler or a drafting compass. The sizes and shapes of many simple pieced designs can be found through paper folding, and it is a great technique to know about when you find the math daunting and graph paper inadequate for the circumstances.

To make a square shape with this method, take the 8½" x 11" sheet of plain paper and measure it with a ruler or hold it up to a finished quilt block or anything whose size you want to match. Start "measuring" at the bottom left corner of the paper and make a pencil mark along the bottom edge to match the desired size. Now fold the paper at a 45° angle from the lower left corner so that the bottom edge comes up to align with the left side. Make a mark on the left side where it touches the mark on the bottom. Unfold the paper. Next fold the excess out of the way: At the mark on the bottom edge, fold the right side back, aligning bottom edges. Similarly fold the top edge back at the second mark, aligning left sides. Now your square is complete.

You can use this square as the basis of a grid to make other shapes, as well. You already have a diagonal fold across the square, indicating the area of an isosceles right triangle. You can fold the square in half lengthwise for a rectangle. You can fold one corner of the rectangle so that the short side touches the long side to make a trapezoid. You can fold two adjacent corners in so that the top edge is along the lengthwise center fold to make a house shape, and so on.

Adding machine tape comes in handy for "measuring" spacer strips and borders and dividing the area into border repeats. See the box on the next page for a paper folding example using adding machine tape.

Paper Folding Example

It sometimes happens that the quilt's center panel has terrible dimensions. The first pieced border builds the quilt center out to a lousy dimension. The numbers are not easily divisible into even border repeats. If, for whatever reason, spacer strips to bring the quilt center and existing borders out to good measurements are not appropriate, you can find a suitable repeat and make simple templates with paper folding.

As an example, let's say that you want to frame a large appliquéd block with a dogtooth pieced border. You have determined that your design looks best with a center block finished at 27¼". This is not a nice number. It doesn't divide evenly by anything! What should you do? A simple paper folding technique will help you find the repeat of the dogtooth pieced border design. Then another bit of paper folding will give you full-sized dogtooth triangles to use for templates.

To find the repeat:

1. Using adding machine tape (a long narrow strip of paper), "measure" the length of the side of your quilt. Do not include seam allowances. Mark each end of the "measurement."

2. Matching the end marks, fold the paper strip in half and make a crease in the center.

3. Fold the paper strip in half again, matching the center crease to the end marks, and crease the folds. This gives you four repeats that will fit evenly along the side of your quilt. Continue folding in half for eight repeats, then sixteen, and so on. Keep folding until you get a space of about the desired size. The space between the creases in the paper is the *running length* of the repeat. Don't worry about the *width* of the repeat at this stage. The width of the adding machine tape is not necessarily the width of your border.

To make the full-size dogtooth triangle:

1. Starting at the bottom left corner of a plain sheet of paper, measure the running length of the repeat along the bottom edge and make a pencil mark.

2. Fold the paper at a 45° angle from the lower left corner. This brings the bottom right corner up and to the left so that the bottom edge of the paper aligns with the left side. Crease. Unfold the paper.

3. Now fold the lower left corner up and to the right so that the existing fold line doubles over itself and a new fold forms diagonally from the mark at the bottom. Crease this new fold, forming an "x" with the previous fold.

4. Unfold the paper to see the two triangles that result. Each is the finished size of the triangle in the dogtooth border. Trace or glue one of these to another sheet of paper to add ¼" seam allowances and make a rotary cutting guide or traditional template.

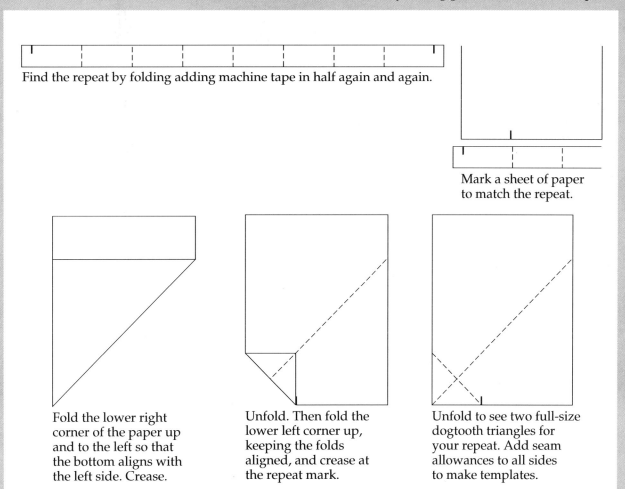

Find the repeat by folding adding machine tape in half again and again.

Mark a sheet of paper to match the repeat.

Fold the lower right corner of the paper up and to the left so that the bottom aligns with the left side. Crease.

Unfold. Then fold the lower left corner up, keeping the folds aligned, and crease at the repeat mark.

Unfold to see two full-size dogtooth triangles for your repeat. Add seam allowances to all sides to make templates.

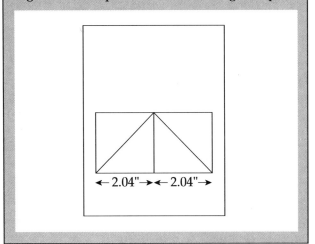
Calculator & Ruler Method

If you are comfortable with a calculator and it doesn't bother you to measure using very small rulings such as ½₂ or ⁷⁄₁₀₀ inch, you can simply use a calculator to divide the projected or measured border space by the desired number of repeats to determine the size of the border repeat. If the resulting number is some odd fraction or decimal, you can still draft it full-size. You won't find these numbers on your standard rotary ruler, however.

After you figure the size of the border repeat on a calculator, you can measure and mark a square or rectangle to correspond to the desired border unit. Draw this on plain paper, or if you are prepared to ignore the lines after the first one or two, use graph paper. Use a gridded ruler or T-square to get a good right angle in each corner. Further divide this space into divisions as needed to draw the appropriate shapes. Divide your overall length by two for two divisions, by three for three divisions, and so on. Make marks corresponding to these measurements, and draw lines from these marks perpendicular to the sides of the square or rectangle.

If you have a ruler with inches and hundredths, you can use the numbers straight from the calculator. The first two digits to the right of the decimal are the number of hundredths. If the third digit is higher than five, round up to the next hundredth. If the third digit is less than five, ignore it.

If your ruler is in inches and ½₂ inches, use our decimal equivalent chart on page 92 to convert your calculations for ruler use.

Computer Method

It is outside the scope of this book to teach you how to use your computer. If you are reading this paragraph, we will assume you have a computer and a drawing or graphics program, and that you know how to use them. We simply want to remind you that a computer can be a viable alternative to graph paper, both for drawing a quilt plan and for drafting full-size pattern shapes for templates or rotary cutting guides.

It's not unusual for printers to distort patterns. Before you rely on your computer for templates, make a test pattern. Draw an 8" x 8" square, print it, and get out your ruler to check the dimensions. Often, the printer stretches a pattern lengthwise but not crosswise. If that is the case, draw long, narrow shapes crosswise to counteract this effect. If your printer is too inaccurate for templates, you can still draw your quilt plan on the computer and use graph paper for translating the plan full size.

Even though most graphics programs and computers have color capabilities, we prefer to make quilt drawings in black, white and shades of gray. We can work out the values in our sketch but select colors and fabrics in the sewing room.

The main difference between drawing on a computer and drawing on graph paper is that on the computer, you must draw a quilt one shape at a time instead of drawing a series of lines that create shapes where they intersect. Each triangle, square or other shape is a separate object, just as it is in sewing a quilt. Individual patches are drawn, shaded or colored, and combined with other shapes to create designs, just as they are in quiltmaking. A computer lets you rotate and duplicate shapes, two functions that can save quilters a great deal of planning time. (Don't you wish you could push a button to duplicate a quilt block in fabric?)

Many drawing programs have grids you can use pretty much the way you use graph paper. Aldus SuperPaint® for the Macintosh® is this type of program. It is relatively inexpensive and very easy to use. Marsha used it for several years before reaching the limits of its capabilities. Though the snap-to-the-grid function makes drawing simple shapes a breeze, the sizes of grids on drawing programs may be limited. You may not be able to draw shapes to the dimensions you need. SuperPaint®, for example, consistently rounds up a ⅛" grid from .125 to .13. If you are interested in more precise work and a program with greater flexiblity, a program that works mathematically is in order. Judy and Marsha use Adobe Illustrator™ to draw shapes defined by precise dimensions and snapped to each other to make a design. This program requires pretty good math skills, is expensive, and takes a lot of computer memory, so it isn't for everybody. However, if you already use it for other purposes, try it for quilt planning. We think it's great.

In Adobe Illustrator™, if you start drawing full size, you can test your pattern shapes as you draw your design. Save the full-size patches to one file and reduce them to 25% in a second file to begin your quilt plan. Keep track of the reduction, so you can add new shapes as needed to relate to the ones on the screen. Zoom in to fiddle with details, and zoom out to see the overall view. Play with the program to practice drawing triangles, diamonds, octagons, and more. If you like scientific precision, don't rely on the pen tool. Try to rely on true shapes and sizes determined using algebra, geometry, and a calculator.

Designing quilts on the computer takes some adjustment. Rather than working with lines and grids, you'll need to think in terms of shapes having specific dimensions. However, once you've made the transition, you can draw patches of any shape and size you desire, whether or not they have a grid basis. On the computer you can quickly design and draft more quilts than you could ever dream of making.

Complete Quilt Patterns

The pages that follow are full of helpful instructions, charts, and illustrations to guide you as you make your quilt. To get the most out of them, read this page first. For each quilt pattern in this book, there is a color photograph (pages 32-43) plus diagrams and directions (pages 101-143) and full-size patterns (pages 148-159). Each quilt is presented in three sizes.

Yardage & Cutting Requirements Chart

Follow the chart to the right to see the yardage and patches needed for each fabric listed on the left. Note that there are three sections to this chart, one for each quilt size. Refer to only the section that describes the quilt size you are making.

The "Yds." column indicates the amount of 44"-wide fabric needed. We allowed for 4% shrinkage in our computations. You won't need to know yardage figures for a scrap quilt, but the yardage listed will give you an idea of the total required.

The "Patches" column identifies the full-size pattern pieces by letter and number and lists the quantity needed of each. If you are rotary cutting patches, the resulting shapes will match the full-size patterns, so they are identified by the same letters. Strip cutting sometimes yields a few extra patches. Compare your strip-cut totals to the totals in the yardage chart, and set aside the extras to avoid unnecessary sewing.

The yardage listed is sufficient for seamless borders. Border strips are listed with exact cutting dimensions, including seam allowances. The "+" indicates that you should cut the strips longer to allow for individual differences in cutting and sewing. Trim the border strips after making your quilt center and measuring it. Cut two strips of each length listed, unless only one length is listed, in which case cut four strips. Sometimes borders are made from random lengths of scraps. Join these pieces to make the total length listed.

At the bottom of the yardage chart is a summary for each quilt size listing the number of blocks, how many blocks are in a row, how many rows there are, and the number of border units needed.

Quilt Construction & Piecing Diagrams

Directions for quilt construction are broken down into steps describing how to make the blocks and units shown in the accompanying diagrams. Where quantities are listed in the text, a series of three numbers separated by slashes refers to the small, medium, and large quilt sizes.

See page 144 for extra help with techniques and shortcuts. We encourage you to embellish your quilting with commercial stencils or other motifs.

Diagrams show patch letters for traditional or rotary-cut shapes. The patches are usually exploded apart to show piecing sequence. Usually, a block is made with two or four sections that are pieced the same. We show one of these sections exploded and others joined. Look at the exploded parts first. Start by joining patches that are shown touching. Then sew the resulting sections together, starting with sections shown close together and progressing to bigger sections shown farther apart.

Multiple Sizes and Drawings to Color

It is often helpful to see the whole quilt to understand the piecing. As we are giving each quilt in three sizes, we show one size in the photographs. Another size is shown in a blank drawing that you can photocopy and color. The third quilt size is presented in a whole quilt piecing diagram that shows where the blocks and units go. With these illustrations to guide you, we think you'll be able to make the quilt in any size.

Full-Size Patterns & Rotary Cutting

The full-size patterns are presented on pages 148-159. Read pages 145-146 for details about our full-size patterns. Specific rotary cutting instructions are on page 146. Charts detailing strip widths, cross cuts and angles for each patch are on pages 147 and 148.

Some patterns are asymmetrical. If you need to cut mirror images, the yardage and cutting chart calls for a patch letter and number and the same notation followed by an "r." Turn the pattern face down for the reversed pieces, indicated by the "r."

Columbia Square

Marsha made this medallion quilt with a 12" Georgetown Circle block and a series of linear and triangular add-on borders that utilize patches and dimensions from the center block for natural fit. Judy took the block and border elements and came up with designs for two bed-size quilts, as well. Within this quilt structure, many variations are possible. Any 12" block could be used in the center, and any 6" block could replace the Ohio Star in the border. A multitude of prints and plaids would yield a scrappy, country look. The color photograph of Columbia Square is on page 32. The full-size templates and rotary cutting chart begin on page 145.

Right, Columbia Square wall quilt, 54¾" x 54¾".

COLUMBIA SQUARE: FABRICS, YARDAGE & CUTTING REQUIREMENTS

All Sizes 12" Blocks	Wall Quilt 54¾" x 54¾"		Twin Quilt 71¾" x 88¾"		Double/Queen Quilt 88¾" x 88¾"	
Fabrics	**Yds.**	**Patches**	**Yds.**	**Patches**	**Yds.**	**Patches**
Navy Prints includes borders (4 each size wall/ queen; 2 each size twin)	2⅛	12 S2, 4 S3, 1 S9, 40 T3, 64 T8, 4 T9, 96 T15 4½" x 56"+	3½	18 S2, 10 S3, 6 S9, 64 T3, 184 T8, 16 T9, 144 T15 4½" x 90"+ 4½" x 73"+	4	20 S2, 12 S3, 9 S9, 72 T3, 240 T8, 20 T9, 160 T15 4½" x 90"+
Rose Prints	½	36 T3, 28 T8	1	60 T3, 92 T8	1	68 T3, 124 T8
Maroon Prints	¾	24 S8, 4 T3, 12 T8, 4 T9, 48 T15	1½	60 S8, 2 S16 24 T3, 44 T8, 4 T9, 72 T15	2	72 S8, 4 S16, 36 T3, 60 T8, 4 T9, 80 T15
Maroon Stripe	½	8 X1	1½	32 X1	1½	40 X1
Dark Beige Prints	1	4 S6, 12 T3, 16 T6, 8 T8, 4 T9	1½	4 S6, 36 T3, 28 T6, 8 T8, 4 T9	2	4 S6, 44 T3, 32 T6, 8 T8, 4 T9
Light Beige Print	1	48 S2, 4 S3, 32 T8, 48 T15, 4 T20	2½	72 S2, 24 S3, 108 T8, 72 T15 10 T20	3	80 S2, 36 S3, 144 T8, 80 T15 12 T20
Binding	¾	1½" x 7 yds.	¾	1½" x 10 yds.	¾	1½" x 11 yds.
Lining	3½	2 @ 30" x 59"	5⅜	2 @ 39" x 93"	8⅛	3 @ 32" x 93"
	1 Block 4 Unit A, 4 Unit B, 4 Unit C, 4 Unit D, 4 Unit E		**6 Blocks** 16 Unit A, 10 Unit B, 4 Unit C, 10 Unit D, 4 Unit E, 6 Unit F		**9 Blocks** 20 Unit A, 12 Unit B, 4 Unit C, 12 Unit D, 4 Unit E, 8 Unit F	

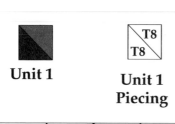

Unit 1

Unit 1 Piecing

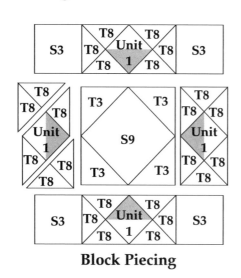

Georgetown Circle Block

S3	T8 Unit 1 T8 / T8 T8 / T8	S3

T8 T8 / T8 Unit 1 T8 / T8 T8	T3 S9 T3	T8 T8 / T8 Unit 1 T8 / T8 T8

S3	T8 Unit 1 T8 / T8 T8 / T8	S3

Block Piecing

1 Referring to the diagram, make 4 (wall)/24 (twin)/36 (queen) Unit 1's from navy and maroon prints.

2 To make the block as shown at left, join four Unit 1's, eight light beige, eight rose and eight navy T8 triangles, four maroon T3 triangles, four light beige S3 squares and a navy S9 square. Make 1/6/9 quilt blocks, depending on your quilt size.

3 Sew two maroon stripe X1's to a navy T9, sewing only to the end of the seam line at the set-in joint. This completes Unit A. Make 4/16/20 Unit A's.

4 From four navy and four rose T8's and three dark beige T3's, make 4/10/12 Unit B's.

5 For Unit C, join one rose and one navy T8 triangle to make a square. Add two dark beige T8's to complete Unit C. Make four Unit C's, regardless of your quilt size.

6 Referring to the Unit D diagrams, join 6 maroon S8 squares, 2 maroon T8's, 6 navy T8's, 6 light beige T8's, a light beige T20 and and a navy S3. Make 4/10/12 Unit D's.

7 Referring to the diagram on page 103, make a Unit 2 from one maroon, one light beige and two navy T15's. Make 48/72/80 Unit 2's.

8 Use four Unit 2's plus one navy and four light beige S2 squares to make a Unit 3. Make 12/18/20 Unit 3's.

9 Join three Unit 3's plus a dark beige S6 square, one T9 and four T6 triangles as shown to make a Unit E. Make 4 Unit E's.

10 For the twin and queen quilt sizes only, sew two dark beige T6's to a Unit 3 to make Unit F. Make 6/8 Unit F's.

11 From navy and rose T3 triangles, make 36/60/68 Unit 4's. (You will have four navy triangles left over.)

12 Separate assembly directions for each size follow. Look for the paragraph for your size.

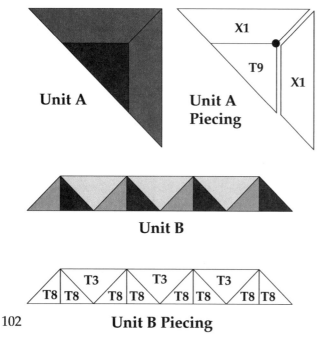

Unit A

Unit A Piecing

X1

T9

X1

Unit B

	T3		T3		T3	
T8	T8	T8	T8	T8	T8	T8 T8

Unit B Piecing

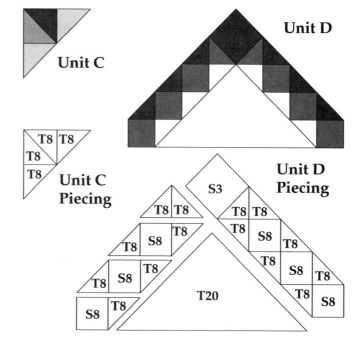

Unit C

T8	T8
T8	
T8	

Unit C Piecing

Unit D

Unit D Piecing

S3

T8 T8 / T8 T8

T8 / S8 T8

T8 / S8 / T8

T8 / S8 / S8 T8

S8 T8 / T20 / T8 S8

For the wall quilt, refer to the color photo. Assemble the units as follows: Sew a Unit A to each side of the quilt block. Sew a Unit B to each side, with the dark beige edge out. Add a Unit C to each corner. Sew a navy T8 to each end of a Unit D to form a large triangle. Repeat for each Unit D. Sew these four units to the sides of the quilt center. Add a Unit E to each corner. Join nine Unit 4's end to end. Add a navy T3 triangle to the rose end. Sew to one side of the quilt. Repeat for the other three sides. Add a maroon T9 to each corner.

For the twin quilt, refer to the coloring drawing. Join two Unit A's to make a large triangle. Repeat to make six of these A-A triangles. (You will have four Unit A's left over.) Sew two A-A triangles to opposite ends of a block. This completes a diagonal row of the quilt center. Repeat. Now sew a maroon S16 square between two blocks. Sew an A-A triangle to one end to make a row. Repeat. Join rows. Add a Unit A to each corner to complete the quilt center. Sew a dark beige T3 triangle between two Unit B's. Sew to the top of the quilt. Repeat for the bottom of the quilt. Join three Unit B's alternately with two dark beige T3's. Sew to the side of the quilt. Repeat for the opposite side. Add a Unit C to each corner. Set in a Unit F between two Unit D's. Add a navy T8 to each end. Sew to the top of the quilt. Repeat for the bottom of the quilt. Set in two Unit F's in a row of three Unit D's. Add two navy T8's, one to each end. Sew to the side of the quilt. Repeat for the opposite side. Add a Unit E in each corner. Join 13 Unit 4's end to end. Add a navy T3 triangle to the rose end. Sew to the top of the quilt. Repeat for the

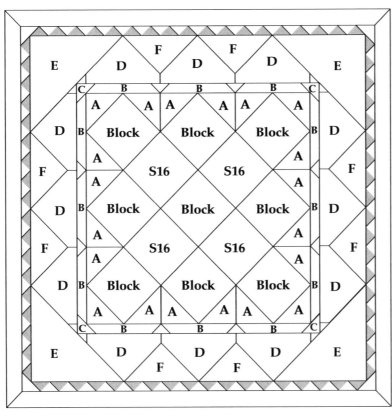

Whole Quilt Diagram, Queen Size

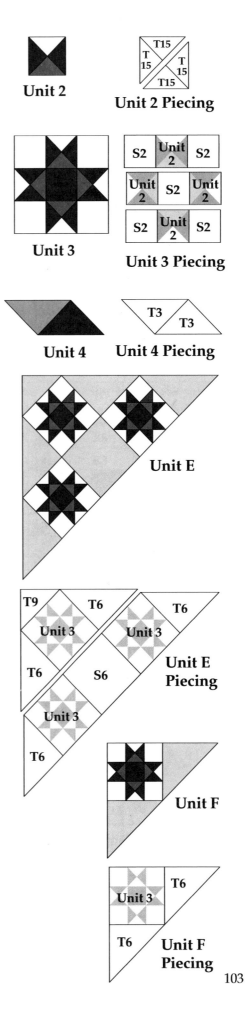

103

bottom. Join 17 Unit 4's end to end. Add a navy T3 to the rose end. Sew to the side of the quilt. Repeat for the other side. Add a maroon T9 to each corner.

For the double/queen quilt, refer to the whole quilt diagram. Join two Unit A's to make a large triangle. Repeat to make eight of these A-A triangles. (You will have four Unit A's left over.) Sew two A-A triangles to opposite ends of a block. This completes the first diagonal row of the quilt center. Repeat for the last row. Now sew a maroon S16 square between two blocks. Sew an A-A triangle to each end to make the second row. Repeat. Sew three blocks alternately with two maroon S16 squares to make the center row. Join rows. Add a

Unit A to each corner to complete the quilt center. Join three Unit B's alternately with two dark beige T3's. Sew to the side of the quilt. Repeat for the remaining three sides. Add a Unit C to each corner. Set in two Unit F's in a row of three Unit D's. Add two navy T8's, one to each end. Sew to the side of the quilt. Repeat for the other three sides. Add a Unit E in each corner. Join 17 Unit 4's end to end. Add a navy T3 to the rose end. Sew to the side of the quilt. Repeat for the other three sides. Add a maroon T9 triangle to each corner.

13 For all sizes, add navy borders, mitering corners. Outline quilt or quilt as desired. Bind to finish.

Columbia Square twin quilt. Photocopy this drawing, enlarging it if desired, to play with colors. It is also handy as a map of blocks and units.

Long May She Wave

This lively scrap quilt with a patriotic color scheme resembles an old-fashioned Ocean Waves quilt in its undulating movement. Now-you-see-them, now-you-don't stars twinkle, thanks to a block coloring that leads the eye to focus on the square block or the bright accents in some places and the stars in others. Judy colored each block basically from two fabrics. However, she substituted other scraps liberally. Some of the substitutions were close to the original fabrics, others were brighter accent colors quite different, although similar in value. Judy is fond of a busy, very scrappy look, which adds interest to a simple pattern such as this. The color photograph of Long May She Wave is on page 33. Full-size patterns and rotary cutting charts begin on page 145.

Right, Long May She Wave lap quilt, 59½" x 72¼".

LONG MAY SHE WAVE: FABRICS, YARDAGE & CUTTING REQUIREMENTS

All Sizes 6⅜" Blocks			Lap Quilt 59½" x 72¼"		Twin Quilt 72¼" x 97¾"		Queen Quilt 97¾" x 97¾"	
Fabrics		**Yds.**	**Patches**	**Yds.**	**Patches**	**Yds.**	**Patches**	
Light Scraps		4	138 S8, 396 T8, 48 T9	6½	222 S8, 660 T8, 96 T9	8½	294 S8, 900 T8, 144 T9	
Dark Scraps incl. border (2 strips of each size)		3	50 S8, 100 T8, 98 X3, 98 X3r 4¾" x 64¼"+ 4¾" x 60"+	4½	98 S8, 196 T8, 164 X3, 164 X3r 4¾" x 89¾"+ 4¾" x 72¾"+	6½	146 S8, 292 T8, 224 X3, 224 X3r 4¾" x 98¼"+ 4¾" x 89¾"+	
Binding		¾	1½" x 8 yds.	¾	1½" x 10 yds.	¾	1½" x 12 yds.	
Lining		3¾	2 @ 39" x 64"	6	2 @ 39" x 102"	8⅞	3 @ 35" x 102"	
			48 Block A set 6 x 8 14 Block B 14 Block C 4 Block D 2 Block E		**96 Block A** set 8 x 12 20 Block B 20 Block C 4 Block D 2 Block E		**144 Block A** set 12 x 12 24 Block B 24 Block C 4 Block D 2 Block E	

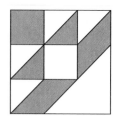

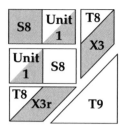

Block A

1 Make Unit 1's from light and dark T8 triangles as shown below. Make 100 (lap)/196 (twin)/292 (queen), according to your quilt size.

2 Make Block A as shown from two Unit 1's, a dark and a light S8, two light T8 triangles, a light T9, and a dark X3 and a dark X3 reversed. Make 48/96/144 A Blocks.

3 Join four A Blocks, turned as shown, to make Unit 2. Repeat for all blocks to make 12/24/36 Unit 2's.

4 Join Unit 2's to make rows; join rows. For the lap quilt, make four rows of three Unit 2's; for the twin quilt, make six rows of four Unit 2's; and for the queen quilt, make six rows of six Unit 2's. Join rows to complete the quilt center.

5 Make border Block B as shown from six light T8's, three light S8's and three dark X3r's (reversed). Make 14/20/24 B Blocks.

6 Make border Block C as shown from six light T8's, three light S8's and three dark X3's. Make 14/20/24 C Blocks.

7 Make border corner Block D as shown from eight light T8's, a light S8, two dark X3's and two dark X3r's. Make four Block D's.

8 For the block corners in the outer border, join two Unit 1's and a light and a dark S8 to make an E Block as shown. Make 2 E Blocks.

9 Note that each border has B Blocks in one half and C Blocks in the other half. Join border Blocks B, C and D as follows: For the side borders join 4/6/6 B's. Add 4/6/6 C's. For top/bottom borders, join 3/4/6 B's. Add 3/4/6 C's. Add a D Block to each end of top and bottom borders. Attach the side borders, then top and bottom borders.

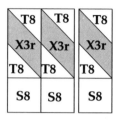

Block A Piecing

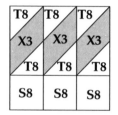

Block B

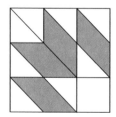

Block C

Unit 1

Block E

Block E Piecing

106   **Unit 2, Four Blocks**

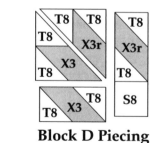

Block D

Block D Piecing

D	B	B	B	B	B	B	C	C	C	C	C	C	D
C	Unit 2	Unit 2	Unit 2	Unit 2	Unit 2	Unit 2	B
C							B
C	Unit 2	Unit 2	Unit 2	Unit 2	Unit 2	Unit 2	B
C							B
C	Unit 2	Unit 2	Unit 2	Unit 2	Unit 2	Unit 2	B
C							B
B	Unit 2	Unit 2	Unit 2	Unit 2	Unit 2	Unit 2	C
B							C
B	Unit 2	Unit 2	Unit 2	Unit 2	Unit 2	Unit 2	C
B							C
B	Unit 2	Unit 2	Unit 2	Unit 2	Unit 2	Unit 2	C
B							C
D	C	C	C	C	C	C	B	B	B	B	B	B	D

E (top right) / E (bottom left)

Whole Quilt Diagram, Queen Size

10 Join dark strips 4¾"-wide by random lengths to make border strips in the lengths listed for your quilt size. Sew an E Block to one end of the top and bottom borders. Add side borders. Then add top and bottom borders to complete the quilt top. Quilt as desired. Bind to finish.

Long May She Wave Coloring Drawing, Twin Size. Photocopy this drawing and use the copies to play with colors. This is also useful as a guide for assembling the blocks and border blocks.

Meadow Lily

Just a touch of appliqué and a striking pieced border make this a memorable quilt. Machine techniques were used for both piecing and appliqué in the 10" Meadow Lily blocks. The big-and-little-chain-of-squares border is built in to the diagonally set quilt with 10" border blocks and pieced edge triangles. The look is complex, but construction is easy, and the fit is natural. The color photograph of Meadow Lily is on page 34. Full-size patterns and rotary cutting charts begin on page 145.

Left, Meadow Lily lap quilt, 45⅜" x 59⅝".

MEADOW LILY: FABRICS, YARDAGE & CUTTING REQUIREMENTS

All Sizes 10" Blocks	Lap Quilt 45⅜" x 59⅝"		Twin Quilt 73¾" x 87⅞"		Double/Queen Quilt 87⅞" x 87⅞"	
Fabrics	**Yds.**	**Patches**	**Yds.**	**Patches**	**Yds.**	**Patches**
Ivory Solid	2	12 R1, 100 S1, 18 S2, 94 T2, 40 T15, 4 T17, 10 X5, 6 X6	4	40 R1, 180 S1, 60 S2, 166 T2, 124 T15, 4 T17, 18 X5, 20 X6	4½	50 R1, 200 S1, 75 S2, 184 T2, 154 T15, 4 T17, 20 X5, 25 X6
Dark Red Prints	1	58 S2, 36 T15, 18 X4	1½	98 S2, 120 T15, 60 X4	2	108 S2, 150 T15, 75 X4
Green	1	100 S1, 4 S2, 18 T2, 6 T4, 12 leaves, 6 bias strips at 1¼" x 11" (stems)	2	180 S1, 4 S2, 60 T2, 20 T4, 40 leaves, 20 bias strips at 1¼" x 11" (stems)	2	200 S1, 4 S2, 75 T2, 25 T4, 50 leaves, 25 bias strips at 1¼" x 11" (stems)
Light Print	1	2 S5, 14 T4, 4 T9, 6 T22	2½	12 S5, 22 T4, 4 T9, 14 T22	3	16 S5, 24 T4, 4 T9, 16 T22
Light Red Print	½	50 S2	½	90 S2	⅝	100 S2
Dark Green Border	1¾	2" x 57⅛"+ 2" x 45⅞"+	2⅝	2" x 85⅜"+ 2" x 74¼"+	2⅝	2" x 85⅜"+ 2" x 88⅜"+
Binding	¾	1½" x 7 yds.	¾	1½" x 10 yds.	¾	1½" x 11 yds.
Lining	3	2 @ 33" x 50"	5⅜	2 @ 40" x 92"	8	3 @ 32" x 92"
	6 Block A, 6 Block B 10 Unit C, 4 Block D		20 Block A, 14 Block B 18 Unit C, 4 Block D		25 Block A, 16 Block B 20 Unit C, 4 Block D	

1 From ivory solid and dark red print T15 triangles, make Unit 1 and Unit 2 as shown. Make 18/60/75 Unit 1's and 18/60/75 Unit 2's.

Unit 1 | **Unit 2**

2 Sew a Unit 1 and a Unit 2 to an ivory solid S2 square. Add a dark red X4 and a green T2 to complete Unit 3 as shown. Make 18/60/75 Unit 3's.

3 Trace the stems and leaves from the full-size X6 template onto the X6 patch. Fold the dark green bias strip in half with right sides out. Stitch down the length of the strip in a ¼" seam. Trim the seam allowance to ⅛". Press the strip to hide the seam allowance. Cut the strip into three pieces for the two curved and one straight stem. Pin in place on the X6 patch, extending the stems into the seam allowances and tucking the curved stems under the straight one. Appliqué by hand or machine. The leaf shape is on the X6 patten on page 158. The outline is the finished size of the leaf. Add a small turn-under allowance by eye when you cut the green leaves for appliqué. Turn under the edges of the leaves, pin, baste, and appliqué in place as marked. Add a green T4 to complete Unit 4. Make 6/20/25 Unit 4's.

Unit 3 | **Unit 3 Piecing**

4 To make an A Block, join three Unit 3's, Unit 4 and two ivory solid R1's as shown. Make 6/20/25 A Blocks.

Unit 4

Whole Quilt Diagram, Queen Size. Use this as a map of the placement of blocks and units.

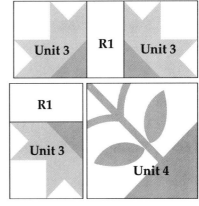

Block A

Block A Piecing

Unit 5

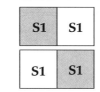

Unit 5 Piecing

5 To make a Unit 5, join green and ivory solid S1's as shown. Make 50/90/100 Unit 5's.

6 To make a B Block, join four Unit 5's, five light red S2's, three dark red S2's, six ivory solid T2's, a light print T22 and a light print T4 as shown. Make 6/14/16 B Blocks.

7 To make a triangular Unit C, join a Unit 5, two dark red S2's, three ivory solid T2's and an ivory solid X5 as shown. Make 10/18/20 Unit C's.

8 To make a D Block, join five light red S2's, four Unit 5's, five dark red S2's, one dark green S2, seven ivory solid T2's, an ivory solid T15, a light print T9 and two light print T4's. Make 4 Block D's.

9 Referring to the quilt photograph, the coloring drawing or the whole quilt diagram, join the blocks and units plus S5 squares in diagonal rows. Flower blocks alternate with S5 squares. Most rows end with a B Block, then a C Unit. Block D's are in the four corners of the quilt. Add an ivory solid T17 triangle to each corner to complete the quilt top.

10 Add dark green side borders, then top and bottom borders. Quilt the motif of your choice in the borders and plain squares. Quilt around the patches. Bind to finish.

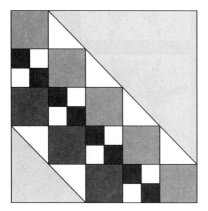

Block B

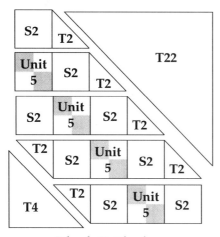

Block B Piecing

Unit C

Unit C Piecing

110   **Block D**

Block D Piecing

Meadow Lily Coloring Drawing, Twin Size.
Photocopy this drawing, enlarging it if desired. Use the copies to play with colors before making the quilt. The drawing is also useful as a reference for seeing how the blocks and border blocks and units are assembled.

111

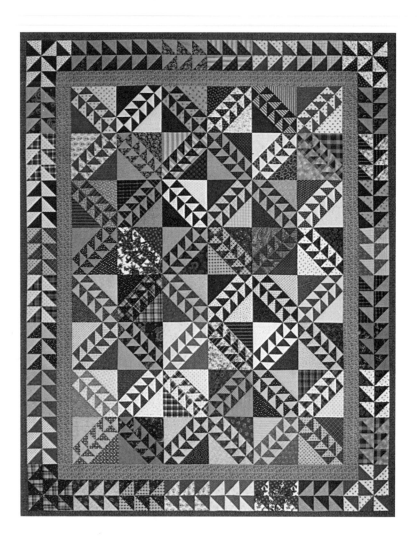

Prairie Rambler

This handsome quilt is related to the old-fashioned Rambler block. It is fun and easy to choose the fabric pairs, and just as fun to play with the scrappy mix of blocks that results. As you cut patches for each block, also cut patches for a border block. Judy made just one block and one border block from each fabric pair, but you could cut sets of two or more if your fabric stash is limited. The color photograph of Prairie Rambler is on page 35. Full-size patterns and rotary cutting charts begin on page 145.

Left, Prairie Rambler twin quilt, 75" x 93".

PRAIRIE RAMBLER: FABRICS, YARDAGE & CUTTING REQUIREMENTS

All Sizes 9" Blocks	Wall Quilt 57" x 57"		Twin Quilt 75" x 93"		Double/Queen Quilt 93" x 93"	
Fabrics	**Yds.**	**Patches**	**Yds.**	**Patches**	**Yds.**	**Patches**
Light Scraps	2	128 T3, 16 T6, 160 T8	4½	200 T3, 48 T6, 480 T8	5½	224 T3, 64 T6, 640 T8
Dark Scraps	2	128 T3, 16 T6, 160 T8	4½	200 T3, 48 T6, 480 T8	5½	224 T3, 64 T6, 640 T8
Brown Border (2 strips each)	1⅜	3½" x 36½"+ 3½" x 42½"+	2¼	3½" x 72½"+ 3½" x 60½"+	2⅜	3½" x 72½"+ 3½" x 78½"+
Red Border (2 strips each)	1¾	2" x 54½"+ 2" x 57½"+	2¾	2" x 90½"+ 2" x 75½"+	2⅞	2" x 90½"+ 2" x 93½"+
Binding	¾	1½" x 7 yds.	¾	1½" x 10 yds.	¾	1½" x 11 yds.
Lining	3⅝	2 @ 31" x 61"	5⅝	2 @ 40" x 97"	8½	3 @ 33" x 97"
	16 Blocks set 4 x 4 8 Unit A 4 Unit B 16 Unit C		**48 Blocks** set 6 x 8 8 Unit A 4 Unit B 28 Unit C		**64 Blocks** set 8 x 8 8 Unit A 4 Unit B 32 Unit C	

1 To make the quilt as shown in the photograph, follow the cutting layout for ½ yards or fat quarters shown here. Select light-and-dark fabric pairs to be used to make blocks. Press, then layer on the cutting mat two fabrics of a pair. Place them with right sides together and selvedges or lengthwise grains aligned. Repeat with a second pair to make four layers. Cut through all four layers as shown in the cutting layout.

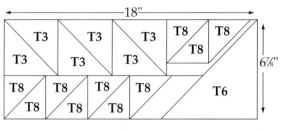

Cutting Layout

Start by making a clean first cut to trim selvedges and even the edge. Measure 6⅞" from this edge and cut off a 6⅞" x 18" strip. Square off the right end. Cut off the corner at a 45° angle to make one 6⅞" T6 triangle. Measure and cut a 3"-wide strip from the shorter long edge. Cut this into three 3" squares and one 3" triangle. Further cut the squares diagonally into T8 triangles.

Cut the remainder of the fabric into three 3⅞" squares, one 3" square and one 3" triangle. Further cut the squares diagonally to make T3 and T8 triangles as shown.

Follow this plan for 16 (wall)/28 (twin)/32 (queen) pairs of light and dark fabrics. From 4 of these fabric pairs (twin/queen), cut one additional 3⅞" square, not included in the 6⅞" x 18" strip. Cut this square diagonally to make the extra two T3's needed for Units A and B in the border corners.

From 4 (wall) additional pairs cut only eight T3's. From 20 (twin)/32 (queen) additional pairs of fabrics, cut the same 6⅞" x 18" piece, but cut only the 3" T8 and 6⅞" T6 triangles, leaving out the T3's.

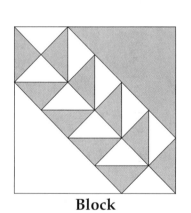

Block

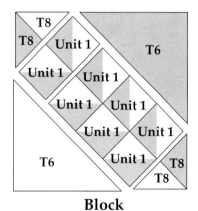

Block

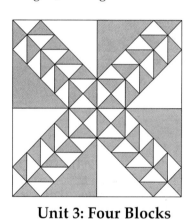

Unit 3: Four Blocks

Unit 1

Unit A   **Unit B**

Unit 2

Unit C   **Unit 2**

Whole Quilt Diagram, Queen Size

2 Leave the fabric layered as you cut. The patches are ready for stitching. Just separate the first pair from the second pair in the layer as you prepare to sew. Make 128/384/512 Unit 1's as shown.

3 Make a block as shown on page 113 from eight Unit 1's, two light and two dark T8's, one light T6 and one dark T6. Make 16/48/64 blocks.

4 Join blocks in groups of four, turned with light always touching dark. This four-block group is shown in Unit 3.

5 Join Unit 3's in rows to complete the quilt center. The wall quilt has two rows of two Unit 3's. The twin quilt has four rows of three Unit 3's. The queen quilt has four rows of four Unit 3's.

6 Add light brown side borders, then top and bottom borders.

7 Make Unit 2 from one light and one dark T3. Make 128/200/224 Unit 2's. Start with the Unit 2's made from the four fabric pairs from which you cut two extra T3's. Use these to make Units A and B. Make eight Unit A's and four Unit B's. Join the remaining Unit 2's in matched sets to make 16/28/32 Unit C's as shown.

8 Join 4/8/8 Unit C's end to end for a side border. (There should be one Unit C for each block along the edge of the quilt.) Add a Unit A to each end. Sew to the side of the quilt. Repeat for the opposite side. Join 4/6/8 Unit C's end to end for the top border. Add a Unit A and a Unit B to each end. Sew this strip to the top of the quilt. Repeat for the bottom of the quilt.

9 Add red side borders, then top and bottom borders. Quilt as desired, and bind to finish.

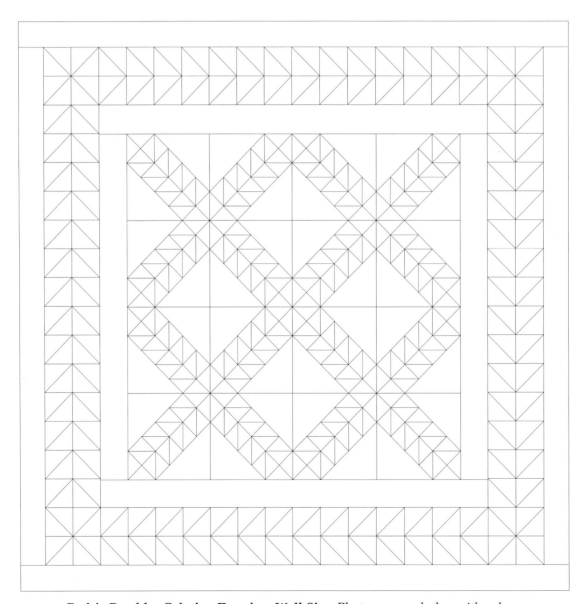

114 **Prairie Rambler Coloring Drawing, Wall Size.** Photocopy and play with colors.

Swing Your Partner

The Swing Your Partner block is a new design in the traditional style. It combines elements of Ohio Star and Bear's Paw blocks. The quilt is attractive either made from scraps or from just a few fabrics. Feel free to add or subtract rows of blocks to make the quilt any size you desire. For each row of blocks, adjust the sawtooth border by 10 repeats, the chain-of-squares border by five repeats, and the inner and outer border lengths by 15". A color photo is on page 36. Full-size templates and rotary cutting details begin on page 145.

Right, Swing Your Partner lap quilt, 66" x 81".

SWING YOUR PARTNER: FABRICS, YARDAGE & CUTTING REQUIREMENTS

All Sizes 15" Blocks	**Lap Quilt** 66" x 81"		**Twin Quilt** 81" x 96"		**Double/Queen Quilt** 96" x 96"	
Fabrics	**Yds.**	**Patches**	**Yds.**	**Patches**	**Yds.**	**Patches**
Dark Blues	1½	12 S9, 8 T7, 256 T8	2	20 S9, 8 T7, 360 T8	2½	25 S9, 8 T7, 420 T8
Light Blues	2	48 R11, 48 S3	3	80 R11, 80 S3	4½	100 R11, 100 S3
Creams	1⅝	50 S7, 82 S8, 238 T7, 96 T8	2½	82 S7, 102 S8, 342 T7, 160 T8	3	102 S7, 112 S8, 402 T7, 200 T8
Reds	1	24 S7, 334 T7	1½	40 S7, 502 T7	2	50 S7, 602 T7
Golds	½	24 S7, 48 S8	1	40 S7, 80 S8	1	50 S7, 100 S8
Light Blue Border (2 ea.)	1⅞	2" x 60½"+ 2" x 48½"+	2⅜	2" x 78½"+ 2" x 66½"+	2⅜	2" x 78½"+ 2" x 81½"+
Dark Blue Border (2 ea.)	2⅛	5" x 66½"+ 5" x 72½"+	2⅝	5" x 87½"+ 5" x 81½"+	2⅞	5" x 87½"+ 5" x 96½"+
Binding	¾	1½" x 9 yds.	¾	1½" x 10 yds.	¾	1½" x 11 yds.
Lining	5	2 @ 36" x 85"	7⅜	3 @ 34" x 85"	8¾	3 @ 34" x 100"
	12 Blocks set 3 x 4, 238 Unit A, 72 Unit B, 2 Unit C, 2 Unit D, 2 Unit E, 4 Unit F		**20 Blocks** set 4 x 5, 342 Unit A, 92 Unit B, 2 Unit C, 2 Unit D, 2 Unit E, 4 Unit F		**25 Blocks** set 5 x 5, 402 Unit A, 102 Unit B, 2 Unit C, 2 Unit D, 2 Unit E, 4 Unit F	

Block

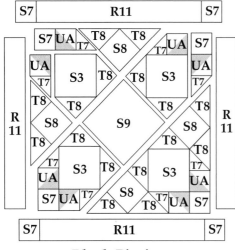

Block Piecing

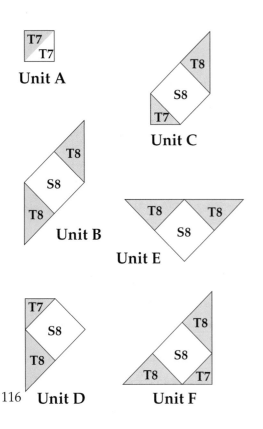

Unit A

Unit C

Unit B

Unit E

Unit D

Unit F

1 From red and cream T7 triangles make Unit A's in the following quantities: 238 (lap quilt)/342 (twin)/402 (queen). These will be used to make blocks as well as borders.

2 Refer to the block diagrams. Join eight Unit A's, a dark blue S9 square, eight dark blue T8 triangles, four light blue S3's, four gold S8's, eight cream T7's, eight cream T8's, four cream S7's, four light blue R11's, two red S7's and two gold S7's to make a block. Make 12 (lap)/20 (twin)/25 (queen) blocks.

3 For the lap quilt, join blocks in four rows of three blocks. For the twin quilt, make five rows of four blocks. For the queen quilt, join five rows of five blocks. Turn blocks so that the red squares touch the gold squares in the block corners.

4 Join remaining Unit A's to make sawtooth borders as shown in the quilt photo and coloring picture. For each side border, join 40/50/50 Unit A's. For each top or bottom border, join 31/41/51 Unit A's. Sew a cream S7 to the red end of the top and bottom borders. Attach sawtooth side borders to the quilt center. Then attach top and bottom borders.

5 Add light blue border strips to the sides of the quilt. Then add light blue borders to the top and bottom.

6 From dark blue T8 triangles and cream S8 squares, make 72/92/102 Unit B's as shown. From dark blue triangles and cream squares also make 2 Unit C's, 2 Unit D's, 2 Unit E's and 4 Unit F's.

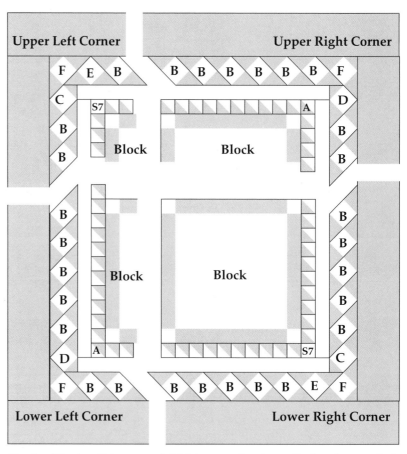

Border Piecing Diagram. Add B's to make the quilt the size needed.

7 Join Unit B's to make chain-of-squares borders. For the side border, join 20/25/25 Unit B's. For all sizes, see the border piecing diagram. Sew a Unit C and a Unit D to opposite ends of the side border. Attach to the quilt center. Repeat for the opposite side.

8 For the bottom border, join 16/21/26 Unit B's. See the border figure. Sew a Unit E to one end. Attach to quilt center. Repeat for the top of the quilt. Add a Unit F to each corner of the quilt.

9 Add dark blue side borders, then top and bottom borders. Quilt and bind to finish.

Swing Your Partner Coloring Drawing. Photocopy, enlarging if desired, and play with different colorings. This drawing is also helpful for visualizing how the blocks and borders are assembled.

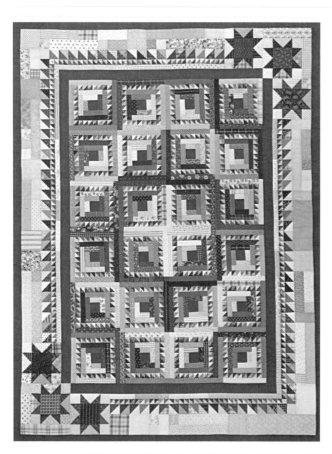

Feathered Log Cabin

Who says Log Cabin quilts don't go with pieced borders? This original design takes the venerable Log Cabin to new heights. The addition of sawtooths within the Log Cabin subtly frames each block. The 10"-wide pieced border makes a bolder statement. The casual, scrappy quality of the quilt center lends itself perfectly to a spontaneous border, randomly pieced in the background and sporting a cluster of stars in just two corners. This quilt is perfect for rotary-cut strips. Because the Log Cabin piecing must fit the sawtooth band in each block, accuracy is important. Rotary cut the logs to the proper length before piecing. The sawtooth units in the blocks and borders can be made from rotary-cut triangles or by using your favorite shortcuts. The color photograph of Feathered Log Cabin is on page 37. Full-size patterns and rotary cutting charts begin on page 145.

Left, Feathered Log Cabin twin quilt, 62" x 82".

FEATHERED LOG CABIN: FABRICS, YARDAGE & CUTTING REQUIREMENTS

All Sizes 10" Blocks			Wall Quilt 62" x 62"		Lap/Twin Quilt 62" x 82"		King Quilt 102" x 102"	
Fabrics		**Yds.**	**Patches**	**Yds.**	**Patches**	**Yds.**	**Patches**	
Light Scraps		3	16 R2, 18 R3, 16 R4, 16 R5, 16 R8, 16 R9, 2 R16, 2 R17, 2 R25, 2 R26, 2 S1, 26 S2, 588 T1, 72 T2, 24 T13 1½" x 32½"+ 1½" x 34½"+ 4½" x 32½"+ 4½" x 34½"+	4	24 R2, 26 R3, 24 R4, 24 R5, 24 R8, 24 R9, 2 R16, 2 R17, 2 R25, 2 R26, 2 S1, 26 S2, 852 T1, 92 T2, 24 T13 1½" x 52½"+ 1½" x 34½"+ 4½" x 52½"+ 4½" x 34½"+	8	64 R2, 66 R3, 64 R4, 64 R5, 64 R8, 64 R9, 2 R16, 2 R17, 2 R25, 2 R26 2 S1, 26 S2, 2092 T1, 152 T2, 24 T13 1½" x 72½"+ 1½" x 74½"+ 4½" x 72½"+ 4½" x 74½"+	
Dark Scraps		2	16 R3, 16 R4, 16 R5, 16 R6, 16 R9, 16 R10, 6 S4, 588 T1, 120 T2	3	24 R3, 24 R4, 24 R5, 24 R6, 24 R9, 24 R10, 6 S4, 852 T1, 140 T2	6½	64 R3, 64 R4, 64 R5, 64 R6, 64 R9, 64 R10, 6 S4, 2092 T1, 200 T2	
Red Solid includes borders (2 ea.) & binding		2⅛	16 S2 2½" x 40½"+ 2½" x 42½"+ 1½" x 60½"+ 1½" x 62½"+	2⅝	24 S2 2½" x 60½"+ 2½" x 42½"+ 1½" x 80½"+ 1½" x 62½"+	3¼	64 S2 2½" x 80½"+ 2½" x 82½"+ 1½" x 100½"+ 1½" x 102½"+	

All Sizes 7" & 14" Blocks	**Wall Quilt** 62" x 62"		**Lap/Twin Quilt** 62" x 82"		**King Quilt** 102" x 102"	
Fabrics	**Yds.**	**Patches**	**Yds.**	**Patches**	**Yds.**	**Patches**
Red Solid, cont'd		1½" x 8 yds.		1½" x 9 yds.		1½" x 12 yds.
Lining	3⅞	2 @ 34" x 66"	5	2 @ 34" x 86"	9¼	3 @ 36" x 106"
	16 A Blocks set 4 x 4 6 Block B 588 Unit 1 72 Unit 2		**24 A Blocks** set 4 x 6 6 Block B 852 Unit 1 92 Unit 2		**64 A Blocks** set 8 x 8 6 Block B 2092 Unit 1 152 Unit 2	

1 From light and dark scraps, make Unit 1's in the following quantities: 588 (wall quilt)/852 (twin)/2092 (king). Some of these will be used in the blocks; the rest will be set aside for the borders.

2 Referring to the diagram for Block A to see which way to turn the units, join 6 Unit 1's to make a log for the left side of the block. Join 7 Unit 1's to make a log for the top of the block. Join 7 Unit 1's to make a log for the right side of the block. Join 8 Unit 1's to make a log for the bottom of the block. Repeat to make enough feathered logs for all 16/24/64 A blocks in your quilt.

3 Referring to the diagram, make Block A as follows: Sew the light R2 rectangle to the red S2 square. Press seams away from the red square. Add a light R3, then a dark R3 followed by a dark R4 to complete one round of logs. Continue adding logs in this order: light R4-R5, dark R5-R6, left, top, right, and bottom feathered logs, light R8-R9, and dark R9 and R10. Make 16/24/64 blocks.

4 For the wall quilt, join the blocks in 4 rows of 4 blocks . For the twin quilt, make 6 rows of 4 blocks. For the king quilt, make 8 rows of 8 blocks. Arrange the blocks in a barn-raising set as shown, or turn the blocks to create a different light/dark pattern, as desired.

5 For the B Blocks, join dark T2's to light T13's. Combine with light S2's and a dark S4 to complete a star block. Make 6 of these B Blocks, regardless of the quilt size.

6 Join light and dark scrap T2 triangles to make Unit 2's as shown. Make 72/92/152 Unit 2's.

7 Sew two Unit 1's to a Unit 2 to make Unit 3 as shown on the next page. Make 34/44/74 Unit 3's. Also make 32/42/72 Unit 4's as shown. You will have 8 Unit 1's and 6 Unit 2's left over for the corners.

8 Referring to the coloring drawing of the wall quilt, the photo of the twin quilt, or the whole quilt diagram for the queen quilt, make the pieced borders as follows. First

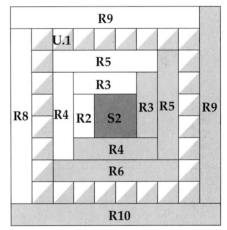

Unit 1

Block A

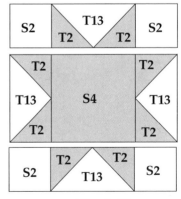

Block B

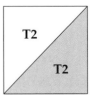

Unit 2

119

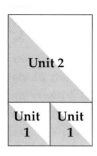

Unit 3

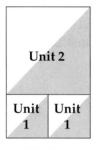

Unit 4

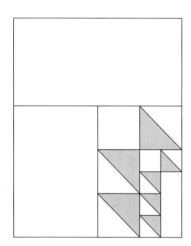

Block C, Border Corner

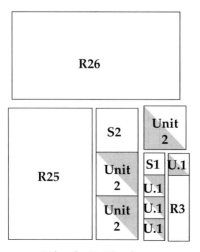

Block C Piecing

make the side borders. Join 6/11/16 Unit 3's. Add 10/15/20 Unit 4's. Join 1½"-wide light strips end to end to make a spacer strip 32½"/52½"/72½" long. Sew to the Unit 1 edge of the side border. Join random strips to make a light outer border 4½" wide and 32½"/52½"/72½" long. Sew to the Unit 2 edge of the side border strip. Add a B Block to the Unit 3 end. Next to the light spacer strip, add a 2½"-wide red spacer strip 40½"/60½"/80½" long. Sew this completed border to the side of the quilt. Repeat for the opposite side.

9 For the top border, join 11/11/21 Unit 3's. Add 6/6/16 Unit 4's. Add a 1½"-wide light spacer strip and a 4½"-wide light border, each 34½"/34½"/74½" long. Add a B Block to the Unit 4 end. Next to the light spacer strip, add a 2½"-wide red spacer strip 42½"/42½"/82½" long. Repeat for the bottom border.

10 Sew a light R16 rectangle, then a light R17 to adjacent sides of one B Block. Sew this star block next to the star at the end of the top border. Repeat for the bottom border.

11 Referring to the diagram for the C Block, join four Unit 1's, three Unit 2's, and one each of light S1 and S2 squares and R3, R25 and R26 rectangles. Make 2 C Blocks for the corners.

12 Sew a C Block to the Unit 3 end of the top border. Attach the completed top border. Repeat for the bottom border.

13 Add red side borders, then top and bottom borders. Quilt as desired, and bind to finish.

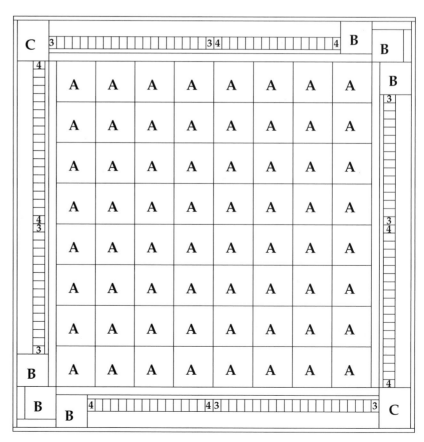

Whole Quilt Diagram, Queen Size. Letters represent blocks. The small units in the borders are Units 3 and 4.

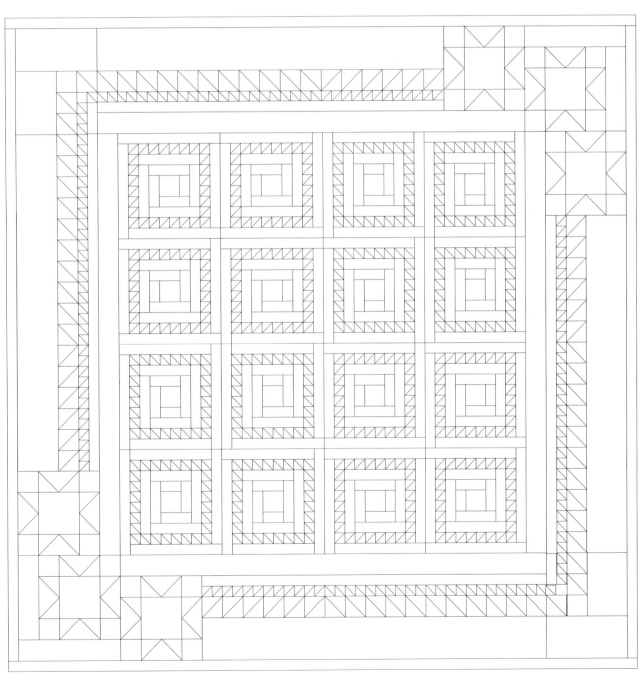

Feathered Log Cabin Coloring Drawing, Twin Size.
Photocopy this drawing, enlarging it if desired, to play with colors. It is also a good reference for seeing how the borders and blocks are assembled.

Italian Tile

This quilt began with a 10¼" Italian Tile block in the center and grew from there. It was not planned on a grid, and some of the border solutions are somewhat organic. For instance, spacer strips of different widths were used between the LeMoyne Star blocks to make them fit both length and width. We give instructions for three quilt sizes. If you want to improvise, feel free to change border designs. It is perfectly in keeping with medallion quilt design to innovate with each new border. The Stock Borders chapter that begins on page 44 is full of ideas you could incorporate here. The color photograph of Italian Tile is on page 38. Full-size patterns and rotary cutting charts begin on page 145.

Left, Italian Tile lap quilt, 52" x 60".

ITALIAN TILE: FABRICS, YARDAGE & CUTTING REQUIREMENTS

All Sizes 10¼" Blocks	Lap Quilt 52" x 60"		Twin Quilt 76" x 92"		Double/Queen Quilt 84" x 92"	
Fabrics	**Yds.**	**Patches**	**Yds.**	**Patches**	**Yds.**	**Patches**
Navy Prints	2	88 D2, 4 D3, 8 R24, 6 R12, 98 S2, 28 T2, 4 T3, 12 T13, 22 T21	4	144 D2, 48 D3, 16 R14, 12 R15, 178 S2, 28 T2, 48 T3, 40 T13, 36 T21	4½	152 D2, 64 D3, 16 R14, 14 R19, 194 S2, 28 T2, 64 T3, 44 T13, 38 T21
Rust Prints including spacer strips (2 ea.)	1⅝	88 D2, 4 D3, 98 S2, 28 T2, 8 T7, 60 T13 1⅜" x 10¾"+ 1⅜" x 12½"+	3½	144 D2, 48 D3, 178 S2, 28 T2, 96 T7, 172 T13 3⅛" x 41½"+ 2" x 36½"+	4	152 D2, 64 D3, 194 S2, 28 T2, 128 T7, 188 T13 2" x 41½"+ 2" x 44½"+
Light Prints	2	88 S11, 4 T4, 24 T7, 88 T11, 20 T13, 18 T21, 4 T22	3½	144 S11, 4 T4, 288 T7, 144 T11, 48 T13, 32 T21, 4 T22	4	152 S11, 4 T4, 384 T7, 152 T11, 52 T13, 34 T21, 4 T22
Binding	¾	1½" x 7 yds.	¾	1½" x 10 yds.	¾	1½" x 11 yds.
Lining	3¼	2 @ 33" x 56"	5⅝	2 @ 41" x 96"	7¾	3 @ 33" x 88"
		1 Block A		12 Block A set 3 X 4		16 Block A set 4 X 4
		12 Block B		40 Block B		44 Block B
		4 Block C		4 Block C		4 Block C
		10 Block D		22 Block D		26 Block D
		22 Block E		36 Block E		38 Block E

1 Note that Marsha mixed a few rusts in with the navies and a few medium shades with the lights in her quilt. From rust and light print T7 triangles, make 8 (lap)/96 (twin)/128 (queen) Unit 1's as shown. To each of these Unit 1's, add two light T7 triangles to make a Unit 2. Make 8/96/128 Unit 2's.

2 Referring to the Block A diagram, set in a Unit 2 between a rust and a navy D3 diamond. Repeat. Join these two sections, and set in another Unit 2 between them. Repeat for the other half of the block. Set in two more Unit 2's, and add a navy T3 triangle in each corner to complete the A Block. Make 1/12/16 A Blocks as shown.

3 For the twin quilt, join A Blocks in four rows of three blocks. For the queen quilt, join A Blocks in four rows of four blocks. Now add the spacer strips to complete the quilt center, starting with the side strips. The side strips are the shorter spacer strips for the lap and queen quilts. For the twin quilt, the side strips are the longer ones. Add the top and bottom spacer strips next. This completes the quilt center.

4 Join one navy and three rust T13's to make a Block B as shown. Make 12/40/44 Block B's.

5 Join a navy and a rust T2 triangle to make a Unit 4 as shown. Make 28 Unit 4's. Set aside 12 Unit 4's for use later. Use the remaining Unit 4's to make four C Blocks as shown.

6 Join rust and navy S2's to make Block D as shown on the next page. Make 10/22/26 D Blocks.

7 See the E diagram on page 124. Join a rust and a navy D2 diamond; set in a light S11 square. Repeat to make four of these sections. Join two of them, setting in a light T11 triangle between them. Repeat. Join halves and set in two more T11 triangles to complete the E Block. Make 22/36/38 E Blocks.

8 Join a light T13 and a rust T13 triangle to make Unit 3 as shown on page 124. Make 20/48/52 Unit 3's.

9 Join a light T21 and a navy T21 to make Unit 5 as shown on page 124. Make 18/32/34 Unit 5's.

10 When joining B Blocks keep in mind that the navy triangles will all touch the quilt center. Join 3/11/11 Block B's. Sew to the side of the quilt. Repeat for the opposite side. Join 3/9/11 Block B's. Add a C Block to each end. Sew to the top of the quilt. Repeat for the bottom of the quilt.

11 Join 5/11/13 Block D's. Sew to the top of the quilt. Repeat for the bottom of the quilt.

12 Join 6/14/14 Unit 3's. Add a rust T13 to the light end. Sew to the side of the quilt. Repeat for the opposite side. Join 4/10/12 Unit 3's. Add a rust T13 to the light end. Sew to the top of the quilt. Repeat for the bottom of the quilt. Sew a light T4 in each corner.

13 Sew 7/15/15 navy S2's alternately with 7/15/15 rust S2's. Add a Unit 4 to each end. Sew to the side of the quilt. Repeat for the opposite side. Sew 5/11/13 navy S2's alternately with 5/11/13 rust S2's. Add two Unit 4's to each end. Sew to the top of the quilt. Repeat for the bottom of the quilt.

Unit 1 **Unit 2**

Block A

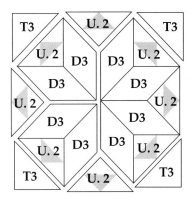

Block A Piecing

Block B **Block B Piecing**

Unit 4 **Unit 4 Piecing**

Block C **Block C Piecing**

Block D

S2	S2
S2	S2

Block D Piecing

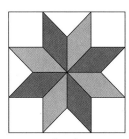

Block E

14 **For the lap quilt,** join five E Blocks alternately with four navy R24's. Sew to the side of the quilt. Repeat for the opposite side. Join four E Blocks alternately with three R12's. Add another E Block to each end. Sew to the top of the quilt. Repeat for the bottom of the quilt.

For the twin quilt, join nine E Blocks alternately with eight R14's. Sew to the side of the quilt. Repeat for the opposite side. Join seven E Blocks alternately with six R15's. Sew another E Block to each end. Sew to the top of the quilt. Repeat for the bottom of the quilt.

For the queen quilt, join nine E Blocks alternately with eight R14's. Sew to the side of the quilt. Repeat for the opposite side. Join eight E Blocks alternately with seven R19's. Sew another E Block to each end. Sew to the top of the quilt. Repeat for the bottom of the quilt.

15 Join 5/9/9 Unit 5's. Sew a navy T21 to the light end. Sew to the side of the quilt. Repeat for the opposite side. Join 4/7/8 Unit 5's. Sew a navy T21 to the light end. Sew to the top of the quilt. Repeat for the bottom of the quilt. Sew a light T22 triangle in each corner.

16 Sew 14/22/22 navy S2's alternately with 14/22/22 rust S2's. Sew to the side of the quilt. Repeat for the opposite side. Sew 13/19/21 navy S2's alternately with 13/19/21 rust S2's. Sew to the top of the quilt. Repeat for the bottom of the quilt.

17 Quilt as desired. Bind to finish.

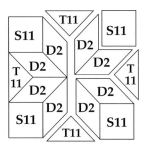

Block E Piecing

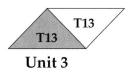

Unit 3

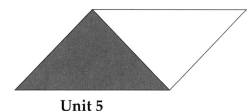

Unit 5

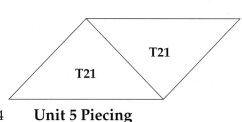

124   **Unit 5 Piecing**

Whole Quilt Diagram, Queen Size

Italian Tile Coloring Drawing, twin size. Photocopy this drawing, enlarging it if desired, and play with different colorings. The drawing is also helpful as a guide for assembling the blocks and units.

Feathered Star

The four-block quilt configuration is a traditional setting used during the last century for oversized blocks. Zigzag borders are often paired with Feathered Stars. Use your favorite shortcuts to make the small triangles that edge the stars. Quick methods such as bias-strip piecing could easily be substituted for rotary-cut triangles in making the Unit 1's and Unit 2's in this pattern. Marsha's book *On to Square Two* gives detailed instructions for this piecing method. The color photograph of Feathered Star is on page 39. Full-size patterns and rotary cutting charts begin on page 145.

Left, Feathered Star twin quilt, 76" x 76".

FEATHERED STAR: FABRICS, YARDAGE & CUTTING REQUIREMENTS

All Sizes 21³⁄₁₆" Blocks	Wall Quilt 50" x 50"		Twin/Double Quilt 76" x 76"		Queen/King Quilt 96" x 96"	
Fabrics	**Yds.**	**Patches**	**Yds.**	**Patches**	**Yds.**	**Patches**
Black Floral includes borders (2 ea.)	2	1 S13, 28 T1, 8 T4, 36 T12, 24 T14, 4 T18, 4 X2, 4 X2r 5½" x 40½"+ 5½" x 50½"+	4	4 S13, 9 S15, 112 T1, 32 T4, 144 T12, 40 T14, 4 T18, 16 X2, 16 X2r 8½" x 60½"+ 8½" x 76½"+	6	9 S13, 16 S14, 252 T1, 72 T4, 324 T12, 56 T14, 4 T18, 36 X2, 36 X2r 8½" x 80½"+ 8½" x 96½"+
Med. Black Print includes 2 ea. spacer strips (wall quilt)	1	4 T5, 24 T14 4¹⁵⁄₁₆" x 21¹¹⁄₁₆"+ 4¹⁵⁄₁₆" x 30½"+	1¼	12 R13, 4 T5, 40 T14	2¼	24 R18, 4 T5, 56 T14
Rose Print	¾	4 S10, 36 T1, 44 T12, 4 T17	2½	16 S10, 144 T1, 176 T12, 16 T17	4½	36 S10, 324 T1, 396 T12, 36 T17
Lt. Green Print	½	24 T14, 4 T18	½	40 T14, 4 T18	1	56 T14, 4 T18
Med. Green Print	½	28 T14	½	44 T14	1	60 T14
Binding	¾	1½" x 6 yds.	¾	1½" x 9 yds.	¾	1½" x 12 yds.
Lining	3⅛	2 @ 28" x 54"	4⅝	2 @ 41" x 80"	8¾	3 @ 34" x 100"
	1 Block 22 Unit A, 24 Unit B		**4 Blocks** set 2 x 2 38 Unit A, 40 Unit B		**9 Blocks** set 3 x 3 54 Unit A, 56 Unit B	

1 Note that you have two sizes of feather triangles; T1's are slightly smaller than T12's. Join a black floral and a rose T1 to make Unit 1 as shown. Make 28 (wall)/112 (twin)/252 (queen) Unit 1's. You will have 8/32/72 rose T1's left over at this point.

2 Join a black floral T12 and a rose T12 to make Unit 2. Make 36/144/324 Unit 2's. You will have 8/32/72 rose T12's left over.

3 To make Unit 3 as shown, join seven Unit 1's, two rose T1's, one rose S10, a black floral X2 and a black floral X2r. Make 4/16/36 Unit 3's.

4 To make Unit 4, join nine Unit 2's, two rose T12's, a rose T17 and two black floral T4's as shown. Use partial seams, stitching from the square end of the large T17 triangle only halfway down its sides. Make 4/16/36 Unit 4's.

5 See the block piecing diagram. Join four Unit 4's, four Unit 3's and a black floral S13 as shown. After joining the top, middle and bottom segments of the block, complete the partial seams at the points of the T17 triangles. Make 1/4/9 Feathered Star blocks.

6 To make Unit A, join a light green and a black floral T14 as shown on page 128. Make 22/38/54 Unit A's.

7 Refer to the coloring drawing (wall)/quilt photo (twin)/or whole quilt diagram (queen). Join 5/9/13 Unit A's. Sew a light green T14 triangle to the black end. Add a black floral T18 to each end to complete a side border. Repeat. Join 6/10/14 Unit A's. Add a light green T18 to the black end and a black floral T14 and a light green T18 to the other end. This completes the top border. Repeat for the bottom border.

Measure your quilt block and your side border. The block should be 21³⁄₁₆" finished or 21¹¹⁄₁₆" from raw edge to raw edge. The border should be 30"/50"/70" finished, from seamline to seamline. If either of these measurements is not as expected, make adjustments to the spacer strips or sashes as described on page 80.

For the wall quilt, add side, then top and bottom spacer strips. **For the twin quilt,** join blocks, medium black R13's and black floral S15's to make two rows of two blocks separated by sashes. **For the queen quilt,** join blocks, medium black R18's and black floral S14's to make three rows of three blocks separated by sashes. **For all sizes,** attach side borders, then top and bottom borders.

8 To make Unit B, join a medium green and a medium black T14 as shown on page 128. Make 24/40/56 Unit B's. Join 6/10/14 Unit B's. Add a medium green T14 to the black end. Sew to the side of the quilt. Repeat for all sides. Add a medium black T5 in each corner.

9 Add black floral side borders, then top and bottom borders. Quilt as desired, and bind to finish.

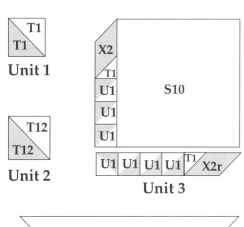

Unit 1

Unit 2

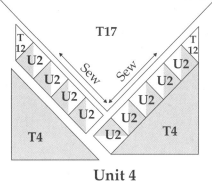

Unit 3

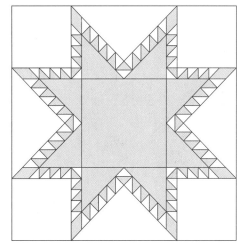

Unit 4

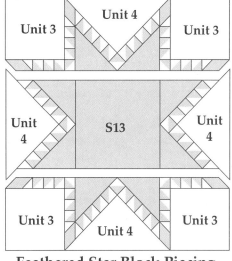

Feathered Star Block

Feathered Star Block Piecing   127

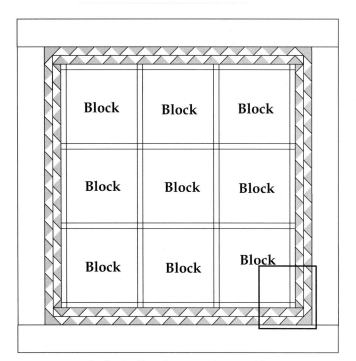

Whole Quilt Diagram, Queen Size

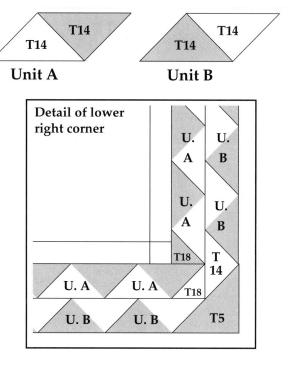

Unit A

Unit B

Detail of lower right corner

Feathered Star Coloring Drawing, Wall Quilt. Photocopy, enlarging if desired, and play with colors.

Devonshire Star

The two star blocks in this quilt are really identical except for coloring. They are colored with the light and dark values reversed, creating an interesting secondary design where the corners of the star blocks come together. Pieces in the triangular edge units of the diagonal set are taken from the block design to create the natural built-in pieced border. The dogtooth add-on border is a natural, too. It utilizes a triangular patch from the quilt block in the same orientation and makes the design look complete. The color photograph of Devonshire Star is on page 40. Full-size patterns and rotary cutting charts begin on page 145.

Right, Devonshire Star lap quilt, 50½" x 63¼".

DEVONSHIRE STAR: FABRICS, YARDAGE & CUTTING REQUIREMENTS

All Sizes 9" Blocks	**Lap Quilt** 50½" x 63¼"		**Twin Quilt** 63¼" x 88¾"		**Queen Quilt** 88¾" x 88¾"	
Fabrics	**Yds.**	**Patches**	**Yds.**	**Patches**	**Yds.**	**Patches**
Dark Blue Prints	1⅝	128 T3, 186 T7, 52 T8	3	212 T3, 372 T7, 100 T8	4	284 T3, 560 T7, 148 T8
Light Blue Plaid (includes borders, 2 each size)	2½	12 S9, 80 T3, 120 T8 4½" x 55¾"+ 4½" x 51"+	4	24 S9, 140 T3, 252 T8 4½" x 81¼"+ 4½" x 63¾"+	5⅛	36 S9, 196 T3, 388 T8 4½" x 81¼"+ 4½" x 89¼"+
Beige Print	1	238 T7	1½	460 T7	1½	672 T7
Light Large Floral	1	6 S9, 20 T3, 56 T8	1½	15 S9, 32 T3, 128 T8	2	25 S9, 40 T3, 208 T8
Binding	¾	1½" x 7 yds.	¾	1½" x 9 yds.	¾	1½" x 11 yds.
Lining	3¼	2 @ 34" x 55"	5⅜	2 @ 34" x 93"	8⅛	3 @ 32" x 93"
		12 Block A 6 Block B 10 Unit C 4 Unit D		24 Block A 15 Block B 16 Unit C 4 Unit D		36 Block A 25 Block B 20 Unit C 4 Unit D

Unit 1   **Unit 1 Piecing**

Block A

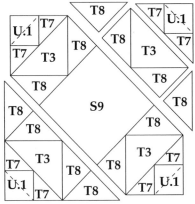

Blocks A & B Piecing

Block B

130   **Unit C**

1 From a dark blue T7 and a beige print T7 triangle, make a Unit 1 as shown. Repeat to make 102 (lap)/204 (twin)/304 (queen) Unit 1's. These will be used in the A and B Blocks and C Units.

2 Make an A Block as shown from one blue plaid S9, eight blue plaid T8's, four dark blue T3's, four dark blue T8's, eight beige T7's and four Unit 1's. Make 12/24/36 A Blocks, depending on your quilt size.

3 Referring to the diagrams, make a B Block from one light large floral S9, eight light large floral T8's, four blue plaid T3's, four blue plaid T8's, eight dark blue T7's and four Unit 1's. Make 6/15/25 B Blocks.

4 Make a Unit C as shown from 3 Unit 1's, 3 dark blue T3's, 2 light large floral T3's, 1 blue plaid T3, 4 beige print T7's and 2 dark blue T7's. Make 10/16/20 Unit C's.

5 Make a Unit D as shown from two dark blue T3's, four dark blue T7's, 1 dark blue T8 and two light large floral print T8's. Make 4 Unit D's.

6 Join a blue plaid T3 and a dark blue T3 triangle to make Unit 2 as shown. Repeat to make 38/56/68 Unit 2's.

7 Refer to the queen-size whole quilt diagram. It will help you see the arrangement of blocks and units for all sizes. Starting in the upper left corner, join blocks and units to make the first two diagonal rows as shown. Repeat for the lower right corner. For the middle rows, proceed as described below for your quilt size.

The lap quilt is made from rows 1, 2, 3, 3, 2 and 1 of the queen diagram, with a slight adjustment. See the photograph. Each row 3 has a D replacing the C at one end. Make rows, join them, and add D's to the remaining two corners to complete the quilt center.

The twin quilt is made from rows 1, 2, 3, 4, 4, 4, 3, 2 and 1 of the queen-size diagram, with adjustments as follows. See the coloring

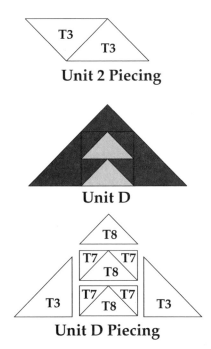

Unit 2   **Unit 2 Piecing**

Unit D

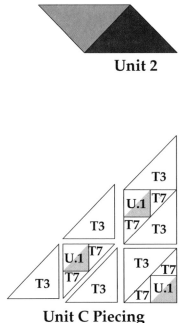

Unit C Piecing   **Unit D Piecing**

drawing. The row 4's are slightly altered for the twin, with a D replacing a C in two row 4's, and one C turned differently in the middle row 4. Make rows, join them, and add D's to the two remaining corners to finish the quilt center.

For the queen quilt, follow the whole quilt diagram. Make rows, join them, and add two D's to complete the quilt center as shown.

8 Join 11/17/17 Unit 2's in a row with plaid touching dark blue. Add a dark blue T3 to the plaid end. Attach to the side of the quilt, with the dark edge touching the quilt center. Repeat for the opposite side. Join 8/11/17 Unit 2's in a row. Add a dark blue T3 to the plaid end. Attach to the top of the quilt. Repeat for the bottom.

9 Join two blue plaid T3's along their short sides to make a triangular unit. Repeat to make four of these triangle units. Sew one to each corner of the quilt.

10 Add side borders, then top and bottom borders to complete the quilt top. Mark and quilt the motif of your choice in the borders and S9 squares. Quilt and bind to finish.

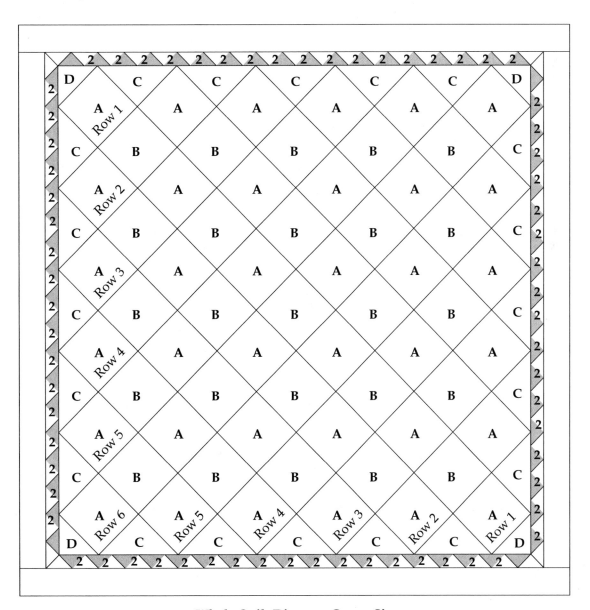

Whole Quilt Diagram, Queen Size

Devonshire Star Coloring Drawing, Twin Size.
132 Photocopy this drawing, enlarging if desired, and play with colors. Make an extra copy to use as a map to guide you in assembling the blocks and units.

Starlight Log Cabin

The Lone Star in this quilt is cleverly built in to the Log Cabin blocks. Judy's fondness for stars and Log Cabins resulted in her popular Colorado Log Cabin design for her book, *Scrap Quilts,* in 1985. That was not her first, nor her last Log Cabin-star combination. The Starlight Log Cabin has more of a medallion effect. The half-starburst blocks echo the diamonds in the quilt center. If you like, you could make a quilt in a Sunshine and Shadows arrangement entirely from these half-starburst blocks. Accurate cutting and sewing are important for this pattern, but this splendid quilt is worth the effort. The color photograph is on page 41. Full-size patterns and rotary cutting charts begin on page 145.

Right, Starlight Log Cabin lap quilt, 55" x 69".

STARLIGHT LOG CABIN: FABRICS, YARDAGE & CUTTING REQUIREMENTS

All Sizes 7" & 14" Blocks	Wall Quilt 55" x 55"		Lap Quilt 55" x 69"		Twin Quilt 69" x 97"	
Fabrics	**Yds.**	**Patches**	**Yds.**	**Patches**	**Yds.**	**Patches**
Light Scraps	2	294 S1, 24 R2, 24 R3, 24 R4, 24 R5, 24 R6, 4 X7, 4 X7r, 4 X8, 4 X8r, 4 X9, 4 X9r, 4 X10, 4 X10r	2	348 S1, 36 R2, 36 R3, 36 R4, 36 R5, 36 R6, 4 X7, 4 X7r, 4 X8, 4 X8r, 4 X9, 4 X9r, 4 X10, 4 X10r	4	522 S1, 84 R2, 84 R3, 84 R4, 84 R5, 84 R6, 4 X7, 4 X7r, 4 X8, 4 X8r, 4 X9, 4 X9r, 4 X10, 4 X10r
Dark Scraps	2	8 S1, 126 R2, 118 R3, 16 R4, 16 R5, 16 R6, 40 R7, 8 X11, 8 X11r, 8 X12, 8 X12r	2½	8 S1, 152 R2, 144 R3, 28 R4, 28 R5, 28 R6, 52 R7, 8 X11, 8 X11r, 8 X12, 8 X12r	5	8 S1, 242 R2, 234 R3, 76 R4, 76 R5, 76 R6, 100 R7, 8 X11, 8 X11r, 8 X12, 8 X12r
Olive Print	⅛	24 D1	⅛	24 D1	⅛	24 D1
Gold Print	⅛	16 D1	⅛	16 D1	⅛	16 D1
Pink Print	⅛	24 D1	⅛	24 D1	⅛	24 D1
Dk. Blue Print	⅛	32 D1	⅛	32 D1	⅛	32 D1
Md. Blue Print	⅛	24 D1	⅛	24 D1	⅛	24 D1
Rust Print	⅛	24 D1	⅛	24 D1	⅛	24 D1
Cream Print	⅛	32 D1	⅛	32 D1	⅛	32 D1

All Sizes 7" & 14" Blocks		Wall Quilt 55" x 55"		Lap Quilt 55" x 69"		Twin Quilt 69" x 97"	
Fabrics		Yds.	Patches	Yds.	Patches	Yds.	Patches
Darkest Scraps		¼	4 S1, 4 R2, 4 R3, 4 R4, 4 R5, 4 R6	¼	4 S1, 4 R2, 4 R3, 4 R4, 4 R5, 4 R6	¼	4 S1, 4 R2, 4 R3, 4 R4, 4 R5, 4 R6
Coral Solid incl. border (2 strips ea. size) & binding		1¾	200 S1 2" x 52½"+ 2" x 55½"+ 1½" x 7 yds.	2	240 S1 2" x 66½"+ 2" x 55½"+ 1½" x 8 yds.	2⅞	372 S1 2" x 94½"+ 2" x 69½"+ 1½" x 10 yds.
Lining		3½	2 @ 30" x 59"	3½	2 @ 37" x 59"	5⅞	2 @ 37" x 101"
		Set 6 x 6 4 Block A 8 Block B 12 Block C 84 Unit D 84 Unit E 2 Unit F 2 Unit G		**Set 6 x 8** 4 Block A 8 Block B 24 Block C 98 Unit D 98 Unit E 2 Unit F 2 Unit G		**Set 8 x 12** 4 Block A 8 Block B 72 Block C 140 Unit D 140 Unit E 2 Unit F 2 Unit G	

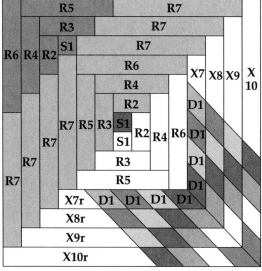

Block A

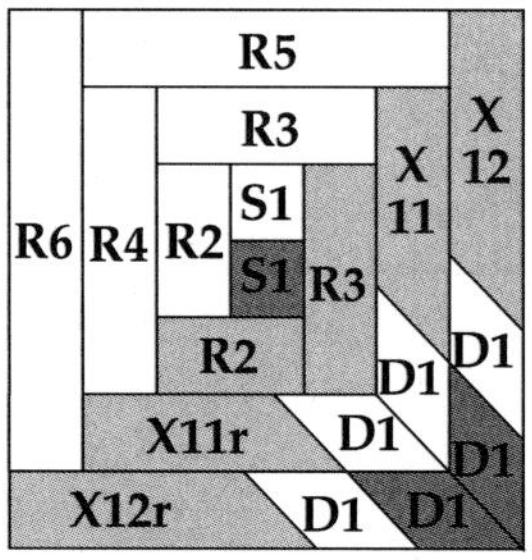

Block B

1. In this pattern, it is important that the Log Cabin blocks be precisely made in order for the Lone Star and starburst elements to fit properly. For more accurate results without any extra work, cut the logs to the needed lengths at the outset. For the best mix of scraps throughout the quilt, cut a variety of different log lengths from each strip.

2. Before making the A Blocks, make logs from patches in a row as follows: Join a light X7 to a rust D1 to an olive D1 to a light blue D1 to a dark blue D1 to make a log. Join the same diamond sequence to an X7r, as well. Join a light X8 to an olive D1 to a light blue D1 to a dark blue D1 to a pink D1. Repeat with X8r. Sew a light X9 to a light blue D1 to a dark blue D1 to a pink D1 to a gold D1. Repeat with X9r. Sew a light X10 to a dark blue D1 to a pink D1 to a gold D1 to an olive D1. Repeat with X10r. Sew an extra-dark S1 to a dark R7. Sew extra-dark R2 through R6 patches to dark R7's.

Now add the logs as follows: Referring to the block diagram, sew a light S1 to a coral S1. Press seams away from the coral S1. Add a light R2, then a dark R2 followed by a dark R3. Continue adding two light logs, then two dark logs, with longer and longer logs. Looking at the diagram, the sequence is a counterclockwise spiral from the center out. After the first dark R7 log, add logs made from D and X patches and logs made from extra-dark patches and dark R7 rectangles. As you add the logs with the diamond patches, attach the long side, but stop stitching at the end of the seam line at the diamond end. This leaves the seam allowance free to pivot at the set-in. Don't miter the corner until all logs are attached. Then you only have one set-in to miter. Make 4 Block A's.

3 Join two Block A's to form a half star. Repeat. Join the two halves to complete the star, pressing the final seam open to distribute bulk.

4 Before making the B Block, make logs from patches in a row as follows: Sew a dark X11 to a cream D1. Repeat with X11r. Sew a dark X12 to a cream D1 to a rust D1. Repeat with X12r.

Now sew the logs together, starting with a coral and a light S1. Add a light R2, then a dark R2 and a dark R3. Proceed in a counterclockwise spiral, adding longer and longer logs. When you add the X-D logs, stitch only to the end of the seam line at the D1 end. After adding all logs, miter the corner. Make 8 Block B's.

5 Make Block C, following the diagram and starting with the coral and light S1 squares.

Add longer and longer logs in a counterclockwise spiral. Make 12/24/72 C Blocks.

6 Join two Block B's to form a half starburst. Make four of these. Arrange all A, B and C Blocks in a barnraising set as shown, or turn blocks in another arrangement if you prefer. Sew a Block C to each end of a half-starburst unit, turned according to your plan. Repeat for each half-starburst unit. Sew one of the resulting sections to the side of the quilt center. Repeat for the other side.

7 Sew an additional Block C to each end of the remaining two half-starburst units, again turning blocks according to your plan. Sew the resulting sections to the top and bottom of the quilt. This completes the quilt center for the wall quilt.

8 **For the lap and twin quilts,** join six Block C's to make a row, turning blocks as needed to make the barnraising pattern or your chosen Log Cabin set. Sew this row to the top of the quilt. Repeat for the bottom of the quilt. This completes the quilt center for the lap quilt.

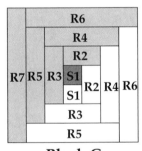

Block C

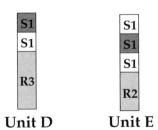

Unit D   **Unit E**

Unit F   **Unit G**

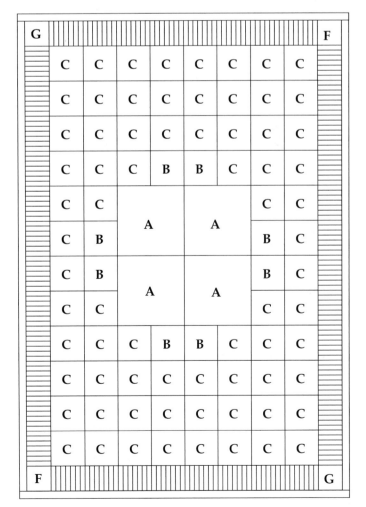

Whole Quilt Diagram, Twin Size

9 For the twin quilt only, make four more rows of six Block C's, turning blocks appropriately. Sew two of these rows to the top of the quilt and two of them to the bottom of the quilt. Also make one row of 12 blocks for each side, again turning blocks to form the barnraising pattern. Attach these last two rows, one to each side of the quilt. This completes the quilt center for the twin quilt.

10 For all sizes, referring to the diagrams, make 84/98/140 Unit D's, 84/98/140 Unit E's, 2 Unit F's and 2 Unit G's. Start with a Unit E and join 21/28/42 Unit E's alternated with 21/28/42 Unit D's to make a side border. Attach with the Unit E at the top of the left border. Repeat for the opposite side, attaching with the Unit E at the bottom of the right border.

11 Starting with a Unit E, join 21/21/28 Unit E's alternated with 21/21/28 Unit D's to make the top border. Add a Unit F to the Unit D end and a Unit G to the Unit E end. Sew to the top of the quilt with the G at the top left. Repeat for the bottom of the quilt, attaching the border with the G and E at the bottom right.

12 Add side, then top and bottom coral borders. Quilt as desired and bind to finish.

Starlight Log Cabin Coloring Drawing, Wall Size. Photocopy this drawing, enlarging if desired, and play with different colorings. Also use this sketch as a guide for joining the blocks and units.

Mountain Vistas

Here is a quilt for the outdoor enthusiast. The colors of earth and trees are always appealing, and the peaks and valleys of this quilt's central panel seem to whisk you off into distant mountains. The almost three-dimensional quality of the image is enhanced by the use of medium values in place of some of the lights and darks. The effect is easy to achieve by clustering mediums in random places to alter the perceived pattern. This is a simple quilt framed with an impressive, but easy-to-sew border. Because of the natural fit, you can make this quilt in many other sizes. Simply add or subtract sets of four rows and/or sets of 2 Unit A's per row in the quilt center. This adjusts the quilt dimensions in 12" increments, to fit the star and triangle borders perfectly. The color photograph is on page 42. Full-size patterns and rotary cutting charts begin on page 145.

Right, Mountain Vistas twin quilt, 72" x 96".

MOUNTAIN VISTAS: FABRICS, YARDAGE & CUTTING REQUIREMENTS

All Sizes 6" Stars			Wall Quilt 60" x 60"		Twin Quilt 72" x 96"		Queen Quilt 96" x 96"	
Fabrics		**Yds.**	**Patches**	**Yds.**	**Patches**	**Yds.**	**Patches**	
Light Scraps incl. border (2 strips of each)		2½	20 R24, 92 S7, 324 T8, 28 T9 2" x 24½"+ 2" x 27½"+	4½	36 R24, 156 S7, 716 T8, 44 T9 2" x 60½"+ 2" x 39½"+	6	44 R24, 188 S7, 1020 T8, 52 T9 2" x 60½"+ 2" x 63½"+	
Dark Scraps incl. border (4 each wall/queen, 2 each twin)		3	24 S3, 16 T3, 192 T7, 172 T8, 56 T9 3½" x 61¼"+	5½	40 S3, 40 T3, 320 T7, 324 T8, 148 T9 3½" x 97¼"+ 3½" x 73¼"+	7½	48 S3, 40 T3, 384 T7, 436 T8, 236 T9 3½" x 97¼"+	
Binding		¾	1½" x 8 yds.	¾	1½" x 10 yds.	¾	1½" x 12 yds.	
Lining		3¾	2 @ 33" x 64"	5⅞	2 @ 39" x 100"	8¾	3 @ 34" x 100"	

8 Rows of 4 A's	**20 Rows of 6 A's**	**20 Rows of 10 A's**
64 Unit A	168 Unit A	256 Unit A
36 Unit B	52 Unit B	60 Unit B
16 Unit C	32 Unit C	40 Unit C
2 Unit D	2 Unit D	2 Unit D
2 Unit E	2 Unit E	2 Unit E

1 Make Unit 1's from dark and light T8 triangles as shown. Make 100 (wall)/220 (twin)/316 (queen) Unit 1's.

2 Add two light T8 triangles to a Unit 1 to make Unit A, as shown. Make 64/168/256 Unit A's, depending on your quilt dimensions.

3 Add two dark T8 triangles to a Unit 1 to make Unit B, as shown. Make 36/52/60 Unit B's.

4 Set aside for borders all of the Unit B's and 32/48/56 Unit A's. Join the remaining Unit A's and dark T3 and T9 triangles to make rows for the quilt center, as shown below. Make 8/20/20 rows.

5 Join rows to complete the quilt center. Join random-length strips cut 2" wide to make two border strips of each of the lengths listed in the yardage chart. First sew the long borders to the two sides of the quilt center. Then add the top and bottom borders, with squared corners.

6 To make Unit 2, sew two dark T7's to a light T8. Repeat to make four of these. Join with a dark S3 and four light S7's to complete Unit 2.

Make 20/36/44 Unit 2's.

7 Add a light R24 to the top of a Unit 2 to make Unit C. Make 16/32/40 Unit C's.

8 Referring to the diagrams for D and E, make a Unit 2 star minus one S7 square. Notice the partial seams indicated by a square mark. Stitch the seam from the S7 to about the square mark. The partial seams will be completed later. Add a light R24 rectangle and a Unit 2 as shown to complete the unit. Make 2 each of Units D and E.

9 Join 5/11/11 Unit C's, turning them so that the rectangles are on alternating ends. Sew to the sides of the quilt, noting that the border extends one S7 square past the plain border on each end and leaving the last couple of inches unstitched at each end. Repeat for the opposite side.

10 Join 3/5/9 Unit C's, turning them so that the rectangles are on alternate ends. Sew a Unit D to the left end and a Unit E to the right end. Sew to the top of the quilt. Repeat for the bottom of the quilt.

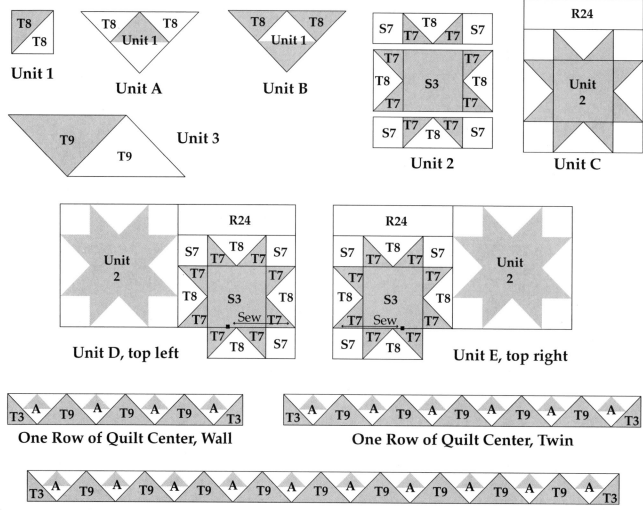

11 Complete the seam that you partially stitched in Step 9 at the ends of each side border. Then complete the seams of the Unit D's and Unit E's to finish the star border.

12 Join dark and light T9 patches as shown to make Unit 3. Make 28/44/52 Unit 3's.

13 Multiple borders are assembled before attaching. For a side border, join 7/13/13 Unit 3's; add a dark T9 to the light end. Join 9/15/15 Unit B's alternated with 8/14/14 Unit A's. Sew to the T9 border. Join 3½"-wide dark strips of random lengths to make a border strip 61¼"+/97¼"+/97¼"+ long. Sew this border to the Unit A-Unit B edge of a pieced border, matching centers. Trim the ends of the plain border at a 45° angle following the line of the pieced border. Sew the completed border to the side of the quilt center,

again matching centers. Sew only to the end of the seam line, not to the raw edge of the patches. Repeat for the opposite side.

14 For top/bottom borders, repeat step 13 for the wall and queen quilts. For the twin quilt, join 9 Unit 3's. Add a dark T9 to the light end. Join 11 Unit B's alternated with 10 Unit A's. Sew to the T9 border. Join 3½"-wide dark strips of random length to make a border strip 73¼"+ long. Sew this border to the Unit A-Unit B edge of the pieced border, matching centers. Trim the ends at an angle. Sew the completed border to the top of the quilt center, again matching centers. Stitch only to the end of the seam line, not to the raw edge of the patches. Repeat for the bottom of the quilt.

15 Miter the corners to complete the quilt top. Quilt as desired and bind to finish.

Mountain Vistas Coloring Drawing, Wall Size. Photocopy this sketch, enlarging if desired, and play with different colors. Also refer to this drawing as a guide for joining the units.

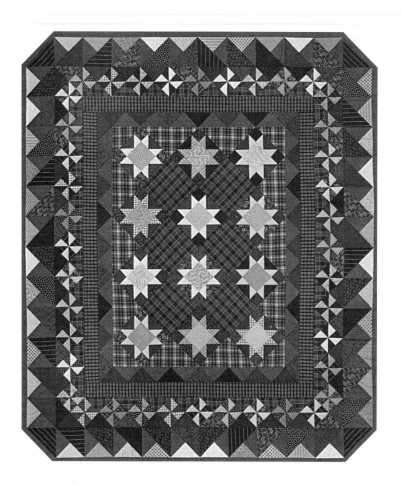

Harvest Time

This straightforward quilt center is framed with three simple add-on borders. Dimensions and patches found in the star blocks in the center of the quilt are used in the borders for a natural fit. The combination of simple shapes is a knockout in the mustard, cinnamon and black fabrics as shown, but the design could easily be made in other colors. Make several photocopies of the line drawing of the quilt on page 143 and experiment with different shadings before choosing your fabrics. The color photograph of Harvest Time is on page 43. Full-size patterns and rotary cutting charts begin on page 145.

Left, Harvest Time twin quilt, 72" x 84".

HARVEST TIME: FABRICS, YARDAGE & CUTTING REQUIREMENTS

All Sizes 8½" Blocks	Wall Quilt 60" x 60"		Twin Quilt 72" x 84"		Queen/King Quilt 96" x 96"	
Fabrics	**Yds.**	**Patches**	**Yds.**	**Patches**	**Yds.**	**Patches**
Black Prints	2½	16 S8, 16 T3, 36 T6, 112 T8, 52 T9	3½	48 S8, 48 T3, 48 T6, 160 T8, 76 T9	4½	100 S8, 100 T3, 60 T6, 208 T8, 100 T9
Mustard Prints	1½	4 S9, 144 T8, 32 T9	2	12 S9, 256 T8, 44 T9	3	25 S9, 408 T8, 56 T9
Big Black Plaid	¾	1 S12, 24 T9	1½	6 S12, 36 T9	3	16 S12, 48 T9
Tan/Black Plaid	⅝	4 T6, 4 T19	1	4 T6, 10 T19	1	4 T6, 16 T19
Small Black Plaid (2 ea. spacer strip)	1⅛	3½" x 30½"+ 3½" x 36½"+	1¾	3½" x 54½"+ 3½" x 48½"+	2¼	3½" x 66½"+ 3½" x 72½"+
Cinnamon Print	1	48 T9	1	72 T9	1½	96 T9
Binding	¾	1½" x 8 yds.	¾	1½" x 10 yds.	¾	1½" x 12 yds.
Lining	3¾	2 @ 33" x 64"	5⅛	2 @ 39" x 88"	8¾	3 @ 34" x 100"
	4 Blocks set 2 x 2 16 Unit A 4 Unit B 4 Unit C 16 Unit D 16 Unit E		**12 Blocks** set 3 x 4 28 Unit A 4 Unit B 4 Unit C 22 Unit D 22 Unit E		**25 Blocks** set 5 x 5 40 Unit A 4 Unit B 4 Unit C 28 Unit D 28 Unit E	

1 Join black and mustard T8's to make Unit 1 as shown. Make 112 (wall)/160 (twin)/208 (queen) Unit 1's.

2 Join four Unit 1's as shown to make Unit 2. Make 28/40/52 Unit 2's, depending on your quilt size.

3 Join cinnamon and black T9 triangles as shown to make Unit 3's. Make 12/24/36 Unit 3's.

4 From two black print T9 triangles, make a Unit 4. Make four Unit 4's, regardless of quilt size.

5 To make the quilt block, sew two mustard T8 triangles to a black T3 triangle. Repeat to make four of these segments. Join as shown with black S8 squares and a mustard S9 square to complete the block. Make 4/12/25 blocks, depending on the quilt size.

6 Join blocks, big black plaid S12 squares and tan/black plaid T19 triangles to make diagonal rows. See the whole quilt diagram for the queen quilt, the color photograph on page 43 for the twin quilt and the coloring drawing for the wall quilt in order to see the way the blocks and triangles are assembled into rows. Add a tan/black T6 triangle to each corner to complete the quilt center.

7 Join 3/5/9 Unit 3's in a row, with black touching cinnamon. Add a cinnamon T9 to the black end. Sew this pieced border strip to the top of the quilt, with the cinnamon edge touching the quilt center. Repeat for the bottom of the quilt. For the wall- and queen-size quilts, repeat two more times for the two side borders. For the twin quilt, join 7 Unit 3's in a row, add a cinnamon T9 and attach to the side of the quilt. Repeat for the opposite side.

8 Add a Unit 4 to each corner to complete the first border. Attach side, then top and bottom spacer strips.

9 Add a big black plaid T9 to one side of a Unit 2 and a black T9 to the opposite side to make a Unit A as shown on the next page. Make 16/28/40 Unit A's.

10 Add two big black plaid T9's to a Unit 2 to make a Unit B as shown on page 142. Make four Unit B's, regardless of your quilt size.

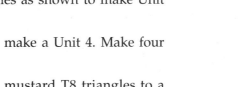

Unit 1   **Unit 1 Piecing**

Unit 2

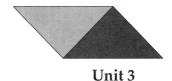

Unit 2 Piecing

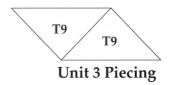

Unit 3

Unit 3 Piecing

Unit 4

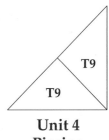

Unit 4 Piecing

Block   **Block Piecing**

141

Unit A

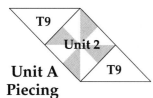

Unit A Piecing

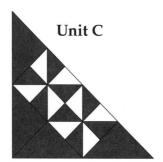

Unit B

Unit B Piecing

Unit D

Unit D Piecing

Unit E

Unit E Piecing

11 Join two Unit 2's and four black T9's as shown to make Unit C. Repeat to make four Unit C's.

12 Join 4/6/10 Unit A's in a row. Add a Unit B at one end. Sew to the top of the quilt. Repeat for the bottom of the quilt. For the wall and queen sizes, repeat this step for the sides of the quilt. For the twin quilt, join 8 Unit A's in a row, add a Unit B and attach to the side of the quilt. Repeat for the opposite side.

13 Add a Unit C to each corner to complete the border.

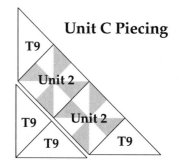

Unit C   **Unit C Piecing**

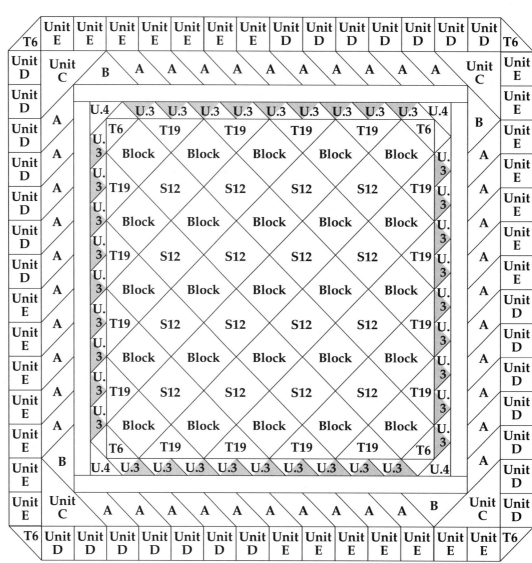

142   **Whole Quilt Diagram, Queen Size**

14 Join a cinnamon T9 to a mustard T9; add a black T6 to make Unit D as shown. Make 16/22/28 Unit D's. Also make 16/22/28 Unit E's from cinnamon and mustard T9's and black T6's.

15 Sew 4/5/7 Unit D's in a row. Similarly sew 4/5/7 Unit E's in a row. Join, with black touching black. Sew to the bottom of the quilt. Repeat for the top of the quilt. Sew 4/6/7 Unit D's in a row. Also sew 4/6/7 Unit E's in a row. Join, with black touching black. Add a black T6 triangle to each end of the strip. Sew to one side of the quilt. Repeat for the opposite side.

16 Mark and quilt the motif of your choice in the large squares and triangles. Outline quilt or quilt in the ditch around patches. Bind to finish.

Harvest Time Coloring Drawing, Wall Size. Photocopy this sketch, enlarging it if desired. Try different colorings before making the quilt. This drawing is also a guide for joining units.

Review of Piecing Shortcuts & Helpful Tips

We recommend washing and pressing fabrics before use.

Study your quilt plan or the piecing diagram in the book to determine the best piecing sequence. Try to sew small patches into units that can be joined in rows without setting in.

Pin seams before stitching if matching is involved or if your seams are longer than about 4". First pin joints that need to be matched, then pin the rest of the seam line. Opposing seams will help you match most joints.

> ### Opposing Seams
> Turn seam allowances in opposite directions at joints. This makes a slight ridge at the joint to help you align seam lines perfectly. It also distributes the bulk evenly. Stick a pin in at an angle across both sets of seam allowances before stitching.

When your seam line joins plain or simple piecing to piecing with points, stitch with the points up. You can then see the "X" formed by the previous seams at each point and stitch through the middle of it. When your seam line joins two pieced parts, point to point, use a positioning pin.

> ### Positioning Pin
> Use a positioning pin to align your patchwork points perfectly for stitching. Carefully push a pin straight through the point of one patch, where the seam allowances cross. Push this pin on through the point of the second patch to align it to the first. Pull the pin tight, with the pinhead against the first patch and your thumb and forefinger holding the second patch directly against the first patch at the pin. Pin the seam normally with another pin before removing the positioning pin.

Set your sewing machine's stitch length at 10-12 stitches per inch. Use 100% cotton thread in a neutral color about the shade of the light fabrics in the project. Stitch using ¼" seams, taping a seam gauge on the throatplate of your machine, if needed. Use chain piecing to save time and thread.

> ### Chain Piecing
> To chain piece, join a pair of patches in a seam, but do not lift the presser foot. Do not take the unit just sewn out of the sewing machine, and do not cut the thread. Prepare the next pair of patches, slide them barely under the tip of the presser foot, and stitch. There will be a little twist of thread between the two units. When all of the patches are chained together, clip threads between units.

For most piecing, sew from cut edge to cut edge, backtacking if you wish. For set-in seams, you must stop stitching at the seamline to leave the seam allowances free to pivot at the corner.

> ### Set-in Seams
> Where three seams come together at an angle, stop all stitching at the ¼" seam line and backtack. (You can mark the spot lightly with a pencil on the wrong side of the fabric.) As each seam is finished, take the work out of the machine, flip the seam allowances and the bulk out of the way of the next seam, then pin and stitch.

Sometimes you can avoid set-in seams with partial seams. We use this technique in Feathered Star patterns, for example.

> ### Partial Seams
> Stitch the seam, starting at one end, but stopping shy of the opposite end. Continue the rest of the sewing, and when the unit or block has progressed far enough that you have avoided the set-in seams, complete the partial seam.

Press seam allowances to one side, generally away from the bulk and toward the darker fabrics wherever possible. When handling and pressing patches, avoid stretching bias edges. After cutting shapes with bias edges, try not to steam press them until all of the bias edges are stitched. Dry press carefully, if you like, simply lowering and lifting the iron rather than sliding it over the fabric. Don't leave it in one place too long. If you must move the iron around, move it following the grain line. Even better, finger press to train the seam allowances to one side before crossing them with another seam.

> ### Finger Pressing
> As you join the patches together, crease the seams to one side using your thumbnail rather than an iron. Lay the piece flat, face up, with the seam allowances turned the proper directions. Run your thumbnail along the seam line.

We have assumed in this book that our readers are well-versed in quiltmaking fundamentals. If you want to learn more about all aspects of quiltmaking, you will find the information you need in our other books, especially Marsha's *Lessons in Machine Piecing* and Judy's *Yes You Can! Make Stunning Quilts From Simple Patterns*. See page 160.

Take care with your cutting, pinning, stitching, and pressing for the best results and a perfectly enjoyable quiltmaking experience.

Master Patterns & Rotary Cutting Details

This chapter includes full-size patterns that serve for the complete quilts on pages 101-143 as well as the stock borders on pages 46-79. The patterns here will fit the needs of most quilters. Use our patterns with traditional or rotary cutting techniques. Our pattern instructions include the information you need for either method.

For rotary cutting, measure and cut patches as listed; then compare your cut patches to the templates in the book to check for accuracy.

For hand piecing, use a stiff template to mark seam lines onto the wrong side of the fabric. Carefully trace the dashed seam lines of each shape onto plain paper or graph paper. Use a glue stick to affix the paper to lightweight cardboard, and cut out the shape. (Trace directly onto stiff template plastic, if you prefer.) Remember to add seam allowances by eye when cutting the fabric shapes.

Bias grain stretches, and straight grain holds its shape, so patches should be cut with the straight grain on the outside edge of the block or border.

For most patches, grain placement is obvious. Cut diamonds with the straight grain along two sides. Some triangles may be used with the grain placed differently in two different patterns. Cut the patches so that the straight grain is on the outside edge of the block or unit. If you want to cut a shape with the grain placed differently from our instructions, the rotary cutting dimensions may be awkward. Use our full-size template as a cutting guide.

With pieced borders, accuracy is especially important. For the best patchwork results, check your work for problems at the outset, so you can correct bad habits early in the process.

The rotary method of cutting squares, triangles and rectangles begins with cutting strips of fabric. Choose Long Strips cut crosswise 40"- 44" long, or Short Strips, cut lengthwise 18" long. Our listed dimensions include ¼" seam allowances.

Long Strips of about 40" are cut along the crosswise grain with cuts perpendicular to the selvedge. Fold the fabric in half, aligning the selvedges and smoothing the two layers. Place fabric on the cutting mat with the folded edge closest to your body. Make a clean first cut perpendicular to the fold. From this edge, measure and cut strips of fabric in the desired width.

Short Strips of 18" length are cut along the lengthwise grain of the fabric with cuts parallel to the selvedge. This method is great for scrap quilts when patches need to be cut from many different fabrics. Start with half yards or fat quarters of fabric 18" long. Layer two to four different fabrics, matching selvedges. Make a clean cut to trim away the selvedges. From this edge, measure and cut strips the full 18" length by the desired width.

A review of how to cut various shapes follows. Trim points for easy matching at trim lines indicated on the template.

Check your cut patches against the master patterns provided to make sure they are the right size.

For squares and rectangles, first cut fabric strips the listed width, which includes seam allowances. Cut across the strips to make patches.

For half-square and half-rectangle triangles (indicated in the rotary charts with a "/"), cut squares or rectangles as listed; then cut these in half diagonally to make two triangles. Our measurements include the extra needed for ¼" seam allowances all around. The resulting triangles will have the two short sides on the straight grain of the fabric and the long side on the bias.

For quarter-square triangles (indicated in the rotary charts with an "X"), cut squares; then cut the squares along both diagonals to make four triangles. Our measurements include the extra needed for ¼" seam allowances. The resulting triangles will have the long side on the straight grain of the fabric and the two short sides on the bias.

To cut diamonds D1-4 and parallelograms X2, X3 and X14, cut a strip the listed width. Make a 45° angled cut at one end. Then make cuts parallel to the angled cut at the listed interval. Mirror images can be cut at the same time by layering fabric right sides facing for X and Xr.

To cut triangles T25-31, trace the template's cutting lines onto paper or a Static Sticker™, cut out, and affix to the back of your rotary ruler with one of the two equal sides on the edge of the ruler. Lay the ruler down over a strip of the listed width, with the base of the patch on the cut edge of the strip. Cut along the ruler's edge. Realign for the next edge to cut triangles down the length of the strip.

For the T33 triangle, cut the strip as listed. Cut a 45° angle for one side, and use a pattern tracing affixed to the ruler to cut the third side.

For trapezoids, such as X1, X4, X5, X13 and X15, cut a rectangle of the listed length from a strip of the listed width. Then cut off both short ends at a 45° angle starting precisely at the corner.

For the X6 shape, cut a square as listed. Trace the pattern, cut out, and affix to the ruler with the angled end on the ruler's edge. Align the patch with the tracing, and cut along the ruler's edge.

For trapezoids, such as X7-12 and X16, cut strips and cross cuts as listed to make rectangles. Cut off one corner at a 45° angle.

For the X17 kite shape, cut a square as listed, then affix a tracing to your ruler with the long side on the edge. Align the square corner of your shape over the square, and trim at the edge of the ruler. Turn over the fabric to cut the other side of the square similarly to complete the kite.

146

ROTARY PATCH CUTTING: DIAMONDS

Patch Letter	Strip Width	Cutting Angle	Cross-Cut Interval
D1	1½"	45°	1½"
D2	1¾"	45°	1¾"
D3	2⅝"	45°	2⅝"
D4	1⁹⁄₁₆"	45°	1⁹⁄₁₆"

ROTARY PATCH CUTTING: RECTANGLES

Patch Letter	Strip Width	Cross-Cut Interval
R1	2½"	4½"
R2	1½"	2½"
R3	1½"	3½"
R4	1½"	4½"
R5	1½"	5½"
R6	1½"	6½"
R7	1½"	7½"
R8	1½"	8½"
R9	1½"	9½"
R10	1½"	10½"
R11	2"	12½"
R12	1¹³⁄₁₆"	6½"
R13	3¹⁄₁₆"	21¹¹⁄₁₆"
R14	2¼"	6½"
R15	2³⁄₁₆"	6½"
R16	2½"	8½"
R17	2½"	10½"
R18	2⅛"	21¹¹⁄₁₆"
R19	2³⁄₁₆"	6½"
R20	2"	3½"
R21	2"	8"
R22	2"	5"
R23	2⅝"	9"
R24	2"	6½"
R25	4½"	6½"
R26	4½"	8½"

ROTARY PATCH CUTTING: SQUARES

Patch Letter	Strip Width	Cross-Cut Interval
S1	1½"	1½"
S2	2½"	2½"
S3	3½"	3½"
S4	4½"	4½"

ROTARY PATCH CUTTING: SQUARES, CONTINUED

Patch Letter	Strip Width	Cross-Cut Interval
S5	10½"	10½"
S6	6½"	6½"
S7	2"	2"
S8	2⅝"	2⅝"
S9	4¾"	4¾"
S10	6⅛"	6⅛"
S11	2¼"	2¼"
S12	9"	9"
S13	8½"	8½"
S14	2⅛"	2⅛"
S15	3¹⁄₁₆"	3¹⁄₁₆"
S16	12½"	12½"
S17	3⁵⁄₁₆"	3⁵⁄₁₆"
S18	3"	3"
S19	1⁷⁄₁₆"	1⁷⁄₁₆"

ROTARY PATCH CUTTING: TRIANGLES

Patch Letter	Strip Width	Cross-Cut Interval	Add'l Cuts
T1	1⅞"	1⅞"	/
T2	2⅞"	2⅞"	/
T3	3⅞"	3⅞"	/
T4	4⅞"	4⅞"	/
T5	5⅞"	5⅞"	/
T6	6⅞"	6⅞"	/
T6	9¾"	9¾"	X
T7	2⅜"	2⅜"	/
T7	3⅜"	3⅜"	X
T8	3"	3"	/
T8	4¼"	4¼"	X
T9	5⅛"	5⅛"	/
T9	7¼"	7¼"	X
T10	7⅜"	7⅜"	/
T11	3¾"	3¾"	X
T12	2"	2"	/
T13	5¼"	5¼"	X
T14	6¼"	6¼"	X
T15	3¼"	3¼"	X
T16	4⁵⁄₁₆"	4⁵⁄₁₆"	/
T17	11¼"	11¼"	X
T18	3⅜"	3⅜"	/
T19	9⅜"	9⅜"	/
T19	13¼"	13¼"	X
T20	9⅞"	9⅞"	/
T20	14"	14"	X

ROTARY PATCH CUTTING: TRIANGLES, CONTINUED

Patch Letter	Strip Width	Cross-Cut Interval	Add'l Cuts
T21	9¼"	9¼"	X
T22	8⅞"	8⅞"	/
T23	2³⁄₁₆"	4⅜"	/
T24	3¹¹⁄₁₆"	7⅜"	/
T25	3⅞"	--	*pg. 146
T26	2"	--	*pg. 146
T27	1¹¹⁄₁₆"	--	*pg. 146
T28	3¾"	--	*pg. 146
T29	6⅞"	--	*pg. 146
T30	1⅛"	--	*pg. 146
T31	1³⁄₁₆"	--	*pg. 146
T32	10¼"	10¼"	X
T33	1¾"	--	*pg. 146

*For additional cutting information, see the second column on page 146.

ROTARY PATCH CUTTING: OTHER SHAPES

Patch Letter	Strip Width	Cutting Angle	Cross-Cut Interval	Add'l Cuts
X1	2⅝"	--	9¾"	*pg. 146
X2	1½"	45°	1⅝"	*pg. 146
X3	2⅝"	45°	2"	*pg. 146
X4	1¹⁵⁄₁₆"	--	6⅞"	*pg. 146
X5	3⁵⁄₁₆"	--	15⅜"	*pg. 146
X6	6½"	--	6½"	*pg. 146
X7	1½"	--	3³⁄₁₆"	*pg. 146
X8	1½"	--	5³⁄₁₆"	*pg. 146
X9	1½"	--	7³⁄₁₆"	*pg. 146
X10	1½"	--	9³⁄₁₆"	*pg. 146
X11	1½"	--	4⁷⁄₁₆"	*pg. 146
X12	1½"	--	5"	*pg. 146
X13	2"	--	7¼"	*pg. 146
X14	2"	45°	4¾"	*pg. 146
X15	2"	--	13¼"	*pg. 146
X16	2"	--	3⅞"	*pg. 146
X17	6½"	--	6½"	*pg. 146

Diamonds D1-D4

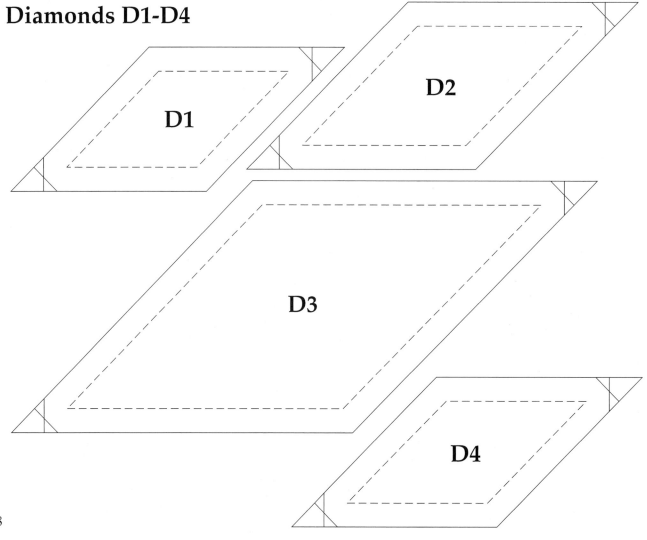

Rectangles R1-R8

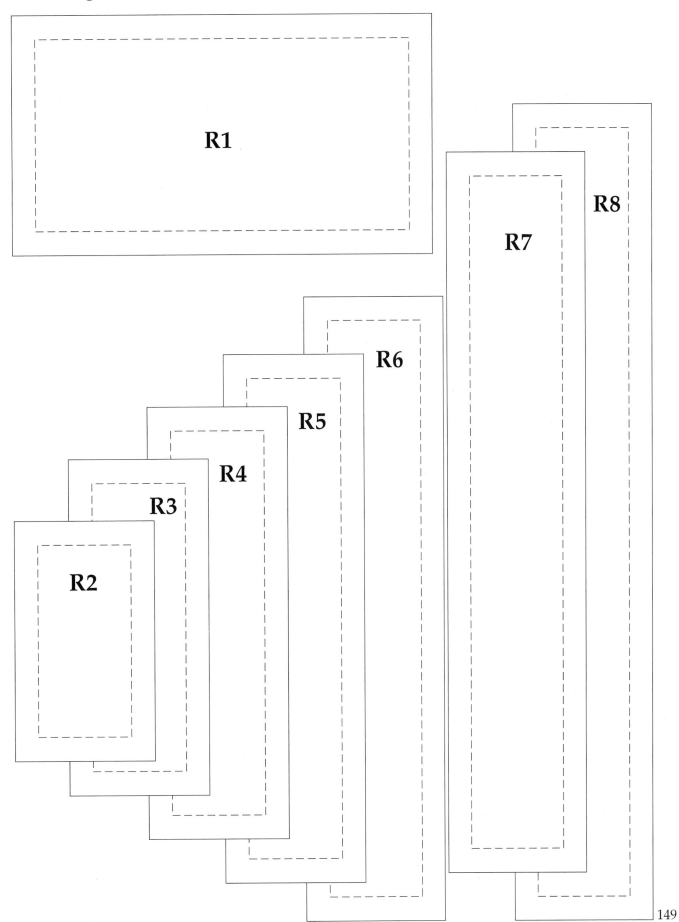

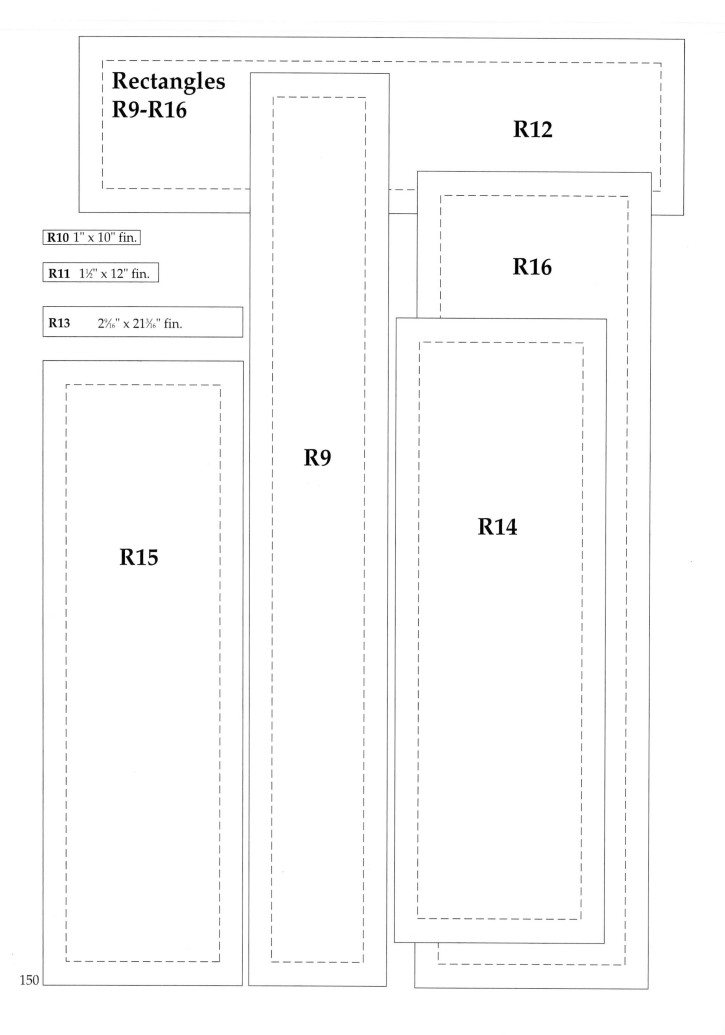

**Rectangles
R9-R16**

R12

R10 1" x 10" fin.

R11 1½" x 12" fin.

R13   2⁹⁄₁₆" x 21³⁄₁₆" fin.

R16

R9

R14

R15

150

Rectangles R17-R26

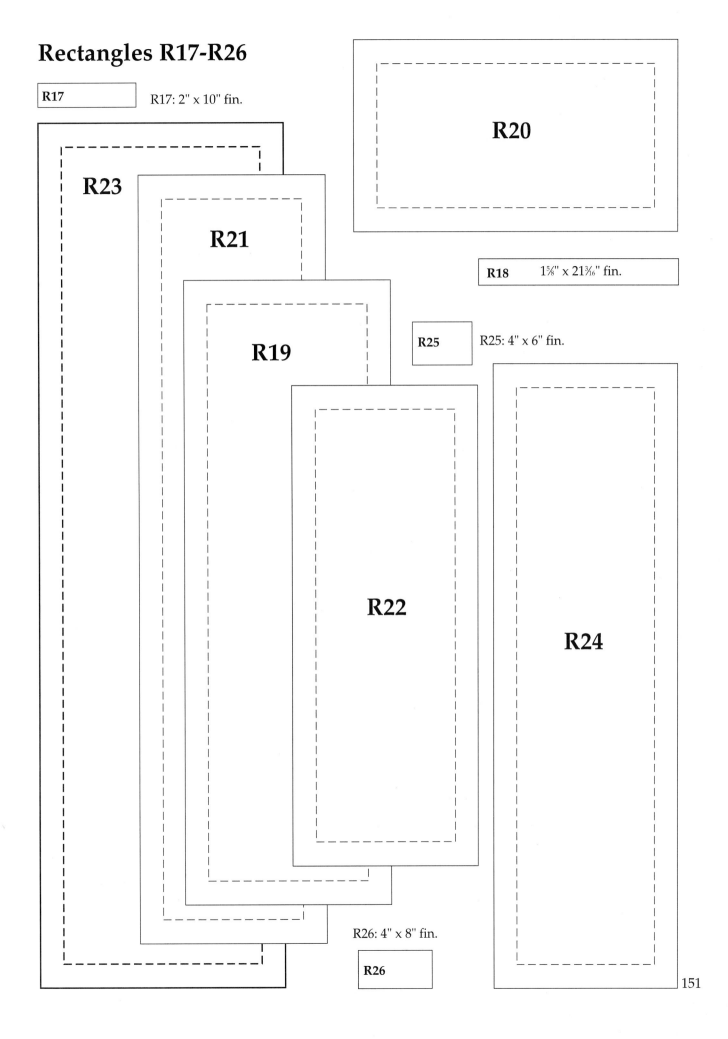

R17

R17: 2" x 10" fin.

R23

R21

R19

R20

R18   1⅝" x 21³⁄₁₆" fin.

R25   R25: 4" x 6" fin.

R22

R24

R26: 4" x 8" fin.

R26

151

Squares S1-S8

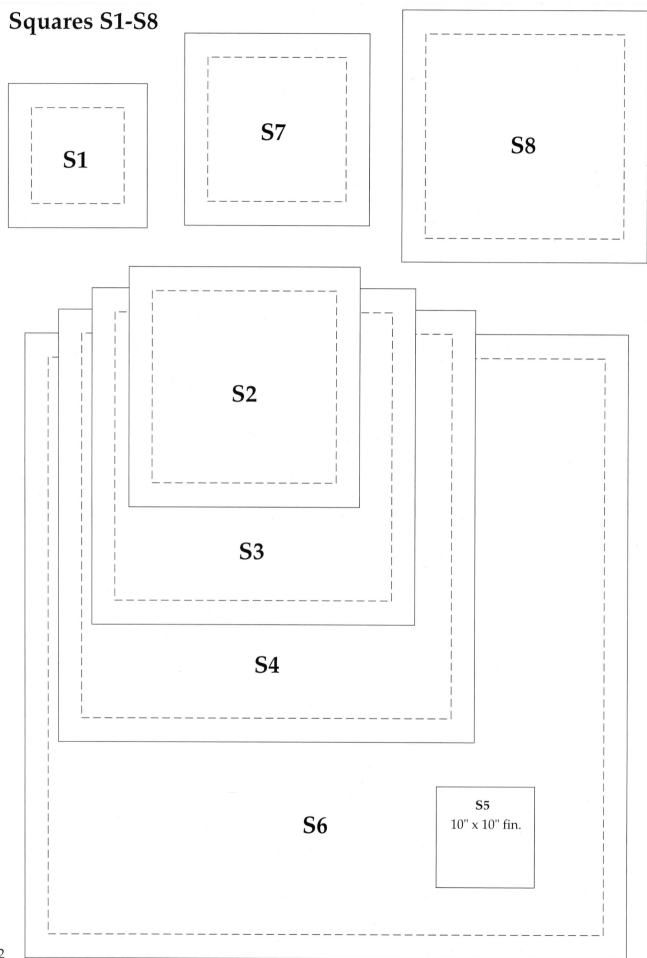

S1

S7

S8

S2

S3

S4

S6

S5
10" x 10" fin.

Squares 9-19

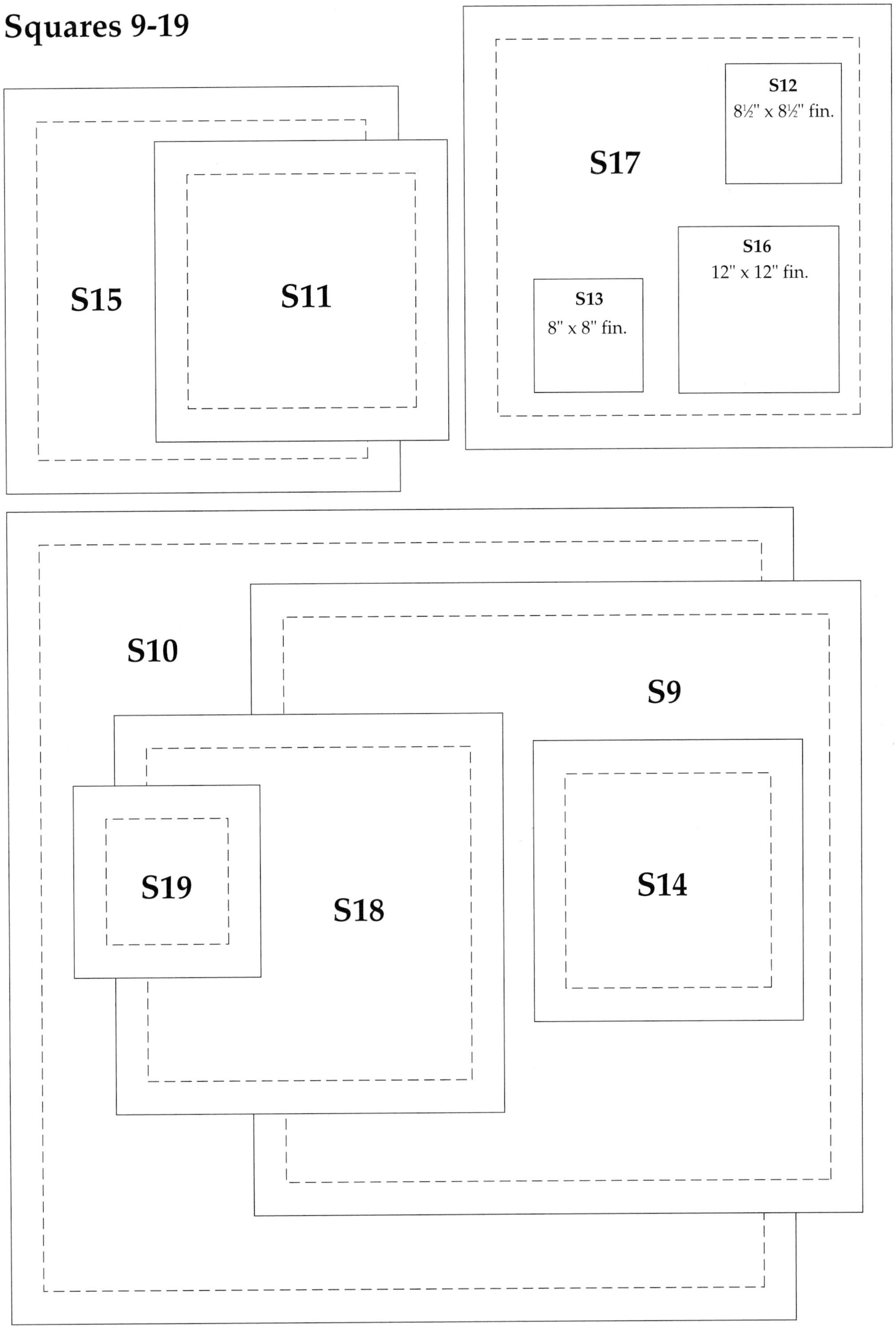

S15

S11

S17

S12
8½" x 8½" fin.

S16
12" x 12" fin.

S13
8" x 8" fin.

S10

S9

S19

S18

S14

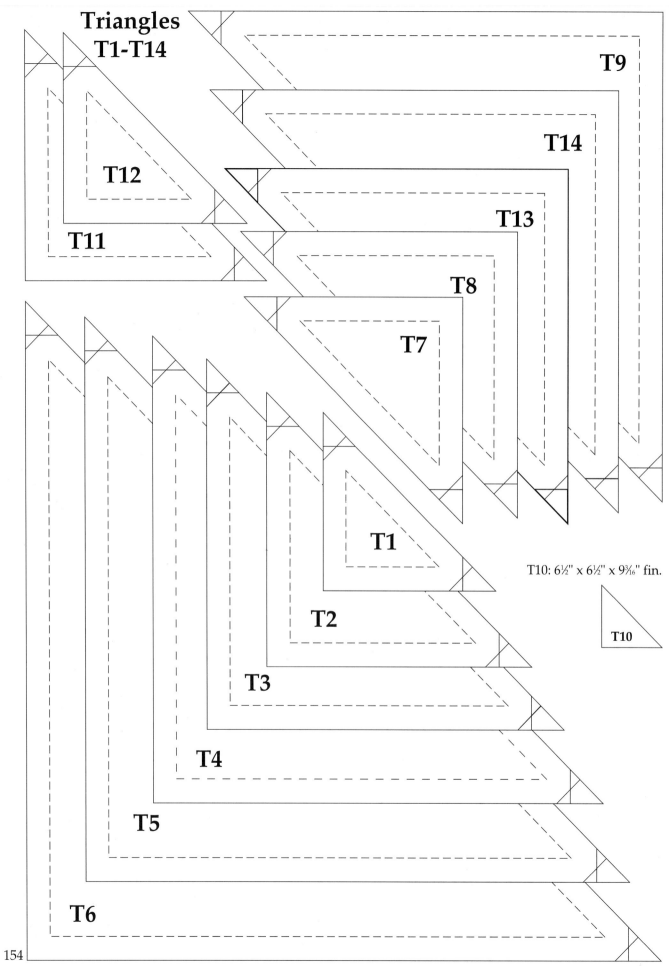

**Triangles
T1-T14**

T9

T14

T13

T12

T8

T11

T7

T1

T10: 6½" x 6½" x 9³⁄₁₆" fin.

T2

T10

T3

T4

T5

T6

154

Triangles T15-T26

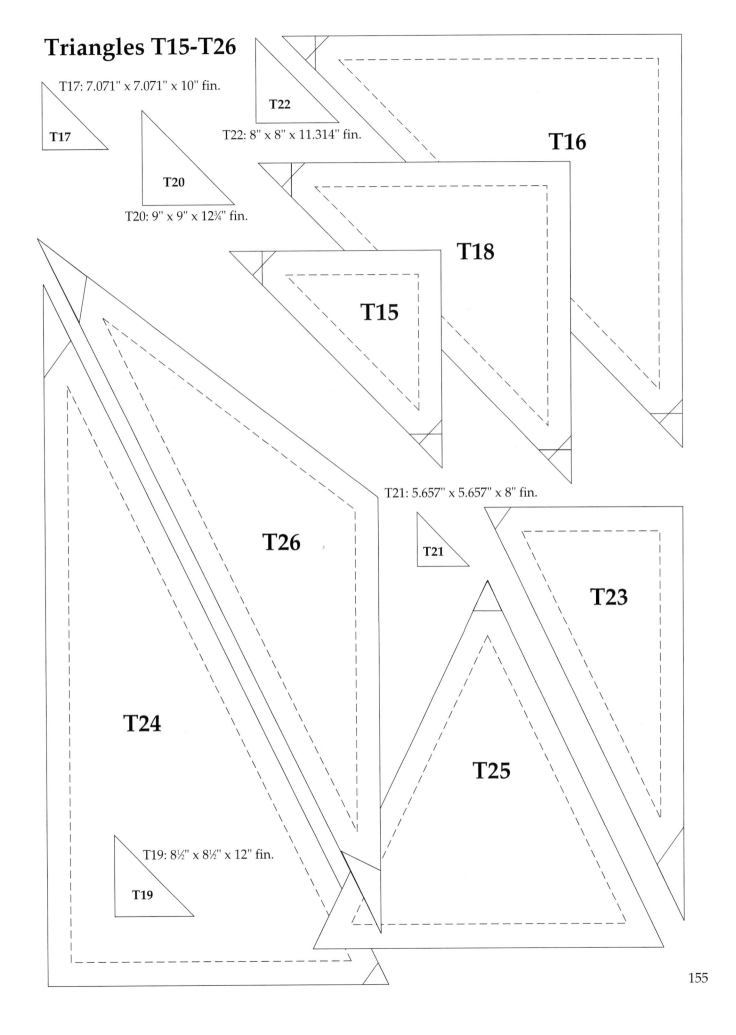

T17: 7.071" x 7.071" x 10" fin.

T17

T22

T22: 8" x 8" x 11.314" fin.

T16

T20

T20: 9" x 9" x 12¾" fin.

T18

T15

T21: 5.657" x 5.657" x 8" fin.

T26

T21

T23

T24

T25

T19: 8½" x 8½" x 12" fin.

T19

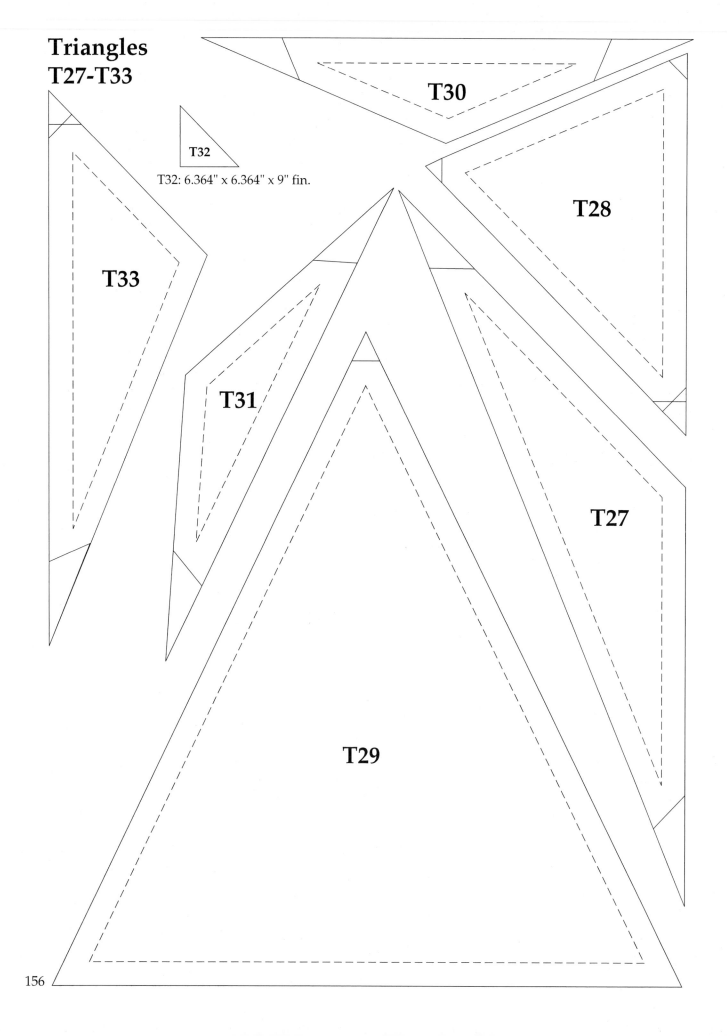

**Triangles
T27-T33**

T32

T32: 6.364" x 6.364" x 9" fin.

T33

T30

T28

T31

T27

T29

156

Other Shapes
X1-X5

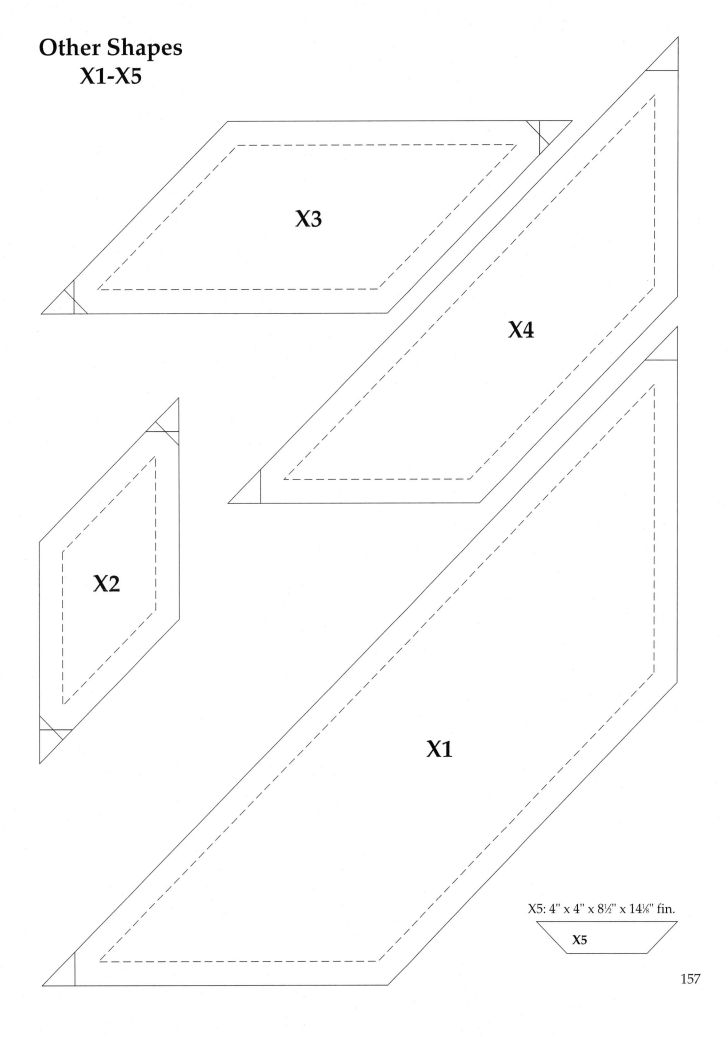

X3

X4

X2

X1

X5: 4" x 4" x 8½" x 14⅛" fin.

X5

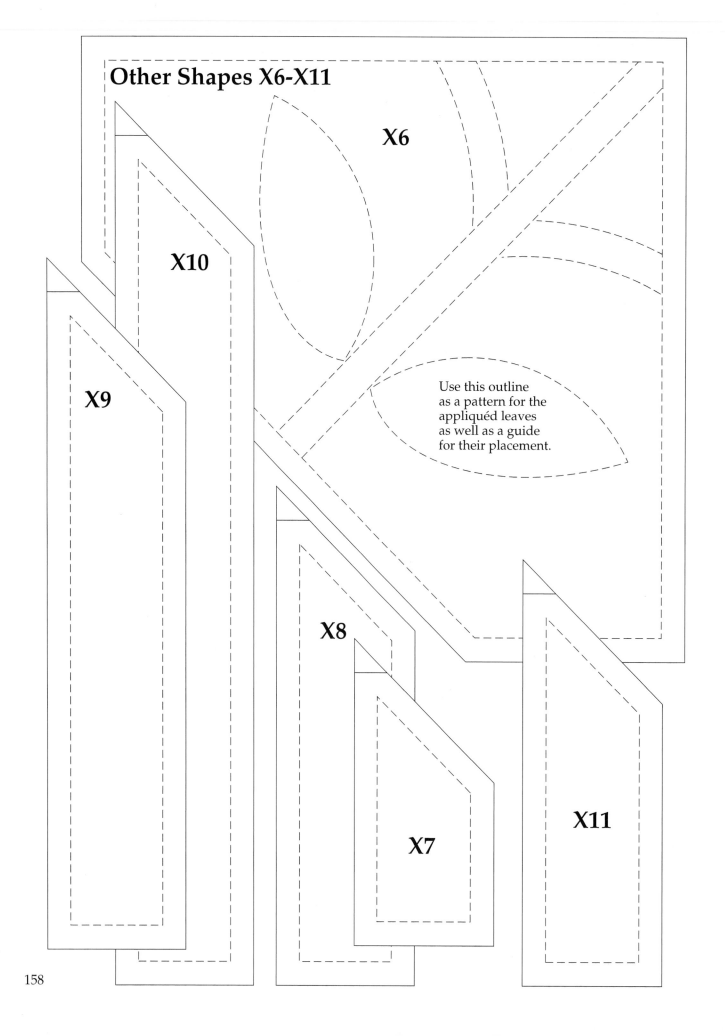

Other Shapes X6–X11

X6

X10

X9

Use this outline
as a pattern for the
appliquéd leaves
as well as a guide
for their placement.

X8

X7

X11

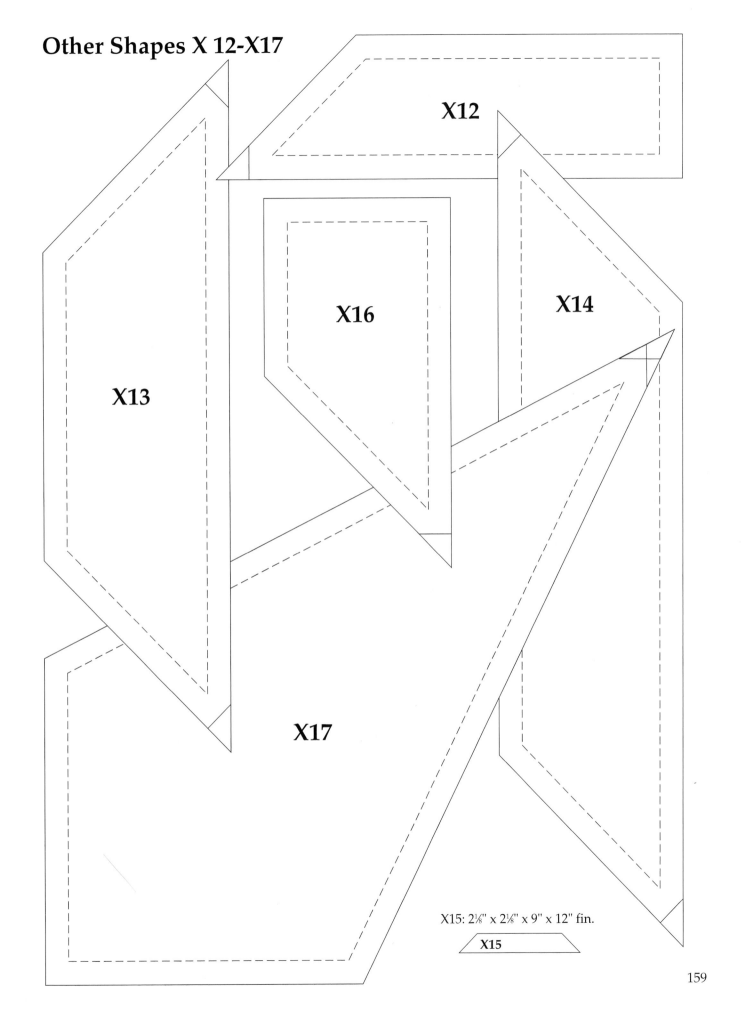

Other Shapes X 12-X17

X12

X14

X16

X13

X17

X15: 2⅛" x 2⅛" x 9" x 12" fin.

X15

Other Books by the Authors

By Judy Martin:

Yes You Can! Make Stunning Quilts from Simple Patterns, *112 pages. Great shortcuts and the most complete patterns ever for 14 easy quilts.*

Scraps, Blocks & Quilts, *192 pages. Color photos and patterns for 200 blocks, 20 quilts. In-depth techniques. Great discussion of fabric choices.*

Judy Martin's Ultimate Book of Quilt Block Patterns, *100 pages. Color photos, block piecing, full-size patterns for 174 quilt blocks. A classic.*

The Rainbow Collection, *43 pages. Patterns and instructions for 10 quilts and 20 blocks featuring rainbow hues.*

Shining Star Quilts, *144 pages. Lone Stars and more, from design ideas to quick techniques. 16 striking quilts with gorgeous quilting patterns.*

Scrap Quilts, *96 pages. One of the most popular quilting books of all time. Everything you want to know about America's beloved scrap quilts. Color photos, 16 great quilt patterns, techniques.*

Patchworkbook, *167 pages. Inspiration galore. Everything you need to know to design and draft original quilts. Easy lesson format.*

By Judy Martin and Bonnie Leman:

Taking the Math Out of Making Patchwork Quilts, *35 pages. Charts for quilt sizes, yardage for just about any shape and size of patch, the indispensable bias binding yield chart, and much more.*

Log Cabin Quilts, *35 pages. America's favorite quilt pattern. Reversible Log Cabin, foundation method, strip method, design ideas, and more.*

By Marsha McCloskey:

100 Pieced Patterns for 8" Quilt Blocks, *64 pages. Smallish blocks for manageable projects. Easy-to-use template format.*

Guide to Rotary Cutting, *22 pages. Concise ready-reference booklet for cutting patches without templates.*

On to Square Two, *80 pages. Bias-strip piecing and beyond. 11 traditional quilts plus 30 blocks using quick rotary cutting methods.*

Lessons in Machine Piecing, *96 pages. Great how-to illustrations. Progressive lessons based on 10 quilts.*

Feathered Star Quilts, *128 pages. Feathered Star history, quilts, blocks and drafting--the classic text on Feathered Star.*

Rotary Cutting Companion for Feathered Star Quilts, *24 pages. Rotary cutting charts for all the Feathered Star block designs and quilt projects in Feathered Star Quilts, plus updated bias-strip and machine piecing techniques.*

Feathered Star Sampler, *24 pages. Feathered Star blocks in a sampler quilt. Revised for rotary cutting.*

Christmas Quilts, *72 pages. Color photos. Christmas lore, quilts and projects for the holidays.*

Wall Quilts, *76 pages. Color photos. 10 traditional pieced Wall Quilts with matching patchwork pillows.*

Small Quilts, *46 pages. A favorite for novice quilters.*

By Marsha McCloskey, Mary Hickey, Nancy J. Martin and Sara Nephew :

Quick and Easy Quiltmaking, *272 pages. 26 projects featuring speedy cutting and machine piecing methods for triangles.*

By Marsha McCloskey and Nancy J. Martin:

Ocean Waves, *72 pages. Color photos. 12 great Ocean Waves quilts made with bias-strip piecing.*

A Dozen Variables, *64 pages. Color photos. 12 star quilts plus design ideas for dozens more.*

For prices, availability & ordering information for Judy Martin's books, write to:

CROSLEY-GRIFFITH
PUBLISHING COMPANY, INC.
P.O. Box 512
Grinnell, Iowa 50112

For prices, availability & ordering information for Marsha McCloskey's books, write to:

Feathered Star Productions
2151 Seventh Avenue West
Seattle, Washington 98119